SCOTCH ON ICE

Scotland's Ice Hockey Heroes

SCOTCH ON ICE
Scotland's Ice Hockey Heroes

DAVID GORDON

This book is dedicated to the memory of my father, Thomas Hunter Gordon (1931-2006), who provided coverage of the Ayr Raiders for *Ice Hockey World* in the early 1950s and who directly developed my subsequent interest in ice hockey as a player, writer and supporter.

Front cover illustration: Colin Shields in action for Belfast Giants. (Michael Cooper Photography)

First published 2006

STADIA is an imprint of
Tempus Publishing Limited
The Mill, Brimscombe Port,
Stroud, Gloucestershire, GL5 2QG
www.tempus-publishing.com

British Library Cataloguing in Publication Data.
A catalogue record for this book is available from the British Library.

ISBN-10: 0 7524 3801 8
ISBN-13: 978 0 7524 3801 6

Typesetting and origination by Tempus Publishing Limited
Printed in Great Britain

Contents

Acknowledgements

There are a number of individuals to whom I am indebted, who gave generously of their time, spoke to me at length, and shared personal photographs and newspaper cuttings. The book would not have been possible without their invaluable assistance.

In terms of featured interviewees, my thanks go to: Bill Brennan of Aberdeen; Alastair Brennan of Irvine; John Carlyle of Falkirk; Bill Crawford of Toronto, Ontario; Scott Neil of Edinburgh; Martin and Colin Shields of East Kilbride; 'Tuck' Syme of Palmdale, California; and the late Tommy McInroy. It was a privilege and a pleasure to meet with all of them.

My thanks must also go to the following individuals who agreed to be interviewed: Mrs Lyn Benko of London, Ontario (daughter of the late 'Tiny' Syme); Gerry Collins of Newton Mearns (cousin of the late Joe Collins); Mrs Shirley Gray of Victoria, BC (daughter of the late Jimmy Foster); Mrs Elizabeth Sneddon of Callander (widow of the late Bill Sneddon); Mr Vernon Neil of Nottingham (son of the late Lawson Neil); Mrs Barbara Waghorn of Nottingham (widow of the late Lawson Neil); Keith Kewley of St Thomas, Ontario; Alan Murphy of Penicuik; Jimmy Thomson of Kinross; Stan Christie of Ayr; Jimmy Agnew of Ayr; the late Jack Siemon of Perth.

The following individuals also provided me with invaluable advice and assistance in the research of the book: Ainsley and Lynn Barwick of Ringwood, Hampshire (nephew-in-law and niece of the late Billy Fullerton, who gave me access to a number of rare materials); Dr Kenneth Collins of Glasgow; Charles Collins of Giffnock; Harold Kewley of St Thomas, Ontario; Martin Harris of London (who responded readily to my many queries and was invaluable in providing statistical data and photographic materials); Ronnie Nichol of Ayr; Tony Allen of London; Stewart Roberts, whose *Ice Hockey Annual* proved indispensable; Tommy Newall of Prestwick; June Dempster of Ayr; John 'Bernie' McCrone of Ayr; T. Kent Morgan of Winnipeg, Manitoba; Rick Brownlee, Executive Director, Manitoba Sports Hall of Fame; Anne Ambler, Abingdon Library; Margaret Shields of East Kilbride; Graeme Farrell of Kirkcaldy; Noel Henderson of Manitoba (late of Dunfermline);George Simmonds of Dunfermline; my late father, Tom Gordon, and uncle, Ian Gordon.

In addition, the ever-helpful staff at the following establishments rendered invaluable assistance:The Mitchell Library, Glasgow;Watt Library, Greenock; Falkirk Library; Dunfermline Central Library; Ayr Carnegie Library; Kirkcaldy Library; A.K. Bell Library, Perth; Personnel staff at RAF Innsworth, Gloucester; National Archives of Scotland, Edinburgh; Strathclyde Area Genealogy Centre, Glasgow.

Sincere thanks, also, to Richard Bath and Tom English of *Scotland on Sunday,* whose use of two of my articles, on Jimmy Foster and 'Tuck' Syme, gave me the impetus to produce the book; and to Rob Sharman at Stadia for making it a reality.

As ever, my gratitude goes to Julie, Emma and Kirsten for indulging me during the research and writing of the book. Thank you, it wouldn't have been possible without you.

Any errors are mine.

David Gordon
Alloway, Ayr
June 2006

The 1976 Great Britain team, Gdansk, Poland. Back From left to right, back row: George Beach (coach), Alfie Miller (Whitley Warriors), Pete Murray (Bristol Red Wings), John Gibson (Ayr Bruins), Jackson McBride (Ayr Bruins), Les Lovell (Fife Flyers), Kenny Horne (Fife Flyers), John Hester (Glasgow Dynamos), Kenny Matthews (Durham Wasps), Jimmy Young (Ayr Bruins), Terry Matthews (Durham Wasps), Chick Cottrell (Trainer), John Pullar (Fife Flyers), John 'Jumbo' Milne (manager). From left to right, front row: Jim Pearson (Whitley Warriors), Martin Shields (Glasgow Dynamos), Keith Havery (Whitley Warriors), Gordon Latto (Västra Frölunda IF, Sweden), Glynne Thomas (Streatham), George Pearson (Whitley Warriors), Lawrie Lovell (Fife Flyers), Willie Kerr (Murrayfield Racers), Alastair Brennan (Fife Flyers). (Martin Shields archive).

Introduction

In writing this book, I was not aiming to produce an objective listing of the best-ever Scottish-born ice hockey players, although it could be argued that those featured would be included in any such compilation. Instead, I wished to profile players whose contribution to the sport has been significant over the past seventy-five years; attempting to provide an evocation, through the personal stories of the players themselves, of how the sport has evolved in both a Scottish and UK-wide context over that time.

I have a particular attachment to the following extract from a poem by Paisley-born author Gordon M. Williams, entitled 'A Scots Burgh Boy's Dream of America':

> Andra Carnegie was a wee Scots laddie who did weel
> for himself in America; that's what we were all going to do,
> probably in Canada where we would play ice-hockey and
> come home in peg-topped trousers and sky-blue raincoats
> and stand about looking dead gallus at Paisley Cross.

The verse is from Williams' 1972 novel, *Walk Don't Walk*, and encapsulates that period when young Canadian hockey players brought glamour and celebrity to the austere, Calvinistic world of post-war Scotland; a period in which such players as Johnny Carlyle, Bill Sneddon, Lawson Neil, the Syme brothers, Billy Brennan and Bill Crawford proved that they could compete successfully with their North American cousins. If the book conveys something of the thoughts and actions of the past by which the present state of the sport could be better understood, offering some pointers as to how its future should be developed, then so much the better.

I also wanted to share something of these men beyond the 'hockey player' label. Where did they come from and what, apart from ice hockey, shaped them? A large part of the premise was, to paraphrase West Indian Marxist C.L.R. James and his famous cricketing reference, 'What do they know of ice hockey, who only ice hockey know?' After all, these are men who lived, or continue to live, interesting lives beyond the narrower confines of the ice rink.

To my mind, these men are all heroes of Scottish ice hockey, with hero defined as a man who is idealised for possessing superior qualities in any field. Individuals like Jimmy Foster, Billy Fullerton and 'Tuck' Syme, for example, deserve to be honoured in the wider pantheon of Scottish sporting achievement that appears to be, sadly, the almost exclusive preserve of football, rugby union, golf, boxing and athletics.

In his book *The Game*, Ken Dryden, the former Montreal Canadiens' goaltender, produced the definitive work on professional hockey. Indeed, for my money, it is the best book ever on any professional sport. Not only is it acutely observed and extremely well written, but it has the authority inherent in Dryden's key role as both the goaltender of a Montreal Dynasty and backstop of Team Canada's epic Summit Series triumph of '72.

Imagine if Roger Kahn had actually been the Brooklyn Dodgers' shortstop of the 1950s before writing the seminal baseball classic, *The Boys of Summer*; or if Hunter Davies had taken the place of Pat Jennings in the Tottenham Hotspur UEFA Cup winning team of 1972 before penning his football classic, *The Glory Game*. That is the measure of Dryden's *opus*.

And yet there is a part of his book with which I take issue, where he writes:

> We are not heroes. We are hockey players. We do exciting, sometimes courageous, sometimes ennobling things like heroes do, but no more than anyone else does. Blown up on a TV screen or a page of print, hyped by distance and imagination, we seem more heroic, the scope of our achievement seems grander, but it isn't, and we're not.

Dryden is not writing under a cloak of false modesty, but I feel he renders himself a disservice. By any interpretation of 'hero' in a hockey context, Ken Dryden fits the bill. And so do those whose stories are recounted here, albeit within the narrower confines of Scottish ice hockey.

Although those included are a subjective choice on my part, I have applied some objective parameters in making the selection. Firstly, they had to have been born in Scotland; secondly, they had to have represented Great Britain in a World Championship. The second criterion was to ensure that those profiled had the necessary playing credentials. It therefore excludes such diverse Scots-born Stanley Cup winners as Edinburgh's Chuck Gardiner and Steve Smith of Glasgow, who had no connection with the sport in their native land.

Unfortunately, it means that a British Ice Hockey Hall of Fame inductee, the Johnstone-born Tommy Lauder, former Paisley and Perth legend, is also omitted. (Inexplicably, despite being one of the finest players of the Canadian-dominated post-war era, Lauder was never selected for the British team.)

There are a number of others whose playing record is on a par with those included. Alas, to keep the book to a manageable twelve chapters at the publisher's request, I had to omit such worthy candidates as Jimmy Spence, Marshall Key, Ian Forbes, Joe Brown, Bert Smith and Jimmy Mitchell. Perhaps their time will come again should a follow-up prove viable.

For a similar reason, I also deemed it appropriate to exclude current players – thus Tony Hand, arguably the most talented player the sport has produced in this country is conspicuous by his absence.

Conversely, my exception to this rule is Colin Shields. I wished to feature Martin Shields as a representative, both as a successful player and coach, of ice hockey from the 1960s through to the 1990s; it would have been illogical not to profile him in tandem with his more famous son.

When I started the research for this book, all the perceived wisdom from previously published sources indicated that Scottish ice hockey originated with the opening of the first Scottish Ice Rink, at Crossmyloof in Glasgow, in 1907, with the sport's outward expansion from Glasgow being delayed until the opening of the Perth rink in 1936. The wonders of digital technology, however, revealed to me that the history of ice hockey's introduction to Scotland would have to be re-written.

Firstly, there was the discovery that an ice hockey match had been played in Edinburgh as early as 27 February 1915, when two teams of Newfoundland soldiers fought out a 1-1 draw at the city's former curling and skating rink at Haymarket. Indeed, hockey was being advertised at Haymarket as early as 1913 (hitherto it had been thought that Haymarket had never staged hockey, with the sport not being introduced to Edinburgh until the opening of the Murrayfield rink in September 1952).

The Scotsman newspaper's digital archive, however, unearthed the following gem of a letter, published in the issue of 17 January 1933, under the heading 'Rink Ice Hockey':

Switzerland, January 12, 1933

Sir – Who introduced ice hockey to Europe is a question now being discussed freely at the Swiss winter sports resorts.

Ice hockey as at present played on small enclosed rinks of either natural or artificial ice with a puck, was first introduced to the Continent of Europe by the Scottish Ice Hockey Club in December 1897.

In November of that year, the secretary of the club received a request from the manager of the Palais de Glace in Le Champs Elysées, Paris, to forward a bundle of hockey sticks, such as the Scottish club used on their artificial rink at the 'Panorama', Glasgow. These were sent, and shortly afterwards a challenge was received to play the match in Paris during the last week of 1897. This challenge was accepted.

The French sportsmen had the opportunity of receiving a certain amount of tuition in the game from Mr George A. Meagher, of Montreal, the then champion figure skater of the world, who was residing in Paris.

The Scottish team left on Christmas Eve, and, after four-days' practice on the French rink, the match came off on the evening of the 31st of December. It resulted in a win for Scotland by twelve goals to one. Mr Meagher captained the French team, and scored the only goal himself, individually; I captained the Scottish team.

Our teams in Scotland were mostly drawn from Edinburgh and Glasgow University students with a sprinkling of students from the engineering schools of Glasgow.

This was the first match played on the Continent of the game as we now know it, and with a puck.

It might be as well for me to also mention that another form of hockey was introduced on the Continent prior to the game in Paris – namely, Fen Country 'bandy'.

Mr Charles Goodmand Tebbutt, the famous international Amateur Speed Champion, took a team of bandy players over to Haarlem in Holland, under the auspices of the Athletic Association there, in the winter of 1891, when he captained the Bury Fen Bandy Club.

This game, of course, is entirely different to present-day hockey, and had been played for many years in the Fens on ice when available; it was played in the open air, and the ground was a right-angled parallelogram 200 yards long and 100 yards wide, the ball used was of solid india-rubber not less than 2¼ in. in diameter – a polo ball was preferable.

Mr Tebbut's Bury Fen team won, I think, by 14 goals to 1.

Mr Tebbut has also to his credit the introduction of bandy to Sweden, Norway, and Denmark.

Hence, Great Britain can fairly claim to have introduced both forms of hockey on the ice to Europe. – I am, &c. W. POLLOCK WYLIE

This letter is of great significance. Not only does it confirm that ice hockey with a puck was being played in Glasgow at least ten years earlier than had first been thought, but indicates that Scottish ice hockey players introduced the sport to continental Europe. It also puts ice hockey in Scotland alongside other 'traditional' team sports like football, cricket and rugby union in terms of establishment in the nineteenth century.

The Panorama referred to by Wylie in his letter was the Glasgow Real Ice Skating Palace, a circular rink on Sauchiehall Street, opened in May 1896 (latterly known as the Hippodrome, hosting Hengler's Circus in the early twentieth century, it became ABC's Regal cinema in 1929).

The Scotsman in December 1896 notes a match at the Skating Palace between the Scottish Bandy Club and Glasgow University, with a Scotland *v.* England match scheduled for January 1897 in London. It reports on a 'Carnival at Glasgow Skating Palace' on 17 March 1897, included in which, 'There were during the evening hockey matches on the ice...'

On 23 January 1897, at Lochwinnoch, the amateur skating championships of Renfrewshire were held. *The Scotsman* reported that: 'About 8,000 people attended the races... A bandy match between teams representing Glasgow and Greenock resulted in a draw – three goals each.'

That such a large crowd made its way to a frozen loch in the middle of the Renfrewshire countryside is astonishing for the period, given that it exceeds by about 3,000 any other attendance for an ice hockey match in Scotland in the subsequent 100-plus years.

By way of a contemporary context, a Rangers *v.* Hibernian Scottish Cup-tie at Ibrox on the same day (Saturday 23 January 1897) attracted a crowd of 12,000; a Morton *v.* Arthurlie friendly football match at nearby Greenock, however, drew only 2,000.

The *Post Office Directory* for Glasgow of the time has an entry for the 'Scottish Bandy Club (Hockey on the Ice)', with the honorary secretary listed as W. Pollock Wylie; he also held this office for the Scottish branch of the National Skating Association.(William Pollock Wylie, the son of a Baptist Minister who had been a former sub-editor of the *Ayr Advertiser* newspaper, was a Glasgow-based journalist and publisher of the 1890s, editing a weekly newspaper, *The Christian Leader,* which had been founded by his late father. Born in Gourock, Renfrewshire in 1869, Pollock Wylie died in Sussex in 1935, aged sixty-six. He was also the Scottish Speed Skating Champion in the 1890s.)

While the confirmation of the sport's even greater Scottish longevity than hitherto supposed is a heartening discovery, it is tinged with a sad irony. Ice hockey is virtually unnoticed by an indifferent Scottish media, who, if they give any kind of thought to it, dismiss it as some kind of passing fad, akin to the 1980s introduction of American football. Yet Pollock Wylie, arguably the first hero of Scottish ice hockey, was himself a member of Scotland's earlier print media, whose latter-day successors shun the sport which he pioneered in Scotland.

Hopefully, in highlighting the achievements of Scotland's ice hockey heroes of a later vintage, it will serve as a fitting tribute to Pollock Wylie's unheralded evolutionary work for ice hockey in Scotland and Europe during the late Victorian age.

1

The Puck Stops Here: Jimmy Foster

The most enduring image from the Nazi Olympics of 1936, courtesy of Leni Riefenstahl's iconic film work, is the triumph of black American athlete Jesse Owens, whose gold medal achievements made a mockery of the host regime's racist ideology.

Riefenstahl's *Olympia* is widely regarded as the supreme example of the documentary form, and has ensured that the dramas of those Berlin summer games have tended to overshadow the 1936 Winter Olympics, held in the twin Bavarian Alpine villages of Garmisch-Partenkirchen in February of that year. An unfortunate corollary is that the story of a unique sporting triumph, the original 'Miracle on Ice' if you will, when the Great Britain ice hockey team won the Olympic title, is now all but forgotten. This lack of recognition is all the more disappointing from a Scottish perspective, as the key contributor to the British team's success was the sole Scot in the line-up; goaltender Jimmy Foster. He has the distinction of being the first Scot to win a gold medal at the Winter Olympics, and was to remain, for over sixty years, the only Scot thus honoured, until joined by Rhona Martin and her curling heroines in 2002.

James Foster was born in a tenement flat at 172 Saracen Street, in the Possilpark area of Glasgow, on 13 September 1905. Some newspaper reports, around the time of the 1936 Winter Olympics, incorrectly describe his birthplace as Greenock, an error which has been perpetuated in some publications ever since. It is unclear how this misconception originated, but the documentary evidence of his birth and early years in Glasgow is indisputable. The anecdotal material is also unequivocal, as his eldest daughter, Mrs Shirley Gray, of Victoria, British Columbia, explained to the writer in January 2006: 'He always said Glasgow was home.'

Jimmy was the youngest child of James Philip Foster and Annie McIntyre, who had married in Govan, Glasgow, on the last day of 1884, in a ceremony conducted according to the forms of the Wesleyan Methodist Church. His parents were both aged nineteen at the date of their marriage, and both lived locally in Govan; Foster's father was an apprentice blacksmith from McLellan Street, while his mother resided at Lambhill Street and was employed as a biscuit packer.

Their origins, however, reflected the melting pot that was industrial Glasgow, the 'Second City' of the British Empire, in the late Victorian age. James Philip Foster had been born at Darlington in north-east England, while Annie McIntyre hailed originally from Ireland, although both had moved to Glasgow as young children.

Nevertheless, as the star of Great Britain's greatest Winter Olympic triumph, it is appropriate that Jimmy Foster's roots spread right across the British Isles. The Foster line of his family tree, however, was decidedly Scottish. William Foster, Jimmy's great-grandfather, was a native of Canonbie in Dumfriesshire, who had moved to work in England, before returning the family north of the border to Glasgow, where he was employed as an engine driver in a Govan factory (Jimmy's grandfather, John Foster, was also an engine driver).

Foster's parents had two children in Govan – William and Margaret – in the first two years of their marriage, before spending an unusual interlude in sunnier climes, as Foster's eldest daughter describes:

> My grandfather did ornamental ironwork, and had been working in Spain for a few years before my Dad was born. Dad had an older brother and older sister. There was something like sixteen or eighteen years between my father's brother and him. My Dad had another adopted elder brother, Uncle Ron, who was a couple of years older than Dad. He was so different to the rest of the family, being tall and thin. I remember saying this to my Dad, and he then told me that Ron had been adopted, but it wasn't something people spoke about back then. His mother had died in childbirth, and my grandmother and grandfather adopted him.

By 1901, the Fosters were back in Glasgow, living in Leyden Street, Maryhill, and had moved across the north of the city, to Possilpark, at the time of Jimmy's birth in 1905. After a brief spell in Paisley, the family returned to Glasgow in 1909, settling in to a tenement flat at 31 Adamswell Street, Springburn, close to the massive Hyde Park Works of the North British Locomotive Company, where Foster's father was a Foreman Blacksmith and his eldest brother worked as a template maker.

The newly-built Hyde Park Public School, a substantial sandstone structure on Mollinsburn Street, was just across the road from Jimmy's home, and he started his formal education there on 16 August 1910, three weeks short of his fifth birthday. Shirley Gray was intrigued to be told of her father's first school:

> It's fascinating to know that he went to a school in Glasgow called Hyde Park, and I bet there wasn't a park nearby! It's like where we lived in London when he played with Harringay. The street was called Green Lanes, but there were no trees to be seen!

Mrs Gray is correct in her assumption, as the Hyde Park Works dominated Jimmy Foster's childhood environment, covering sixty acres and employing a workforce of 8,000.

The Adamswell Street tenement flat, comprising a room and small recessed kitchen, was home to Foster's parents, his grown up elder brother and sister, as well as himself and his adopted brother. The rest of the three-storey building was equally overcrowded and representative of the 'respectable' working-class of the Edwardian era. The 1911-12 Valuation Roll shows that the Foster's neighbours – all 'up the one close' at number 31 – included a bricklayer, an electrician, a car conductor, a fitter, a machineman, an inspector, a tuber, an engineer, a machinist, a waiter, a restaurateur, and two clerks.

As previously mentioned, Foster's parents had already experienced working abroad, having spent several years in Spain in the 1890s, so it is unsurprising that emigration to a new life in Canada was a consideration for them. That they chose this option at the relatively advanced age of forty-seven was, perhaps, unusual for the time.

For the six year-old Jimmy Foster, his last day at Hyde Park School would be Friday 10 May 1912. His 'Cause of Leaving' is recorded in the School Register with a single word: *'Canada'*. He would not return to Glasgow for more than twenty-three years, by which time he was an Olympic gold medallist.

His father had decided to swap work in the locomotive works of his native city to take up employment with the Canadian Pacific Railway at their Winnipeg rail yards; the largest in the world at that time. The Foster family sailed the Atlantic just a month after the sinking of the *Titanic*, heading for their new life in Manitoba.

Back in 1912, Winnipeg was a bustling, growing city with immigrants flooding in. It was only about an eighth the size of the Fosters' native Glasgow, but was described at the time as the 'Chicago of the North.' Winnipeg was undoubtedly booming, and it still had the feel of a lively frontier town.

Cartoon of Jimmy Foster, 1936/37. (Martin C. Harris archive)

Foster's daughter Shirley described her father's early years in Winnipeg:

> My father was six when he moved to Winnipeg, that's when he started to skate and play hockey. I think my grandfather was looking for work, I knew he was a blacksmith. My grandfather worked for the CPR [Canadian Pacific Railway], I guess something to do with the ironworks at the rail yards in Winnipeg. I think they lived in the north end of Winnipeg, close to the CPR rail yards. By the time I was born, we had moved to the west end.
>
> It would have been in the north end of Winnipeg that Dad went to school. I know that my mother went to St John's High School, but I don't know if she met Dad there.

Young Jimmy grew up, literally, on the wrong side of the tracks in Winnipeg's north end, around Selkirk Avenue and the CPR rail yards, skating and playing hockey on the frozen ponds of the harsh Manitoba winter.

He started out in organised hockey as a seventeen year old with the Winnipeg Argonauts, of the Winnipeg Junior Hockey League, in 1922, and would go on to earn a reputation as the world's finest goaltender. His first two seasons with the Argonauts gave no indication of what was to come. Jimmy conceded 55 goals in 14 games, with the Argonauts winning only once and losing twelve.

Foster's next club was the University of Manitoba Juniors, where his illustrious predecessor between the pipes had been fellow Scot, Chuck Gardiner. A year older than Foster, Edinburgh-born Gardiner would go on to backstop the Chicago Black Hawks to their first Stanley Cup in 1934, while racked with a chronic tonsil infection which, tragically, claimed his life immediately after the finals. He was aged just thirty.

Foster, like Gardiner, also backstopped the University of Manitoba to a Junior Provincial Championship in 1925, although his eligibility to represent the varsity squad appears to have been somewhat tenuous, as his daughter recounts:

> He certainly didn't attend the University of Manitoba; they must have needed a goalie for him to have played for them!
>
> My Mom and Dad married in 1926 in Winnipeg, at St Jude's Church. My Mom's own name was Pearl Fooks. I'm seventy-eight, he was twenty-one when I was born in 1927. I had a younger sister, Pat, born in 1934, and a brother, also Jimmy, born in 1943.

Jimmy had stepped up to senior hockey for the 1925/26 season, representing Brandon Regals in the South Saskatchewan Senior Hockey League. He was also an integral part of two quaintly named Manitoba Senior Championship-winning teams – the Winnipeg Winnipegs of 1927, and the 'Steamer' Maxwell-coached Elmwood Millionaires in 1930 – having spent 1927/28 with the University of Manitoba Senior team, in the Manitoba and Thunder Bay Hockey League, and assisted Winnipeg CPR of the Winnipeg Senior League in 1928/29 (a teammate on the CPR team was Gus Rivers, who would win a Stanley Cup with the Montreal Canadiens in 1930).

Foster fractured a leg in two places when playing with Elmwood, and it was even feared that his hockey career might have been over. His daughter Shirley recalls the incident:

> I remember my mother talked about that. She was not in the rink when it happened; I guess she was looking after me at the time, as I was about two. She said they could hear the crack all over the ice. I remember watching a hockey game in Winnipeg years later and we got talking to a chap who had been there when Dad broke his leg, and he also said that the crack was heard all round the building.
>
> I also remember the doctor came to the house many times to check him. One time I was sitting playing around on the piano, and the doctor asked me what I was playing, not thinking I would know; and I replied: 'Sally of My Dreams', which was a popular song at that time!

In 1931, after a long lay-off due to his injury, he was persuaded by fellow Winnipegger Percy Nicklin to move east to New Brunswick and the Moncton Hawks, of the Maritime Senior Hockey League. Nicklin was to coach the Hawks, and he and Foster were to work successfully together over the next eight years, with Nicklin coaching the British team to their unlikely Olympic triumph in 1936. The Moncton Hawks were Allan Cup Champions in both 1933 and 1934, the trophy being awarded to Canada's amateur hockey champions.

The amateur aspect, however, seems to have had quite a liberal interpretation, particularly when there were then such supposedly rigid lines of demarcation separating paid and unpaid sportsmen. Nicklin left for Britain in 1935 amid a controversy surrounding 'sham-amateurism', describing his former charges in Moncton as, 'The highest-paid group of amateur hockey players ever to chase a puck.'

Jimmy Foster's eldest daughter recalls her father's employment status when playing in Canadian 'amateur' hockey of the early 1930s:

> I was only four when we moved to Moncton, and in the summer Dad was working for the fellow who owned the Moncton Hawks hockey team, Henry White, who also owned an orange crush bottling plant (I could never drink orange crush again, we got so much of it!). He sold orange crush, and I know he got it into Eaton's department store in Moncton, which was a big thing then. It was more like what we'd call PR today, as they had to retain their amateur status.

In the 1932 Allan Cup, Foster posted the first ever back-to-back shut-outs in the competition and went a staggering 417 minutes without conceding a goal, although Moncton failed to reach the final. With Jimmy Foster between the pipes, and also captaining the side, the Hawks went on to claim the Allan Cup in 1933 and again in 1934. They were the first club to win successive Allan Cups with the same roster, and the first team from Canada's Maritime Provinces to become Allan Cup Champions. In those three seasons, he missed only one of Moncton's 220 games, saving an estimated 6,000 shots.

The 1933 finals were held in Vancouver, and the Hawks were pitted against the Saskatoon Quakers. Foster was unbeaten in the two games which gave Moncton the cup. The Hawks won the opening game 3-0, and tied up the series with a 2-0 victory in Game Two, with second-period goals from Duke McDonald and Bert Connelly in front of 9,000 fans.

In the 1934 finals, Foster and the Hawks had the opportunity to showcase their skills in two of the sport's great, iconic amphitheatres: the Montreal Forum and Toronto's Maple Leaf Gardens. In the quarter-finals, the Hawks recorded two 3-1 wins in the Forum to defeat the hometown McGill University Redmen. In the final, Moncton would need three games to see off the Fort William Thundering Herd in Maple Leaf Gardens. Hawks were shocked in the series opener, as Fort William won 3-2. Game Two saw Moncton edge it 4-2, and the cup was retained with an emphatic 5-1 Moncton victory in Game Three. The triumphant Hawks were greeted by 15,000 fans in Moncton on their return from Toronto with the cup in 1934.

Foster's popularity in Moncton was to endure, as his daughter was to discover years later:

> My husband, Bob Gray, was a hockey player as well. Bob played in Charlottetown and I remember they had a story in the local newspaper describing me as 'Bob's wife, Jimmy's daughter.' The people in the Maritimes are very friendly and never forget. My Dad liked that. 'It's always nice to be remembered,' he used to say.

With a second daughter, Patricia, having arrived in 1934, and with his thirtieth birthday approaching, Foster took the momentous decision to return to the UK for the first time in over twenty years, turning his back on the National Hockey League. He spent 1935/36 in south-west London with Richmond Hawks, coached by Percy Nicklin.

Daughter Shirley didn't travel to London with her parents, remaining at school back in Winnipeg:

> I didn't go with them when they first went to England. They came back and picked me up in 1937, and we came back to Winnipeg on a summer holiday in 1939. War was declared, and Dad never went back. I remember once when my daughter and I were watching figure skating on TV. It was Torvill and Dean, and they were skating at Richmond, and I cried out: 'Gosh, that's the rink that my Dad played in!'

Foster backstopped Hawks to a runners-up slot in the English National League, finishing level on points with champions Wembley Lions. His abilities were recognised with an All Star 'A' team selection.

Nicklin, in tandem with the astute general secretary of the British Ice Hockey Association, J.F. 'Bunny' Ahearne, had scouted Canada for other British-born hockey players, like Foster, eligible to represent the national team in the upcoming Olympic tournament. This ensured that relations between the British and Canadian governing bodies would become increasingly acrimonious as the Olympics beckoned, with a residue of Canadian resentment still remaining seventy years on.

The ire of the Canadian Amateur Hockey Association had been aroused by players under its jurisdiction allegedly joining teams overseas without permission, and it suspended sixteen English National League players for this supposed breach. Two of the sixteen were key components of Great Britain's Olympic team: Jimmy Foster and winger Alex Archer. In the case of Foster, however, the Canadians also threw in, for good measure, the further, doubtful, allegation that he was also ineligible through having supposedly represented Canada, when appearing for Moncton Hawks against a Detroit team of the USA in 1934. Foster's daughter Shirley recalls the dispute vividly:

> There was a big fuss at the time, and the Canadians didn't want my Dad and Alex Archer to play in the Olympics. I was an eight-year-old kid in Winnipeg, listening to it on the radio, and I remember thinking: 'my gosh, are they not going to let my Dad play?'

Ironically, Foster could have represented Canada in the Olympics – at boxing. As a welterweight, he had won several YMCA titles back in Winnipeg and took part in Olympic trials in the 1920s, before concentrating on hockey. He was a fine all-round athlete, also assisting the Canadian Pacific Railway team to a Manitoba commercial soccer championship, as his daughter relates:

> I know my Dad was a good, all-round athlete, and was a good boxer with the 'Y' in Winnipeg. I remember my Dad saying he had done some boxing, and my daughter, Laurie, remembers her grandpa showing her how to skip, he did fancy skipping like a boxer would.

On 5 February 1936, the very eve of the opening ceremony, the Ligue Internationale Hockey sur Glace (LIHG) sat down in Garmisch to resolve the Canadian-British wrangle. Last minute politicking saw the Canadians lift their suspension, and Foster and Archer were able to take part in the tournament, but it was hardly the ideal preparation for the British team, anxiously awaiting the decision in their small *pension* in the centre of Garmisch.

Foster was nicknamed 'The Parson' by his teammates, and newspaper reports of the time suggested it was because his father had at one time wanted him to enter the church. His daughter, however, finds such a suggestion amusing:

> They did call him 'The Parson', I do remember that, but I don't know where that came from! My Dad liked to have a good time, so perhaps it was tongue-in-cheek! We certainly went to the Anglican Church, but, apart from that, he wasn't particularly religious. No, he never gave any indication along those lines about entering the church! They all liked a good time, and they all had a good time! They were all a very close-knit team at Harringay.

That notwithstanding, Nicklin ensured that any good time being had by the British team was confined to the rink for the duration of the Olympic tournament. No alcohol was permitted, and cigarettes were rationed, with a smoking ban in the dressing-room. Nicklin also imposed a 10p.m. curfew on his team, and expected them to be in bed by that time, with no telephone calls allowed after bedtime.

Coach Nicklin adopted a tight-checking, defensive game for the GB team, playing to its strengths and reliant heavily on the nigh-impregnable Foster in goal. On the open-air Olympic rink in Garmisch, in the cold of a Bavarian winter, the dream was realised.

It was never, however, an impossible dream, and the 'Miracle on Ice' parallels perhaps do an injustice to a talented and very well-coached group of players. That is not meant as an underestimation of what was, undoubtedly, Britain's greatest Winter Olympic achievement, but the triumph should be considered in context. Those journalists covering British ice hockey at the time had actually been pondering on the possibility of a British Olympic success for some weeks prior to the commencement of the Games. The possibility of such success was further helped by the fact that internal dissent was to impact on the Canadian preparations.

Canada was to be represented not by the previous year's Allan Cup Winners, the Halifax Wolverines (as was the usual practice), but by their defeated opponents, the Port Arthur Bearcats. The Canadian Amateur Hockey Association claimed that the Wolverines had broken the strict player residency rules then in place, and had thus denied them the opportunity to represent Canada at the Olympics. Four of the Wolverines were added to the Port Arthur roster but, two weeks prior to the departure for Europe, these four players were dropped from the team, having had the temerity to ask for payment for time lost from work during their three months' absence representing Canada.

With each of the English National League clubs containing a nucleus of British-born but Canadian-trained players, Percy Nicklin was able to build a very well-organised and hard-working team; professional in approach (unsurprisingly, as the majority of the players were, at the very least, semi-professional – a somewhat incongruous situation, at odds with the Olympian amateur ethos of the time). And Nicklin knew that in Jimmy Foster, he had, to borrow the terminology from a later hockey era, a match-winning 'money goalie'.

Foster appeared in all seven games played by Great Britain, posting four shutouts and conceding just three goals, turning aside 219 shots for a save percentage of 98.7. His was a massively significant contribution to the British squad's not entirely unexpected annexation of the Olympic crown, together with the World and European titles, to complete a triple triumph. Team manager 'Bunny' Ahearne, in a final interview before his death in 1985, paid the ultimate compliment to Foster's Olympic goaltending: 'There was only one way he could have been improved upon and that's if we had put a metal sheet across the goal.'

On 6 February 1936, overlooked by the Zugspitze, the highest mountain in Germany, a crowd of 20,000 watched the competitors from twenty-eight nations march past Adolf Hitler at the Games' opening ceremony. For the first time at the Winter Games, the Olympic Flame was lit, and the protracted formalities were held in the large arena at the base of the ski-jump. The weather was overcast with flurries of snow. Carl Erhardt, the patrician captain of the British team, remembered the ceremony for *Ice Hockey World* some twelve years later: 'Whereas most teams, particularly the Continentals, were uniformly dressed to look something like a team we, of course, looked rather ragtime...'

With the host nation determined on building prestige for the Nazi state, the Garmisch Games had the financial backing that allowed a Winter Olympics to be organised on a scale unmatched up to that point. With Alpine skiing included as an event for the first time, and with Norway's Sonja Henie securing her third gold medal in figure skating, the fourth Winter Olympic Games were a great success, drawing over 500,000 spectators to the seventeen events.

But it was the ice hockey which was to produce the greatest drama, and upset, of the Games. In the ice hockey qualifying pool, the British opened against Sweden on 7 February, in Garmisch's open-air Olympia-Kunsteis-Stadion (and on natural ice). The game faced-off at 6.15p.m., and Brenchley gave the British an early lead. Foster had to be on his toes in the second period as the Swedes pressed for an equaliser, but Great Britain held on to win 1-0.

The next day, the British team headed a mile or so south of Garmisch for their only appearance on the picturesque Riessersee rink, located on a frozen lake, on a pine-clad hill, above the village. They were to play a morning match with Japan in this idyllic setting, with the temperature a bracing -7°C. Despite the cold, first period goals from Chirp Brenchley and Sandy Archer put the British in command, and a late breakaway from Jimmy Borland secured a comfortable 3-0 victory and qualification for the semi-final pool.

The Great Britain Olympic team, pictured on the Riessersee, outside Garmisch, February 1936. From left to right, standing: Jimmy Chappell, Archie Stinchcombe, Alex Archer, Gordon Dailley, Percy Nicklin (coach), Jack Kilpatrick, Carl Erhardt (captain), Johnny Coward, Gerry Davey. Front row: Jimmy Borland, Art Child, Jimmy Foster, 'Chirp' Brenchley. (Martin C. Harris archive)

The team had a three-day rest before the first semi-final match, which was against favourites Canada, whose team comprised mainly of players from Port Arthur Bearcats. The Canadians had never been defeated in Olympic competition, and were shocked when Gerry Davey put Great Britain ahead after forty seconds. In front of a 10,000 crowd, a titanic struggle unfolded. Ralph St Germain equalised for Canada at 13.40, but with Jimmy Foster in superb form, and his endeavours inspiring his hard-skating teammates, the Canadians couldn't get another goal. Then, with just ninety seconds remaining, the British netted a sensational winner; a Gordon Dailley shot rebounded off the pads of Canadian goalie 'Dinty' Moore, and 'Chirp' Brenchley followed up to slot home. Great Britain 2, Canada 1, and Jimmy Foster was the hero of the hour.

The next match was the following evening, against the hosts, Germany, and, despite three full periods of overtime, the game finished 1-1. Gerry Davey had netted the British goal in the second period of normal time, with the Germans equalising in the third, to set up the marathon overtime session.

After their late-night overtime exertions against Germany, the last thing the British team needed was a match the next morning. Fortunately, Hungary were not difficult opponents, and Great Britain eased to a comfortable 5-1 win in an uninspiring game to move into the final pool, to be joined by Canada, USA and Czechoslovakia. Adolf Hitler was in attendance at this match (the first event he had attended since the opening ceremony). It had been suggested to the players that they should give the Nazi salute. They voted to do so, but only if it was clear that they were saluting the German people. At the end of the game, they saluted Hitler, and then turned round and gave the salute to the other side of the rink, to a tumultuous reception, being heiled off the ice by the German crowd.

Further controversy surrounded the format of the final pool, which stipulated that teams who had already met in an earlier round of the tournament were not required to play each other again in the final pool. Instead, they would be credited with whatever points, and goals for and against, which had been earned in the earlier game. Canadian efforts to have this predetermined method replaced by a round-robin final were rejected. Thus Canada was denied the opportunity to avenge the defeat by Great Britain, and started the final pool two points adrift of the British.

Foster kept another clean sheet in the first match of the finals on 14 February, as Britain picked up the European title when beating Czechoslovakia 5-0 in a night-time match. The following evening, the British met the USA, knowing that a win would give them the gold medal. The night temperature was around 5°C, so the ice plant was required in the Olympic rink.

In another tense struggle, dominated by both defences, the game finished 0-0, and a further three periods of overtime failed to produce a goal. Foster had again produced a brilliant display of goaltending, his jaws moving rhythmically as he constantly chewed gum through 120 minutes of pressure hockey. He was calm and collected, dealing with whatever came his way, which included a puck driven hard into his face, but he continued to give a 'masterful display'.

The match had been broadcast live by the BBC, and had overrun its allotted time by some forty-five minutes when the commentary of Canadian journalist Bob Bowman was faded out during the second overtime period. Even the national news, that holy of holies, had been held back. Despite this, the BBC still received a staggering 600 telephone calls the next day, along with countless letters and telegrams, complaining about the termination of the ice hockey commentary on the wireless. The team's exploits had caught the imagination of the nation, and the groundswell of interest in ice hockey would sustain the sport in the UK for the next twenty years.

There was still a chance that Britain could be pipped by the Americans, who needed to beat the Canadians without losing a goal, or by more than 5-1, to take the title. A tired US squad, understandable after their marathon match with the British, went down to Canada by a single goal the following night. The Great Britain ice hockey team were Olympic Champions, in no small measure due to the brilliance of their Glaswegian goaltender.

Strangely, Jimmy Foster did not receive his gold medal at the Games' closing ceremony on the evening of Sunday 16 February 1936, as he had a train to catch! Along with coach Nicklin, Foster and two others had to leave Garmisch during that afternoon in order to be back in London on the Tuesday for matches with their club sides. The four, however, 'received an equally great send off at the station'. The *Glasgow Herald* noted that Foster was '...well-known in the west of Scotland and... has been the greatest favourite with the crowd for his wonderful saving...'

In the home of hockey, however, the Canadians were smarting at their defeat. In a country where it is not just the national sport, but the national passion, the events of seventy years ago still resonate today, as Jimmy Foster's daughter can testify:

> Every time the Olympics are on, they bring up footage of 1936 and show it here on TV, because it was the first time Canada had been beaten. There's always a lot about my Dad on TV at the time of the Winter Olympics, with film of him leading the British team onto the ice.
>
> We kept it a family secret, because it didn't go down too well with a lot of Canadians! Until Canada won the last couple of times in the Olympic hockey, we told the kids don't dare tell anybody that your grandfather was the British goalie in 1936! With Canada losing in the Olympics [in 2006], I had to say to my grandson: 'my gosh, Travis, here's another time when you can't say who your great-grandfather was!'
>
> My father was very humble about that sort of thing; he was not one to do bragging. It was always amazing to him, and us, when people did make a thing about it.
>
> I don't think he was troubled by playing against Canada. If he was, I never heard it. He was so totally into the game, and winning. That would overshadow anything else, when you're that competitive. And he always had a British passport.

Less than two weeks after the ending of the Winter Games, the sanitised facade of the Nazi state, which had been maintained for the duration of the Games, was starkly exposed. German troops marched into the demilitarised Rhineland region, in flagrant breach of the post-First World War Treaty of Versailles. It was against the backdrop of this worrying new political landscape in Europe that Foster returned home to his native Glasgow. A month after the Olympics, he would represent Scotland against England at the old Crossmyloof rink, on Titwood Road, on Saturday 14 March.

Scotland *v.* England, Glasgow, 14 March 1936. From left to right, standing: J.R. Gilmour (hon. secretary, SIHA), W.L. Macdonald (referee), P. McPhail, W.S. Montford, J.C. Kelly, J. Kenny (all Scotland), J. Coward (England), J. Fullerton, W. Fullerton (both Scotland), E.J. Ramus, J. Shannon (both England), R. McAlpine (Scotland), A. Dick (referee), G. Fraser (coach, SIHA). Seated: S. Cameron, R.O. Macdonald (both Scotland), C.A. Erhardt (England), J. Foster (Scotland), A. Child, J. Groome, E. Brenchley, A. Archer, J. Kilpatrick (all England). (Billy Fullerton archive)

As the hero of the Olympic triumph, he was very much the star attraction. The English team contained most of his Olympic teammates from the previous month, but the underdog Scots gained a hard-earned 1-1 draw in front of a capacity 3,000 crowd. A contemporary report stated that: 'Foster in goal played a heroic part by his magnificent work, time and again turning aside apparently certain scoring shots.'

With the Scots trailing to a 'Chirp' Brenchley goal, Foster turned the match late in the third period, as the *Glasgow Herald* recorded: 'All seemed lost for Scotland when Brenchley went clean through, but a spreadeagle save by Foster relieved matters.' This kept the Scots in with a shout, and 'Scotty' Cameron grabbed a late equaliser on a solo rush.

Foster's daughter was aware of his Glasgow 'homecoming':

> I remember Dad telling me that he was back in Glasgow after the Olympics, playing hockey. He went back to visit the place where the family had been staying before they went to Canada. He couldn't believe the conditions; he was absolutely blown away.
>
> The only time I was in Glasgow was in 1996, when we went over to the British Open at St Andrew's. I went round some of the museums and art galleries in Glasgow, and it was wonderful. I didn't know that my Dad was the first Scot to win a gold medal. I remember watching those women curlers from Scotland winning the gold medal in 2002, it's incredible.

In the autumn of 1936, Foster followed his mentor, Nicklin, to the newly-opened, 10,000-capacity, Harringay Arena in north London. Owned by the Greyhound Racing Association company, and modelled on Toronto's Maple Leaf Gardens, the Arena adjoined the Stadium which housed greyhound racing and speedway. The Arena was to be home to two new hockey clubs – the Greyhounds and the Racers, each liveried in blue and yellow – and it was reckoned that the English National League of this period in the latter 1930s provided the highest calibre of hockey outwith the NHL.

Jimmy Foster, Harringay Greyhounds, 1937/38. (Martin C. Harris archive)

With the reputation as the best goaltender in ice hockey following his Olympic heroics, Foster was well rewarded for his time with Harringay Greyhounds, as his daughter describes:

> He did get offers from the NHL, but at that point there wasn't the good safety net for the players. I remember seeing a contract from the Montreal Maroons, but beyond that I don't know what happened. By the standards of the time, it was big money in those days he was getting for playing in England.

It was big money indeed. With the maximum wage restricting top English footballers to a comfortable £8 per week, the ice hockey players of the English National League in the late 1930s earned around £12 per week. A major star such as Foster would probably have commanded £20. Some of Foster's colleagues from the Moncton Hawks had gone on to play in the NHL, but most astute observers were of a mind that Foster benefited better financially than any of them.

By this time, daughter Shirley was with her parents in London:

> I remember we lived in Richmond, on Cresswell Road, and then we moved back to Harringay, and we lived in a new apartment block on Green Lanes, down from the Arena;

> what you'd call flats. I vaguely recall a circular thing in the centre that cars could drive around. I remember the butcher boy would deliver, and the grocery girl and the milkman as well; that was quite a novelty! We had a coal fire in the living room, and electric heaters on the walls in the other rooms.
>
> I remember my Dad worked at the track next to the Arena, with the greyhounds, once in the summer. I remember my Mom and I going to watch the dogs once!
>
> Harringay was a fantastic arena. I skated there, and they had a restaurant, it was quite a posh place. It's sad to think that it's all gone now. Percy Nicklin was the coach. I remember Percy and his wife, Lil, they were good friends of my Mom and Dad; they would come up to the apartment in London to visit a lot.
>
> When we came back to Canada, we remained friendly. I remember Percy's wife visiting us in Winnipeg.
>
> Our son got Jeff Nicklin's electric train set, which was quite unique at that time. Jeff was Percy's son who was killed in action during the war.

Foster assisted Britain in retaining the European titles in the next two years, but the World crown was reclaimed by Canada in February 1937, when the tournament was held in London, at Harringay and Wembley.

Foster was in outstanding form in 1937, keeping a clean sheet in the first six games of the Championship. He was still unbeaten in the first two matches of the final round, as Britain defeated Switzerland 2-0 and Germany 5-0. The world title was lost, however, in controversial circumstances at Harringay, when Canada, represented by Kimberley Dynamiters, won 3-0. At one point during the heated match, with spectators hurling coins and programmes onto the ice, order was only restored when the Arena band struck up 'God Save the King'!

In February 1938, the Championships were held in Prague, in the famous rink located on Stvanice Island in the middle of the Vltava River. Great Britain finished top of their qualifying group, edging the USA on goal difference, with Foster again in fine form, having defeated Germany 1-0, Norway 8-0 and Latvia 5-1, but drawing 1-1 with the Americans.

The semi-final 'A' pool saw the British matched with Poland and Sweden. The Poles were defeated comfortably (7-1), and Sweden were narrowly beaten (3-2), as the British progressed to meet the host Czechoslovakians. A 1-0 victory set up a Canada-Great Britain final. The Canadians were represented by Sudbury Wolves and they proved too strong, winning 3-1.

Foster's last taste of international hockey came in the Zurich World Championships of 1939, and it was a British team now much less reliant on its Canadian-trained players. It finished a disappointing eighth, but this was actually better than either Foster or coach Nicklin had expected, as Frank Butler, legendary *Daily Express* sports journalist, wrote at the time:

> Goalminder Foster, skipper of the team, chuckled to me before he left London: 'Say, I'm hiring a kid in Switzerland at sixpence a day. He can pick the puck out of the net when I get tired – and he'll probably earn that sixpence.'

As it was, Foster only conceded 8 goals in Britain's 5 games, but it wasn't enough to earn qualification for the final round.

The team spirit of the much-maligned British squad was personified by their gutsy showing against Canada; represented by the highly fancied Trail Smoke Eaters, in the opening match of the semi-final round at Zurich, on 7 February 1939. The game remained scoreless until the final five minutes, when the Canadians scored four goals to give them a deserved, though flattering, victory. The result was all the more creditable from the British perspective, given that Jimmy Foster had broken a skate blade during the first period. Foster tied the blade together with a strap of his goal pads, and played the final two periods with this restriction.

A 1-0 defeat the next day to Germany ensured that Britain would not progress to the final pool. Thus Jimmy Foster's last match for Great Britain was a 0-2 defeat by Czechoslovakia, on the afternoon of Thursday 9 February 1939, on the open-air Dolder rink, high above Zurich.

In total, he played in thirty Olympic and World Championship matches for the British team over four years, posting shut-outs in an incredible 16 games.

Back in London, the season finished on a successful note, as he captained Harringay Greyhounds to an English National League and London Cup double, and gained an All Star 'B' team nomination. Foster and his family spent the summer of 1939 back in Winnipeg, amid the worries of the worsening international situation back in Europe. He was never to return to the land of his birth, and the outbreak of war with Germany, in September 1939, made him think back to the events in Garmisch three years earlier and his unease at being part of a team which had given the Nazi salute, as his daughter remembers:

> He said that even in 1936 it was obvious that things weren't as open as the Nazis were pretending. My Dad told me that he and some of his teammates had taken the hats from some SS, or storm troopers, they had met on the street. They put the hats on and were fooling around, but were told that it was a very stupid thing to do. He had Hitler's autograph, which he tore up the day war was declared!
>
> He went to Prague in 1938 for the World Championships. He said that it wasn't until he was in Prague and heard those Czechoslovakian people singing their national anthem, and you were carried away with the fervour and emotion, that he really understood about patriotism.
>
> We only came back to Winnipeg for the summer in 1939, as my Dad was to have played for Brighton in 1939/40. I remember that I was in school in London, and they were talking about evacuation. Mom and Dad went up to the school and told them that I didn't need to be included, as we'd go back to Canada if war broke out.
>
> I was only twelve when we came home to Canada from London. My late husband and I were visiting London a few years ago, and we went on the Underground. Seeing station names like Finsbury Park brought back such memories of those old 1930s tube trains!

Jimmy Foster was denied the opportunity of assisting the British in the defence of their Olympic title in 1940. Those Winter Games had originally been scheduled for Sapporo in Japan but, with the Japanese Empire engaged in a brutal war of colonisation in China since 1931, demands grew for a venue change. The International Olympic Committee bowed to international pressure in July 1938, re-assigning the games to St Moritz. However, a dispute between the Swiss organising committee and the IOC in June 1939 saw the venue changed once again. Ironically, had the 1940 Games gone ahead, they would've taken place back in Garmisch-Partenkirchen.

Having achieved 24 shut-outs in his four seasons of English National League hockey, Foster played out his career with three seasons back in Canadian senior hockey. He played 29 games for the Quebec Aces of the Quebec Senior League in 1939/40, as daughter Shirley remembers: 'When he played in Quebec, my mother went with him. I was in school in Winnipeg, and didn't go with them.'

'Doc' Brodrick, a Canadian who came to Britain to study medicine and played hockey for London-based Streatham, had watched Jimmy Foster play for the Quebec Aces. He described Foster's goaltending style in his 1951 book *Ice Hockey*:

> He would stop a high shot on the back of the stick hand and smother the puck with the other hand as it hit the glove. It demanded flawless timing and the way Jimmy did it with a graceful upsweep of both arms was pretty to watch. But then Jimmy had style.

Foster then moved to the Cape Breton Senior League, spending the 1940/41 season with the Glace Bay Miners, backstopping them in 38 regular season games (21 wins, 15 losses). Foster was one of four official imports allowed in the Cape Breton League, but Glace Bay

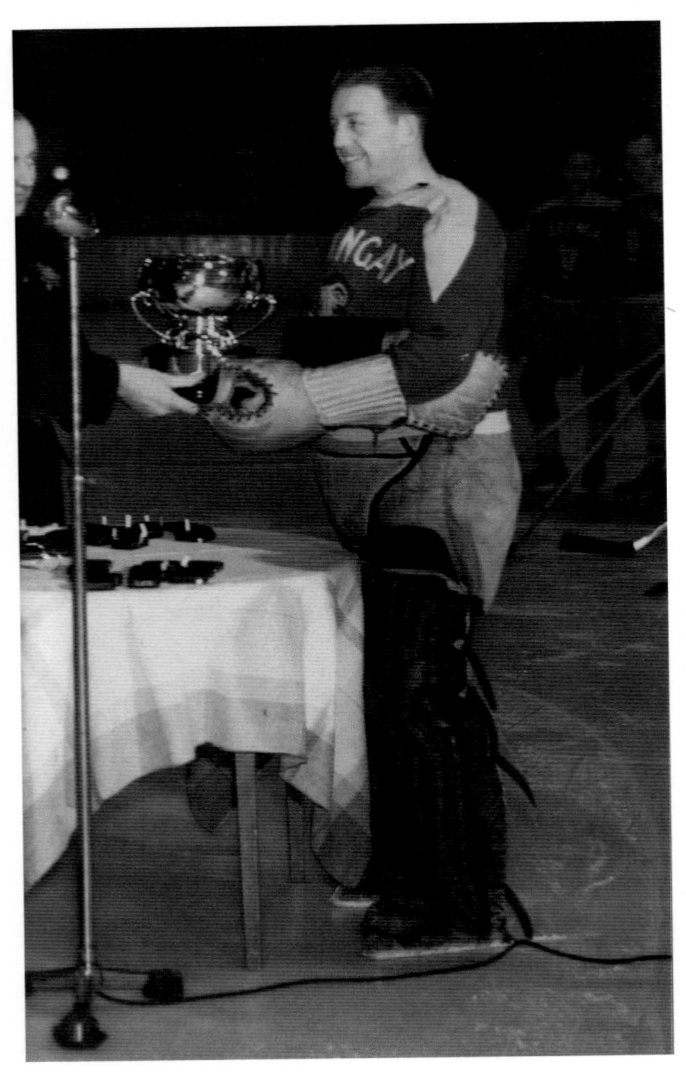

Jimmy Foster, as captain of Harringay Greyhounds, is presented with the London Cup, 1938/39. (Martin C. Harris archive)

manager Martin 'The Ape' MacDonald spared no expense in building his team, employing ten imported players, claiming that six of them were in the mining and steel town because of 'job transfers' from non-existent companies in other parts of Canada.

The League, however, would have its revenge on MacDonald – but at the expense of Jimmy Foster. Due to an administrative error, Foster was not included on the list of players submitted by Glace Bay as eligible for the play-offs. The duplicitous MacDonald, not wishing to be reliant on his inexperienced back-up netminder, gave the hapless reserve $100 and a train ticket to Montreal, telling the local press that he'd joined the army, thus allowing him to borrow an experienced 'keeper! Glace Bay went on to upset the favourites, Sydney Millionaires, with three straight wins. The Millionaires discovered MacDonald's nefarious subterfuge and, on appeal, had Glace Bay's series victory annulled.

The local rivalry between Glace Bay and Sydney, always fierce, reached new levels of intensity following the dispute. Jimmy Foster was not to be part of it, however, as he signed for North Sydney Victorias, also of the Cape Breton League for 1941/42, in what was to be his final season of hockey.

The Victorias were not a strong club, and Foster conceded 152 goals in 36 regular season games, followed by 26 in 7 play-off games. It was his poorest return, over a season, in twenty years of hockey. At thirty-six, perhaps age had finally caught up with him.

Foster returned to Winnipeg in 1942 to do war work in an aircraft factory, followed by many years as a travelling salesman across Canada's Midwest. Daughter Shirley thinks he played his last ever hockey match back in Winnipeg:

> I vaguely remember him playing an exhibition game during the war back in Winnipeg. I think that was the last hockey match he played in. We continued to live in Winnipeg, and during the war Dad worked in the MacDonald aircraft factory. After the war, he worked as a travelling salesman for T.H. Estabrook, selling tea, coffee, spices.
>
> I worked as a secretary at CPR, married at twenty-one, and in those days women had to give up work on marriage. My sister Pat also worked as a secretary, and also gave up after marriage, although we both went back to work years later. My brother, Jimmy, taught school after graduating from the University of Manitoba, but he died young too. My sister, Pat, passed away three years ago.
>
> Mom and Dad had five grandchildren, three from my sister, and two from me. My sister had three boys, and I had a boy and a girl, Bruce and Laurie. My brother had two children, but they were born after my Dad died.
>
> He was a very, very nice person. He was very fond of his family, he was a great man. We had a wonderful, close family relationship, especially for the age I was brought up in, because I could talk to him about anything.

Jimmy Foster's achievements were recognised with his induction to the British Ice Hockey Hall of Fame in 1950, but his hockey involvement had ended by that time, as his daughter relates:

> There were a couple of guys he kept in touch with from his hockey. Walter Monson was one, because he was in Winnipeg, another was Len Burrage, and Fran Heximer was another one.

A fit and healthy man, looking forward to an active retirement with his five grandchildren, Foster was cruelly stricken by cancer in late 1968, as his daughter remembers:

> He passed away with cancer on 4 January 1969, just before he was to retire. He died in hospital in Winnipeg. He was sixty-three. He was in really good physical condition when he was first diagnosed, and the illness took him quite quickly. I had married and moved to Vancouver at the time of his death.
>
> He was a terrific father, and a terrific grandfather to my two kids.

His prized Olympic gold medal is now in the safe possession of one of his grandchildren, as daughter Shirley describes:

> My father gave his Olympic gold medal to my sister's son, Rick Banks, in London, Ontario. Ricky was about eight or nine at the time when he asked Dad for it. Dad was happy to just give it to him.
>
> My late son, Bruce, got a couple of World Championship and European Championship medals, we've still got those. But we lost a lot of pictures and things in a flood at my sister's house some years ago. I remember a terrific picture in the *Daily Mirror*, when he played for Harringay, with my sister and myself watching.

Foster's widow, Pearl, was to survive him by thirteen years:

Mother died in 1982 in Vancouver. We had moved there, and she moved out and had an apartment. She stayed on there when we moved over to Victoria.

My late husband, Bob, thought Dad was the absolute living end. Bob was a chartered accountant, but had played Senior 'A' hockey and so admired Dad for his hockey achievements. Bob passed away in 1997, but we were always very grateful for what hockey gave to us.

My daughter Laurie works with autistic children, and my son-in-law is a tax accountant. My daughter and granddaughter figure skated, and my grandson Travis plays hockey. Travis is in a private school here in Victoria, and is totally wishing he could be a hockey player and is fascinated to know about his great-grandfather.

Sadly, Jimmy Foster is without honour in his native land, and it is astonishing that Foster's decisive contribution to the greatest British success in the history of the Winter Olympics has been overlooked by the Scottish Sports Hall of Fame since its inception in 2001.

His posthumous inclusion in the Manitoba Hockey Hall of Fame took place as long ago as March 1992. Hopefully, it will not be too long before his error of omission is righted by its Scottish equivalent. It would be a fitting tribute to the Scot who starred at 'Hitler's Games' more than seventy years ago.

Career Record (in English Professional Hockey)

	GP	W	L	T	Min	GA	SO	GAA
Jimmy Foster (Harringay Greyhounds)1937-1939	78	40	24	14	4,680	187	8	2.40
(Records unavailable for 1935-1937)								
Great Britain 1935-1939	30	22	5	3	–	22	16	0.73
Scotland 1935-1936	1	0	0	1	60	1	0	1.00

2

The Flying Mohawk: Billy Fullerton

The usual image created in the mind's eye by the term 'war graves' is one of identical stone headstones, stretching into the distance in the now-green fields of France and Flanders. So, it's difficult to reconcile that stereotypical picture with a municipal cemetery in the south-west corner of Glasgow.

Eastwood New Cemetery straddles the city boundary where Glasgow merges with Thornliebank in East Renfrewshire. Surprisingly, this relatively small, suburban cemetery contains over 200 graves looked after by the Commonwealth War Graves Commission, and reinforces the scale of the sacrifice made in two World Wars. The writer found himself there on a sunny day in early March 2005, with only the occasional dog walker for company amidst the neatly tended borders and gravel paths.

Your narrator was specifically interested in only one of these war graves and, after a lengthy search, the simple, rectangular headstone of grey granite was discovered. At the top, the emblem of the Royal Air Force is engraved, incorporating the Latin motto 'Per Ardua ad Astra' (through struggles to the stars). Underneath is the following inscription:

PILOT OFFICER
W. FULLERTON
PILOT
ROYAL AIR FORCE
17TH JANUARY 1941 AGE 27

At the bottom, there is a simple cross, and the phrase: 'At the going down of the sun and in the morning we will remember.'

It is the final resting place of Billy Fullerton, and preserves the memory of a young man who died in the service of his country. But Fullerton also deserves to be remembered for his sadly unrecognised achievements as one of Scotland's finest winter sportsmen, as both a Scotland and Great Britain ice hockey internationalist, as well as being the Scottish and British Speed Skating Champion. Not for nothing was he called 'The Fastest Man on Ice' and 'The Flying Mohawk'.

Sadly, if the name Billy Fullerton stirs any past echoes in Scotland today, they are likely to be those of the not-so-secret shame of sectarianism. The other, infamous, Billy Fullerton was leader of the eponymous Billy Boys; the notorious Protestant gang from Glasgow's Bridgeton of the 1920s, whose violent anti-Catholic bigotry found a wider outlet into the 1930s through membership of Oswald Moseley's British Union of Fascists.

The ice hockey-playing Billy Fullerton (no relation) from that same period of Glasgow's history is more deserving of remembrance than the distasteful activities of his namesake. If the term role model had been in use in the 1930s, it would certainly have applied to the young stockbroker's clerk from Newlands on Glasgow's south side. Not only was he a champion on

A young Billy Fullerton in a Mohawks uniform. (Billy Fullerton archive)

the ice, but as a Pilot Officer in the RAF he was to die in the service of his country during the Second World War.

Tall and slim-built, Fullerton was a fast right winger and excellent stick-handler, being noted for his clean play in an era when Scottish ice hockey was moving from an amateur recreation of the wealthy to a popular professional sport. It is a measure of Fullerton's abilities that he was able to develop as the standard of the sport improved, and could hold his own with the increasing number of paid Canadian imports. Fullerton was also a two-way player, and the *Ice Hockey World* noted that his backchecking was, 'as good as any Canadian'.

This is borne out by his performances for the British team at the 1939 World Championships in Zurich, with the *Ice Hockey World* of the time reporting on how the locals viewed the quality of the Great Britain team: 'In general, the Swiss press considers Foster, Dailley, Kelly and Fullerton are the players of international class…' His being bracketed in such company makes it a fair assumption that he must have been the finest British player of his era, as the first three named were all Canadian-developed players of the highest calibre; interestingly, both Foster and Kelly, like Fullerton, were Glaswegians.

Curiously, although Fullerton's ability kept apace as the standard of the sport increased dramatically, he still favoured an outdated skate throughout his career; the *Ice Hockey World* in January 1939 noted that he was, 'One of the few hockey players today who disdains hockey tubes for the old-fashioned "Automobile skate"…'

A contemporary of Fullerton's, ideally qualified to assess his talents, was Sid Montford. As a member of Glasgow's Kelvingrove team, Montford was a regular opponent of Billy Fullerton, who starred with the Mohawks, but he also played with him on a number of occasions for Scotland. Additionally, he had a unique critical perspective, being also a respected sports journalist (his son, Arthur, is now the elder statesman of Scottish sports broadcasting). Sid Montford paid the following tribute to Fullerton on his untimely death:

Billy was a universal favourite and was admired as much for his fine sense of sportsmanship as for his genius as a player. It was as the 'Flying Mohawk' that he became best known to the fans. His speed and dash on the right wing earned him many a brilliant goal. Billy shared in all the triumphs of the Mohawks team, under the captaincy of his brother John.

William Fullerton was born on 23 November 1913, at Darnley Mains Farm, Nitshill, then in Renfrewshire's Eastwood Parish. It has long since been swallowed up by Glasgow's expansion and a DIY warehouse now stands on the site of Fullerton's birthplace. The M77 motorway runs through what remains of the fields of the onetime farm.

He was the youngest of five children born to Alexander Fullerton and Jane Adams, who had married in Glasgow on Christmas Eve, 1902. His father was a dairyman, hailing from Pollokshaws Road on Glasgow's southside, while his mother was the daughter of a house painter, from nearby Nithsdale Road.

The Fullertons resided on Pollokshaws Road for several years, but by 1912 had moved to Darnley Mains Farm, where their father was the tenant farmer. By 1916 the family had moved again, to Paper Mill Farm on Earlspark Avenue, in the Newlands area of Glasgow. It was in this somewhat incongruous environment that Billy Fullerton grew up. The small dairy farm was set amidst Victorian and Edwardian terraces, and provided the products which were sold in the Fullerton's dairy outlet on Pollokshaws Road (this farm, too, is no more, with 1960s housing on Earlspark Avenue occupying the site).

Where Fullerton was educated remains a mystery. His elder sister, Jean, had received her primary education at nearby Langside School, before moving on to Shawlands Academy, but the school Admissions Register contains no details of Billy or his elder brothers, John and Alec. At that time, the school leaving age in Scotland was fourteen, and Ainsley Barwick, the husband of Billy Fullerton's niece, Lynne, thinks this is the age when the brothers completed their education: 'All the boys left school early, and didn't have any other education. Only Jean had her secondary education paid for.' But where Billy received his education is still a puzzle. His name doesn't appear on Langside School's 'Roll of Honour', listing those pupils killed in the Second World War, nor does it appear on similar memorials at Shawlands, Allan Glen's and Queen's Park Schools. This would indicate the strong possibility of his attending the former Holmlea Public School, a red sandstone building on Cathcart's Holmlea Road, the nearest school to his home. Unfortunately, the school's records no longer exist, so the speculation cannot be confirmed.

What is known is that he didn't enter the family dairy business on leaving school. Instead, he took up employment with a firm of stockbrokers, Messrs George Wingate & Sons, of West George Street in Glasgow's city centre, becoming an accredited stockbroker's clerk.

Around about the same time that the young Billy Fullerton was leaving school and entering the world of stocks and shares, work was ongoing at the new Scottish Ice Rink at Crossmyloof, Glasgow, less than a mile from the Fullerton family farm on Earlspark Avenue. This is where the Fullerton family would excel.

Glasgow's Scottish Ice Rink, or 'Crossmyloof' as it was more commonly known, first opened in January 1929, just a couple of months after Billy Fullerton's fifteenth birthday, and it was there that he developed his skating and ice hockey abilities, alongside his elder brothers, John and Alec. All three Fullerton brothers would represent Scotland at ice hockey during the 1930s, but it was the youngest sibling who was to have the greatest impact. The Crossmyloof rink possessed a massive ice pad, reputedly the largest in Europe at 225 feet by 97 feet, and seating for spectators in an upper balcony surrounding the ice.

In terms of ice hockey, the first Scottish League was competed for during 1929/30, with ten teams playing out of the Glasgow rink. The players were mainly wealthy individuals, many of whom had been introduced to the sport during winter holidays in the Swiss Alps. A small number of expatriate Canadians, based in the Glasgow area, augmented several of the participating teams. The Fullerton brothers, being the sons of a Pollokshaws dairy owner, were in the vanguard of the sport's widening appeal to Glasgow's middle classes.

John Fullerton, at twenty-six, the eldest of the three brothers, was a member of the Mohawks team which won the Scottish Championship that first season. Indeed John Fullerton played in the very first competitive Scottish League match, at Crossmyloof, on 4 Oct 1929, scoring Mohawks' goal in their 2-1 defeat by Bridge of Weir.

The development of young talent was not neglected, however, as the *Glasgow Herald* of 10 January 1930 reported: 'The invitation given to the enthusiastic young skaters of the Crossmyloof Rink, Glasgow to form a boys' club has not been long in being taken full advantage of.' The middle-class background of the aspirant hockey players can be gauged from the schools which, in the main, provided the players: Glasgow High School formed the Junior Mohawks; Queen's Park, Shawlands and Hutcheson's Grammar formed Junior Queen's, while Glasgow Academy and Kelvinside Academy supplied the Mohicans.

The sixteen-year-old Billy Fullerton was a member of Queen's, and it is likely that his first hockey match took place on Saturday 22 February 1930, as Glasgow's *Evening Times* noted: 'The first of a series of boys' League matches for the silver puck which it has been decided to present to the winners was played at Crossmyloof, Glasgow this morning.' (Queen's beat the Sioux 1-0).

A Canadian, Andy Gray, writing in the *Ice Hockey World* of November 1938, looked back on the start of junior hockey in Glasgow, and provides an insight into the formative years of Fullerton's ice hockey:

> ...We got a league of four junior teams going. I was the only Canadian and was considered pretty hot...
>
> In Scotland I helped – although they won't admit it now – stars such as Joe Collins, Billy Fullerton, Billy Turnbull, Donald Edwards, Kenny Hurll and many others, get a start in the game. Later we had a coach, Gordon Rowley, who is now a doctor in Edinburgh.
>
> Despite conditions we made fast progress. We were given practices from 8 till 8.30 on a Saturday morning at the price of a shilling. We didn't mind paying this, for later on, during the school children's skating hour, we could swagger round in hockey sweaters and receive the worship of the fair sex... but that's another story.
>
> We had to buy our own equipment, and in most cases it was inferior. It had to be because hockey stuff cost a lot in Glasgow then. We made our own pads, pants, and our mothers made us sweaters and stockings. Some fellows had hockey skates, most had figure skates.

Despite his later connections with the Mohawks club of his elder brother, Billy's first games in Scottish senior hockey were with Queen's as a sixteen year old. Indeed, his first recorded appearance came early in the second season of Crossmyloof hockey, when he was one of Queen's three substitutes in their 3-1 loss to Glasgow Skating Club on Tuesday 21 October 1930.

His burgeoning talent was first noticed against the strong, and hitherto unbeaten, Bridge of Weir side, in a Mitchell Trophy match, on Friday 12 December 1930. The *Glasgow Herald* noted that '...Bridge of Weir began full of confidence, but they received a rude shock when young Fullerton took advantage of slackness on Rowley's part to give Macfie a hard drive to save... For Queen's, Tingley, Fullerton, and Bazin were outstanding.'

Fullerton's development at this time was no doubt assisted by playing alongside several Canadians in the Queen's team, notably Art Tingley and A.S. Bazin, who both represented Scotland. These itinerant Canucks happened to be in Glasgow, either studying or working; they had not been imported for the purposes of playing hockey, as the sport was still a wholly amateur affair at Crossmyloof at that time.

Billy received his first representative honour having just turned seventeen, being chosen for the Glasgow Select to play the West of Scotland Select on Friday 2 January 1931.

Over the next few seasons, the standard of play gradually improved, as the number of teams reduced through amalgamation, and capacity crowds of 3,000 were drawn to the Crossmyloof rink on a regular basis. The Scottish National League was, essentially, a Glasgow house league,

At Loch Leven, January 1933. From left to right: Billy Fullerton, Jean Fullerton and Johnny Fullerton. (Billy Fullerton archive)

with all the clubs based at Crossmyloof; the introduction of a succession of professional Canadian coaches, however, helped the development of new local talent.

Fullerton's further development was also noted early in the 1931/32 season, with the *Glasgow Herald* commenting '...but Fullerton – a greatly improved player – was the most prominent for Queen's', who defeated Glasgow Skating Club 4-0 on Friday 23 October 1931.

His final year with the Queen's club was 1932/33, and they opened that season in unusual circumstances, defeating Kelvingrove 3-2, whilst icing only a goalie and four skaters! The *Herald* reported that '...Fullerton and Tingley were so brilliant in attack that the absence of a third forward was minimised to a large extent... Fullerton cut right through and scored a magnificent goal.' This was Queen's second goal, tying the game at 2-2 early in the third period. Interestingly, Billy was opposed by his other elder brother, Alec, who was on the Kelvingrove blueline.

Fullerton first appeared for Scotland on 26 November 1932 at Crossmyloof, just three days after his nineteenth birthday. The opponents were the Edmonton Superiors, touring Europe in preparation for the 1933 World Championships in Prague, when they would represent Canada. A contemporary newspaper report described the contest as:

> ...one of the finest games seen at the Scottish Ice Rink, Glasgow... While there was plenty of heavy body-checking, the game was clean, and not a single player came under the ban of Referee Hugh Reid. The rink was packed, and from the first face-off the thrills crowded one on top of another.

The Scots made a sensational start, taking the lead inside the first minute, when Johnny Fullerton fired home a rebound given up by the Edmonton goaltender from an Art Brady shot. The powerful Edmonton squad, who would go on to claim the Silver Medal at the World Championships, came back strongly to earn a comfortable 8-1 victory. The Scots were not disgraced, however, and the press noted that 'young Billy Fullerton made no mistakes.' The Scotland side was: Dave Cross (Kelvingrove); Gordon Rowley (Juniors, Captain); Jock Gilmour (Bears); Johnny Fullerton (Mohawks); Dr Art Brady (Mohawks); Jackie Easton (Glasgow University); Billy Fullerton (Queen's); Art Tingley (Queen's); and Johnny Campbell (Kelvingrove).

With the disbandment of Queen's, Billy teamed up with brother John's Mohawks for 1933/34, assisting them to a 2-0 win over Juniors in his debut on 17 October 1933.

There was a decidedly familial feel to the Scotland side which met London's Richmond Hawks, at Crossmyloof, on 29 December 1934. All three Fullerton brothers were in the line-up, and all did well, despite the Scots' 8-1 defeat by the Canadian-dominated visitors. Scotland's goal was scored by eighteen-year-old Pete Stevenson, a local lad who had learned the game in Port Arthur, Ontario. He was to earn a berth on the Great Britain team which won a Bronze Medal at the 1935 World Championships in Davos.

Billy Fullerton didn't get to the World Championships, but he did make his first appearance for Great Britain against the Canadian side which had picked up the World crown of 1935. The Winnipeg Monarchs played their fifty-fifth, and final, match of their four-month European tour against a Great Britain team, at Crossmyloof, on Friday 15 March 1935. Although Winnipeg won 7-2, *The Scotsman* described how 'A crowd of 3,000 witnessed one of the most stirring ice hockey contests ever seen at the Scottish Ice Rink, Glasgow... The game was clever, fast, and clean. Remarkable speed and uncanny accuracy in stickhandling and shooting were the salient features of a really notable game.'

Billy was on international duty again – but this time for Scotland – the following night, when he and his brother Johnny were in the Scotland side which went down 6-3 to England at Wembley's Empire Pool.

Johnny and Billy Fullerton were the mainstays of the Mohawks side which won the Scottish National League in 1935/36 and 1936/37 (although Alec didn't make the switch from Kelvingrove to join his brothers until 1937/38).

Mohawks defeated Kelvingrove 3-0 on 17 January 1936 in the replayed 'President's Pucks' final, with the *Herald* describing how 'W. Fullerton used his speed on the wing, and sent a good pass to Welch, who scored.' Billy himself sealed the victory with Mohawks' third goal late in the game. Two months later, on 14 March 1936, he was a member of the Scotland team, backstopped by Britain's Gold medal-winning Olympian Jimmy Foster, which tied 1-1 with England at Crossmyloof, with the *Daily Record* noting that '...Jim Kenny and Billy Fullerton were outstanding' for the home side.

A week later, on 21 March 1936, he netted three of the 'Scottish Canadians' goals in a 5-5 tie at Manchester, with the *Record* again commenting that the '...outstanding player for the Glasgow team was undoubtedly Billy Fullerton, the British speed skating champion, who at times led the Englishmen a merry dance.'

The Olympic success of the Great Britain ice hockey team at the 1936 Winter Games in Garmisch-Partenkirchen, together with the opening of the large London ice arenas at Wembley, Harringay and Earl's Court, undoubtedly led to a significant rise in public interest in this 'new' sport of ice hockey.

Billy Fullerton's performances in March 1936, particularly against England, prompted London's Earl's Court Rangers to offer the twenty-three-year-old winger an immediate

Billy Fullerton with the Scottish Outdoor Mile Speed Skating Championship Cup, 1935. (Billy Fullerton archive)

professional contract. He was reluctant to give up his job with a Glasgow stockbroking firm, however, and he declined the offer from the Empress Hall outfit.

In Scotland, the growing interest in ice hockey manifested itself with the opening in October 1936 of the new Central Scotland Ice Rink in Perth, having cost £26,000 to complete. It would be the precursor of a series of similar small arena-type rinks across Scotland in the next three years. The Fullerton brothers were soon to be in great demand as the sport's popularity was to spark a plethora of new Scottish teams desperate for players.

Billy played in the first match at the Perth rink, on 1 October 1936, with the *Perthshire Advertiser* noting that he '...was outstanding, and his bursts of speed were always dangerous to the Kelvingrove defence.' Mohawks lost 2-1 to rivals Kelvingrove in a friendly encounter, with Johnny Fullerton on the scoresheet for 'hawks.

His electrifying pace was still his greatest asset the following season, with *The Scotsman* describing Mohawks 2-0 win over rinkmates Mustangs on 21 December 1937:

> W. Fullerton, the speed-skating champion, was again in great form, and repeatedly left his opponents standing, as he flashed through. He engineered the opening goal... threw the Mustang defence out of position and passed nicely to Kenny, who scored with a first-time shot.

Another example of Fullerton's standing in the sport was his selection to the Scottish Select touring team which played several matches in Germany over Christmas and New Year 1937/38. Fullerton was the only Scottish-trained player in the thirteen-strong squad.

The fifteen-year-old Gerry Collins was a member of the Junior Mohawks in 1938 and during the summer of 2005 he remembered Billy Fullerton: 'He was a good player, was fast and could stickhandle. He wasn't one of my mates, as he was about ten years older than me.'

1938 also saw the second expansion of the sport in Scotland, with new rinks opening in Dundee, Kirkcaldy and Falkirk, and this predicated the ending of Billy's connections with Mohawks and the Crossmyloof rink.

Billy and his brother Alec were persuaded to join the newly-formed Fife Flyers in September 1938, in readiness for the opening of the Kirkcaldy rink the following month. Alan Murphy was, at that time, a fifteen-year-old schoolboy in nearby Burntisland. He and his parents became regular spectators during the first season of hockey at Kirkcaldy. He soon took up the sport, and made a few appearances for the post-war Flyers before his work as a Mine Surveyor took him way from Fife. He was good enough, however, to take part in trials for the 1948 British Olympic team and in early 2005 he recalled Billy Fullerton's season with the Flyers:

> Billy Fullerton was a very fast skater. He didn't get involved in fights; he was a clean player – not a dirty player. He was quite a tall chap, and not very well made, slim-built.
>
> His brother, Alec Fullerton, was a defenceman, and played alongside Jack Stover and George Horn with the first Flyers. Alec was a heavier build than Billy.

As well as his new commitments with the Flyers, Billy had other flying obligations in 1938. The increasing threat posed by Nazi Germany had prompted the British government to initiate the Civil Air Guard Scheme in the summer of 1938 in an effort to train pilots for possible future military service. Fullerton was the first Scot to pass the Civil Air Guard examinations, and trained as a pilot at the Scottish Flying Club's Moorpark aerodrome in Renfrew. The *Daily Record* commented that '…it was remarked that his astonishing sense of balancing and timing – assets which made him an ice hockey star – marked him out as a "natural" airman.'

September 1938 also saw Billy admitted to the Incorporation of Fleshers, a prestigious charitable body of the Trades House of Glasgow, through his father's sponsorship. The entrance fee was £5, a substantial sum in 1938.

Fullerton's Kirkcaldy career didn't have the best of starts, as he sustained a broken collar bone following a hefty body-check in a pre-season practice. He thus missed the Flyers first game, a 5-2 reverse on 30 September 1938 in the inaugural match at Dundee's Kingsway rink; the injury meant he was also an absentee the following day, when Dundee spoiled the Kirkcaldy rink's opening night with a 4-1 victory.

His delayed debut for Flyers came on 11 October 1938, ironically, on his home ice at Crossmyloof, where Fife picked up their first point in a 2-2 tie with Kelvingrove. Billy was on Flyers' first line alongside Canadians Norm McQuade and Len McCartney.

His first goal for Fife came on 20 October 1938 at Kirkcaldy, netting a twelfth-minute opener in an 8-1 rout of Kelvingrove: 'Billy Fullerton scored a lovely goal, picking up Norm McQuade's shot, taking it behind the net, and squeezing it past Cross', according to the *Ice Hockey World*.

Elder brother John, who had hung up his skates to become Mohawks President, came out of his brief retirement aged thirty-five, firstly helping out Perth Panthers before joining the new Falkirk Lions in December 1938.

Over at Kirkcaldy, Billy's success with the Flyers continued. Fife secured the Anderson Trophy at Kirkcaldy on 19 January 1939, defeating Perth 1-0. Fullerton broke the deadlock after fifty-five minutes, following up on a George Horn shot to slot the rebound past 'Scotty' Milne in the Perth net.

His fine form saw him honoured with selection for the Great Britain team in the 1939 World Championships in Zurich. This was a belated recognition for Scotland's finest player, as a dispute between the British and Scottish Associations had previously denied him the opportunity of appearing on the World stage with the GB team.

Great Britain *v.* Germany on Zurich's Dolder rink, 8 February 1939. Jimmy Foster is on his knees in goal and the other dark-shirted British players are, from left to right: Bob Wyman, Tommy McInroy, Gordon Dailley, Billy Fullerton and Jimmy Kelly. (*Ice Hockey World* photo)

Billy was to score on his British debut on Zurich's outdoor Dolder rink, during a 3-1 win over Belgium, on the evening 4 February 1939. It was a period of transition for Great Britain, with the phasing out of the Canadian-trained players who had secured the Olympic title three years earlier. It was not to be a successful tournament for the British, who failed to retain their European title. One positive aspect was the performance of Britain's first forward line, centred by Wembley's Glasgow-born Canadian Jimmy Kelly, alongside Flyers' Billy Fullerton and fellow Scot Tommy McInroy (sadly, war was only a matter of months away, and it would claim the lives of both Kelly and Fullerton).

Fullerton certainly showed the London media that his previous absence from the British team was unjustified. The BBC's Stewart Macpherson, writing on GB's 0-2 loss to Czechoslovakia on 9 February 1939 for the *Daily Sketch*, reported that:

> The British team gave a plucky display and paced by Fullerton, of the Scottish League, they gave the Czechs many anxious moments... To say that the British team has surprised their critics is to put it mildly. No one, including myself, ever thought that they would do as well as they have done. Fullerton gave a grand display today and was ably supported by the three National League players, Dailley, Kelly and Foster.

Fullerton was unlucky not to double his goal tally for the tournament against the Czechs when, with Britain trailing by a goal, he rounded the Czech goalminder but shot against the post.

The British team, having failed to qualify for the final pool, decided to withdraw from the Pool to determine fifth to eighth. Sid Montford, in the *Sunday Mail* of 12 February 1939, revealed he received:

> ...a letter from Billy Fullerton who says the British team, after their exertions in the Championships, were going up to Engelberg for three days to try their hand at ski-ing. He remarks that he and his Scottish colleagues are having a glorious time amid sunshine and snow.

It certainly benefited Fullerton, as Glasgow's *Evening News* noted that a 'sun-tanned and fit Billy Fullerton' arrived back in Glasgow on 14 February 1939.

Fullerton's final match for Fife Flyers was a 5-2 victory over Perth Panthers at Kirkcaldy on 27 April 1939. The *Ice Hockey World* noted that 'Outstanding in a well-balanced team were Kerr, Stover, Billy Fullerton, and McCartney.'

With the new Ayr rink having opened the previous month, the *Sunday Mail*'s Sid Montford predicted that 'Bill Fullerton, Mickey Shires and 'Biff' Smith are all likely to be Ayr Raiders next season.' Indeed Fullerton, guesting for Perth Panthers, played at the Ayr rink on 3 May 1939, notching two of Perth's goals in a 5-3 exhibition loss to Dundee Tigers. It was, however, to be his only appearance at Ayr, as his RAF commitments were to preclude him from joining the newly formed Raiders later that year.

Fullerton's sporting prowess on skates was not confined solely to hockey. His speed-skating career had run in tandem with his ice hockey, the sport having been introduced to Crossmyloof in October 1930. A stylish competitor, he first claimed the Scottish outdoor mile title at Loch Leven in 1935, and retained the title on 15 February 1936, with a Sunday tabloid featuring a front-page photo of him being carried shoulder-high off the ice. The skating Fullerton family could boast two other champions: elder brother John won the Scottish half-mile outdoor title in 1933, and sister Jean was the Scottish Ladies Champion.

Billy Fullerton first challenged for the British One Mile Indoor Championship in May 1935, but was runner-up to the Australian champion, Ken Kennedy. Fullerton's revenge, and the highpoint of his speed skating career, came on 29 February 1936, when he won the British One Mile Indoor Championship at Streatham, London in three minutes and thirteen seconds. Leading throughout, he finished six yards ahead of runner-up H.V. Tipper of Aldwych to

Pilot Officer Fullerton, at home on leave, 1940. (Billy Fullerton archive)

claim the Hewett Challenge Cup. His main rival Kennedy, surprisingly, had been eliminated in a qualifying heat. Fullerton's winning time was good, considering that a public skating interval had badly cut up the ice prior to the final. His success was all the more commendable, given that he had only been practising indoor speed skating for two weeks prior to the finals due to hockey commitments. The Crossmyloof Speed Skating Club honoured him with honorary life membership after his British triumph.

The following year, Kennedy regained the title at London's Harringay Arena, with Fullerton disappointed at a fourth place finish.

Twenty years were to elapse following Fullerton's success before another Scot would capture the British Indoor Championship; Ayr's Alex Connel taking the title in 1956. A fund was set up in 1946 to raise funds for the purchase of a speed skating trophy in Fullerton's memory. The Scottish Ice Hockey Association donated an initial £16, a significant figure then, and a mark of the esteem in which Fullerton was held. The William Fullerton Trophy was awarded to the winners of a three-mile inter-club relay championship.

With the coming of war in September 1939, Fullerton enlisted into the Royal Air Force Volunteer Reserve on 19 September 1939. The following day he was accepted for immediate pilot training. His RAF record describes him as being 5ft 10in, having brown hair and brown/hazel eyes and a thirty-four inch chest. A scar on his left cheek is noted; possibly a result of a hockey injury?

His sporting interests were now a secondary consideration, but he still managed to fit in some ice hockey at the Brighton rink, scoring for Sussex Tigers in a 4-5 loss to Earls Court Marlboroughs on 12 May 1940.

Following training on Tiger Moths and Oxfords, he was granted a commission as Pilot Officer on 19 October 1940 and commenced night bomber training.

His last recorded ice hockey match came in late 1940, as described by Sid Montford in January 1941:

> His last appearance on Scottish ice was a month or two ago when he scored five goals for a service team against the Paisley Pirates at the Paisley stadium. The crowd gave him a magnificent reception.

On 17 January 1941, Pilot Officer Fullerton was at the controls of a twin-engine Whitley bomber which was approaching RAF Abingdon, near Oxford, in a snowstorm. An engine had cut out due to icing, and two crew members safely baled out. The aircraft, however, crashed on the Wooton Road, next to the airfield, killing the remaining four airmen, including Billy Fullerton. He was aged twenty-seven.

His funeral took place on the afternoon of 21 January 1941, at New Eastwood Cemetery. His elder brothers, who were also his ice hockey teammates, were two of the eight pall-bearers. John Fullerton, of Mohawks and Scotland fame, was a Timber Merchant then serving as a Sub-Lieutenant in the Royal Naval Volunteer Reserve. He passed away in February 1991 at Mudeford in Dorset, aged eighty-seven; Alec Fullerton, an original Fife Flyer and also a Scotland internationalist, was a Demolition Contractor, and died aged thirty-eight, in February 1947, at Greenock in Renfrewshire.

It is a terrible irony that Billy Fullerton, the man known as 'The Flying Mohawk', and whose last club was the Fife Flyers, was to die tragically in a flying accident. The irony is sadly compounded in that the death of Scotland's outstanding skating sportsman was attributable to 'icing'.

Career Record (in World Championships)

	GP	G	A	Pts	PiM
Billy Fullerton					
Great Britain 1939	5	1	0	1	Unknown

3

The Kalinsky Prospect: Joe Collins

When examining the best of Scottish ice hockey over the past eighty years, it is noticeable that there is a disproportionate number of fine defencemen in comparison to clever forwards. Granted, there have been outstanding Scottish playmakers and goalscorers, such as Billy Fullerton, Marshall Key, Jimmy Spence and Bert Smith and, of more recent vintage, Tony Hand, Ronnie Wood, Scott Neil and Colin Shields.

But consider the quality of Scottish defensive talent to have represented Great Britain: 'Tuck' and 'Tiny' Syme, Lawson Neil, Johnny Carlyle, Bill Sneddon, Jimmy Mitchell and Joe Brown – a 'Magnificent Seven' who emerged to brighten that austere post-Second World War era, when twelve-player rosters were dominated by ten paid Canucks.

Yet there is one man always overlooked, who was, for a too brief spell in the late 1930s, at the vanguard of this outstanding crop of home-bred blueliners – Glasgow's Joe Collins. His hockey career ended prematurely with the outbreak of war in 1939, when he was aged just twenty-four. But his impact was considerable, and his abilities deserve belated recognition.

After all, this was a man whose career had begun in Crossmyloof's Corinthian dawn, before blossoming briefly at a time when Scottish ice hockey was developing into a hard, competitive circuit stocked with Canadian pros. A man, too, who was described by Sid Montford, writing in the *Daily Record* back in January 1939, as 'to my mind, the best ice hockey player ever developed in this country.' Montford was referring to Scotland, but Collins' reputation has a greater endorsement, provided by Bob Giddens, Canadian Editor of the *Ice Hockey World,* who stated in December 1938 that '...he was of the opinion that Joe Collins is probably the best player Britain has ever produced.'

A name like Joe Collins is suggestive of origins within the thousands of Irish immigrants to nineteenth-century Scotland. It is misleading, however, as Joe's family roots lay not in the west of Ireland, but some 1,500 miles from Glasgow in Eastern Europe.

Joe was born Joseph Kalinsky, on 12 September 1915, in a tenement flat at 93 Gorbals Street, Glasgow; a younger son for Solomon Kalinsky and Golda Pockerofski, who had married in London in 1904. His father was born Solomon (or Shama) Kagarlitsky in the village of Kovshevata in the Ukraine, some sixty-five miles south of Kiev, in 1882. The Kagarlitskys were a Jewish family in the then czarist Russian Empire, where anti-Semitism manifested itself in brutal pogroms, prompting massive Jewish emigration to Western Europe and the USA. Solomon Kagarlitsky was one of these emigrants, and he moved to London as a young man, where his surname became modified to Kalinsky.

He worked for a number of years in the cap-making industry, before moving north to Glasgow in 1912, setting up his own cap-making business in a cramped Oxford Street workshop in the city's Gorbals area.

A newspaper caricature of Joe Collins, in his Kelvingrove uniform, 1938/39. (*Sunday Mail*)

With increased demand brought about by the First World War, Solomon Kalinsky established factory premises in the Renfrewshire town of Barrhead, just outside Glasgow, to accommodate increased production. With the surname now anglicised to Collins, the family relocated in 1916 to a house in Renfrewshire, next to Kennishead Station, near Thornliebank. The young Joe Kalinsky – or Joseph Hyman Collins as he'd become – grew up in a then-rural Kennishead, in the new family home named Goldina. Now part of suburban Glasgow, five twenty-two-storey tower blocks stand on the site of the Collins' family's former home. As befitted the son of a now-prosperous middle-class family, Collins was educated at the fee-paying High School of Glasgow, then sited in the city centre at Elmbank Street.

Joe's younger cousin, Gerry Collins, was to follow him at Crossmyloof, representing Scotland at ice hockey in the post-war period. He retains fond memories of his elder cousin:

> Everybody knew Joe Collins – he was the kindest person I'd ever known, I never heard anyone say a bad word about him.
>
> He was brought up at Kennishead; I remember there were five big houses down the lane there, at the railway station. I believe he had a huge operation when he was little, and was a tender young man and was very ill.
>
> Joe and I were as close as any two fellows could be – we went on holiday a lot together. The Collins family were as close as a bunch of bananas! There were three girls and three boys in Joe's family. Moira was the youngest; Alf, his elder brother, was a GP. Moira and his other two sisters – Ann and Sarah – were all heavily involved in charity work.

Joe had played rugby union at Glasgow High School but, due to a lung problem, had been advised by his doctor to give it up as being too strenuous – so he took up ice hockey as a replacement!

In 1929, the newly opened Scottish Ice Rink conveniently adjoined Crossmyloof station, just a couple of stops by train from Joe's Kennishead home. Gerry Collins recalled that time:

> Skating was the in thing – it was new. I should imagine that was how it developed for Joe (as he would have been thirteen when the Crossmyloof rink opened.) I was eight years younger.
>
> Joe played for Kelvingrove. He was my idol, and I started playing more or less as soon as I could skate. The whole thing was going to watch Joe play, that's what got me playing. On a Saturday morning, when the juniors were having a game, four or five of us would play with a puck in a corner. I was about twelve at the time. I'd be going to the rink at 6a.m. on a Saturday morning, then away out to Bishopriggs to play rugby for Allan Glen's School, so that by the time I went home in the afternoon I was exhausted. So I gave up rugby and concentrated on the hockey.
>
> Joe was probably one of the toughest, not roughest, on the ice. He was a good defenceman and a great body-checker; he stood on the blueline and tried to bounce people, a strong, strong defenceman. He was strong on his skates, but he wasn't a stickhandler or scorer, by any means. But that was the way the game was then, defencemen defended.
>
> Joe was so popular, he was the player on the ice most loved by the spectators; and he was built like a battleship. Rest assured that anybody that came near him was flattened!

The first published record of Joe Collins playing ice hockey is a *Glasgow Herald* report of a junior match at Crossmyloof, on Tuesday 30 December 1930, between Andrew Gray's team (Queen's Juniors) and Jack Johnstone's team (Mohawks Juniors). The fifteen-year-old 'J H Collins' was a substitute for Gray's team, which triumphed 1-0, with the *Herald* noting that, 'The keenness of the young puck-chasers was the feature of the game… Several were smart individually, but the lack of combined effort was always evident.'

His progress can be measured almost a year later in a report of another junior match on 6 November 1931. The 'A' Team defeated the 'B' Team 3-0, with the sixteen-year-old 'J H Collins' scoring two of the goals.

A left-hand shot, the young Collins was playing as a forward at that time, and had already been introduced to senior hockey with Kelvingrove of the Scottish League. Exactly a week after his brace of goals in the junior match he was on the scoresheet for Kelvingrove in their 2-1 loss to Queen's, as a contemporary report described: 'Kelvingrove scored first, Collins putting the puck past Carty from close range.' His linemates on that Kelvingrove team of 1931/32 were Sid Montford and Johnny Campbell. The 'grove goaltender was the Scottish internationalist Dave Cross, a Glasgow policeman who turned to refereeing in the post-war years, as did another member of that Kelvingrove team, forward Bert Gemmell.

On 4 December 1931, he was included in a Kelvingrove and Bearsden select team, which lost 0-5 to the Scottish international team, who were preparing for the match with England the following week (he was on a Kelvingrove line with Sid Montford and Ken Hurll).

Collins' defensive capabilities, however, had already been spotted. *The Bulletin*, reporting on Kelvingrove's 2-1 win over Bridge of Weir on Friday 22 January 1932, commented that 'The defence, Andy Dick and young Joe Collins are a… steady pair.' Interestingly, it also noted that 'The two juniors, Collins and Hurll, "mixed it" with the best and gave as much as they got.'

He was obviously relishing his new role on the blueline, as *The Bulletin* reported in February 1932: 'Young Collins is a great little defence player, who uses his head, and, besides being fast and able to check well, is blessed with a liberal dash of "devil".' This was emphasised in Kelvingrove's 4-1 defeat of Bearsden on 19 February 1932, with *The Bulletin* stating that 'Collins again heavily checked Adams – too heavily for the referee's liking – and he was given time to "reflect" on the boards.'

Joe Collins, February 1939. (*Glasgow Evening News* photo)

A team comprising of Crossmyloof's best junior talent entered the senior Scottish League in October 1932, mentored by Canadian medical student Gordon Rowley, who partnered the seventeen-year-old Joe Collins on the blueline.

After two seasons with Juniors, Collins joined Dennistoun Eagles for the 1934/35 season, and was first selected for Scotland in December 1934. He was originally to have made his international debut against Wembley Canadians, in London, on 22 December that year. He and Alec Fullerton were selected as the Scottish defencemen, with contemporary reports mentioning that Bridge of Weir's international defensive pairing of M.D. Brennan and W.G. Macdonald were unable to travel because of their Edinburgh University studies. It transpired, however, that the Bridge of Weir men were available, so Joe Collins had to make way.

He had only a week to wait, however, before pulling on a Scotland sweater. London's Richmond Hawks came north to Crossmyloof on Saturday 29 December 1934 to face a confident Scotland team. Unfortunately, the Scots were disadvantaged by the unexpected absence of 'Scotty' Milne, the Glasgow-born, Canadian-trained goaltender who had returned to his native city from Prince Albert a few weeks earlier with a reputation primarily as a football goalkeeper (he had trained with Glasgow Rangers).

According to the *Evening Times*, 'The Scots gave a plucky display, but Billy Turnbull, the 17-year-old 'keeper, called in to substitute for Milne, found the occasion a little too much for him.' The Canadian-dominated Richmond outfit won 8-1, with Hymie McArthur grabbing four goals; for Scotland, according to the *Evening Times*, '...Collins and the Fullertons came out best on the evening's showing.'

Joe joined the Glasgow University team for 1935/36, aged twenty, but he wasn't a student, as his cousin Gerry recalls:

> Joe didn't study at Glasgow University; he went from school into the family business. I was invited to play for Cambridge University ice hockey team once after the war, but I never

> studied there! In the same way as that happened to me, Joe would have been invited to play for the Glasgow University team.

It was another example of the rationalisation process taking place in the then Crossmyloof-based Scottish League. With a reduced number of teams, the better players – like Collins – were in demand, lesser players dropped out, and the standard continued to improve.

His first match for 'The Students', on 15 October 1935, was a 5-1 loss to Mohawks. Despite this, *The Scotsman* was able to report on 'J Collins's defensive work being a feature of the match.' He had his first goal for his new club a week later, scoring from close in during the University's 5-0 defeat of Crossmyloof Lions.

Collins returned to Kelvingrove for 1936/37, netting for 'grove in the opening match at the new Perth rink in a friendly defeat of Mohawks, his goal being set up by Canadian Les Tapp, coach of the new Perthshire Panthers (as they were originally named, before dropping the 'shire').

Ironically, with the league's expansion from its Glasgow starting point, Collins became a love-to-hate opponent for the new audience in Perth. After a joust with Les Tapp in early 1937, the *Perthshire Advertiser* dubbed Joe 'Public Enemy No.1.' While the adoption of American phraseology, obviously borrowed from Hollywood gangster movies of the period, is an interesting social history aside in the context of a transatlantic sport's introduction to 1930s Scotland in tandem with other American cultural influences, it is also confirmation of Collins' status as a player feared and respected by opponents.

His popularity with the Perth public would not have been improved with Kelvingrove's annexation of the Coronation Cup on 30 April 1937, on Perth ice. A running commentary was broadcast on the BBC's Scottish Service, and Collins gave 'grove an early lead against Mohawks. The game finished 1-1, but Jack Johnstone won the cup for Kelvingrove with a goal in the second extra period.

Like his contemporary Billy Fullerton, Collins thrived as the standard of Scottish hockey improved. Going in to the 1938/39 season, he and fellow Scot Bill Turnbull, the goaltending dental student, were the only non-Canadians in the Kelvingrove line-up. Twenty-three-year-old Collins partnered Bert Forsythe on the 'grove defence that year, in what was to be the peak of his hockey career. Though linked with a move to the newly-formed Falkirk Lions, he remained an amateur, loyal to Kelvingrove and the Crossmyloof rink.

His cousin Gerry, though referring to his own experiences in post-war hockey, offers an insight to the rather blurred amateur/professional status of Scottish ice hockey of the time:

> They called us juniors; I was never too happy with that. We were amateurs. I remember at a select game, they handed me an envelope. I said, 'What's in that?', and was told it was 'wages for playing.' I told them that I was an amateur, and wouldn't take it. I was playing golf at the time as well, and didn't want to affect my amateur status. The other players weren't very happy with me; they wanted me to have taken the money and shared it out with them!

Unusually, Joe Collins always wore a rudimentary leather helmet of the time when playing. But his play, and not just his headgear, started to get him noticed by the Great Britain selectors, as the *Ice Hockey World* noted: '...Collins, Jewish Scots boy with Kelvingrove, has the makings of a great defenceman. I'd recommend him with enthusiasm to Great Britain's Selection Committee. He's a blocker, and a heavy body-checker. Two weeks under Nicklin, and his rough edges will be smoothed.' The unnecessary use of the adjective 'Jewish' is a reminder of how less tolerant British society was in 1938; especially as this insensitive comment appeared just days after Germany's notorious *Kristallnacht* which saw widespread attacks on Jewish premises.

This contemporary need to mention his religion in a sporting context was continued by the *Daily Record* in January 1939: 'Collins, by the way, has the distinction of being the only Jewish

The Great Britain team arrive at Zurich, February 1939, photographed in front of the Swiss Airlines Dakota DC-3 in which they had flown from Croydon that morning – the first British representative ice hockey team to travel by air. From left to right, standing: Billy Fullerton (on steps), Tommy McInroy, Percy Nicklin (coach), Arthur Green, 'Pip' Perrin, Art Ridley, Pete Halford, Stan Simon, Tommy Grace.

player in Scotland.' Thankfully, however, his hockey abilities were all that mattered, and these were encapsulated by *Ice Hockey World* editor Bob Giddens, who watched Collins at Kirkcaldy in December 1938: '...he was hitting so hard and sure against Flyers that the wise ones were going out of their way to avoid him... Send Collins and Fullerton to London and I am sure Nicklin is going to like Joe if he plays the hockey he's been dishing up with Kelvingrove.'

Collins, along with fellow Scots Fullerton and McInroy, travelled south to Harringay for a Great Britain trial match on Sunday 15 January 1939. All three went to Switzerland in February 1939 for the World Championships. It is believed Collins may have been carrying an injury going in to the tournament, given Sid Montford's disclaimer in the *Daily Record*: 'Joe will step on to the ice at Zurich 100 per cent fit.'

That notwithstanding, Collins played in four of Great Britian's World Championship matches, being one of only three defencemen iced, alongside Gordon Dailley and Bob Wyman.

The British played all their games on the outdoor rink adjoining the Dolder Grand Hotel, considered then, as now, to be one of Europe's finest. Situated atop a fifty-acre wooded promontory in a residential area of Zurich, 1,988 feet up above the city, it is connected to the centre of Zurich by a funicular. The outdoor hockey rink is still in use today, overlooked by the magnificent backdrop of the Hotel, part medieval fortress, part Renaissance chateau, and part nineteenth-century Palace.

Victories over Belgium and Hungary saw Britain advance to the semi-final pool. The British held out against Canada for over forty-five minutes in the first semi-final match, before losing four late goals. The *Daily Express* noted that:

> While the margin rather flattered Canada, the victory was deserved. Kelly was the outstanding player for Great Britain, although the defence which included Collins of Kelvingrove, also played well and until the last 15 minutes bore up well under the fast Canadian raids.

The next afternoon, 8 February 1939, the British faced Germany in front of a 10,000 capacity crowd. What must have gone through the mind of Joe Collins as he lined up to face the team representing the Nazi state? Here was he, a Scottish Jew, appearing for Great Britain

The Great Britain bench during a World Championship match at Zurich's Dolder rink, February 1939. Joe Collins (no. 5) has his back to the camera on the left; others pictured are Jimmy Kelly (with baseball hat) talking to BBC commentator Stewart MacPherson (right); behind Kelly are Art Ridley (with helmet) and Pete Halford. (*Ice Hockey World* photo)

against Germany, a country where anti-Semitism had become, by this point in February 1939, incorporated in the very fabric of German life.

After two goalless periods, the Germans scored the game's only goal through Jaenecke after forty-six minutes to effectively eliminate Great Britain from the Final Pool.

Collins sat out the next day's 0-2 loss to Czechoslovakia, which ended the British involvement in the tournament. It also signalled the end of the international hockey career of Joe Collins, together with that of fellow Scots Fullerton and McInroy (and of the two Scots-Canadians, Kelly and Foster). Indeed, just over a month later, Czechoslovakia was seized by Nazi Germany, and matters other than ice hockey would be foremost in the minds of the five in the coming months.

Collins' Great Britain sweater is now framed and displayed in the home of his son in the Glasgow suburb of Giffnock, as Gerry Collins comments:

> Joe was extremely proud to have played for Scotland and to have represented Great Britain in the World Championships, oh yes! Goodness gracious, I also played for Scotland at ice hockey, and nothing – in any kind of athletics – can beat the thrill of wearing your country's shirt.

Sid Montford, in his *Sunday Mail* column of 12 February 1939, revealed that 'In an interesting letter from Switzerland, Joe Collins tells me that Billy Fullerton and Tommy McInroy played really splendid hockey in the championships, in the face of "great odds".' It also reveals Collins' spirit of generosity that he would take the trouble to write from a World Championship in praise of his two Scottish colleagues.

With the recent opening of the new Ayr rink in March 1939, and the impending opening of rinks in Aberdeen, Dunfermline, Edinburgh and Paisley, only one team was to be required from the Crossmyloof rink for 1939/40. Kelvingrove were to be sacrificed, and their distinctive green, white and black uniform, with the large 'K' on the sweater, would disappear from the hockey scene. They disbanded at the end of 1938/39 after ten years.

Their last game on Crossmyloof ice came on Tuesday 25 April 1939, and saw the 'grove defeat Falkirk Lions 7-4. *The Scotsman* reported that Kelvingrove '...had in goal 16-years-old Angus Macdonald, but he was so well protected by Collins and Seafred that, apart from the early stages of the game, he was never in trouble.'

It wasn't known at the time, but this final appearance of Kelvingrove's on their home ice was also to be the last time Joe Collins would play ice hockey in the rink where he had been such a favourite.

His – and Kelvingrove's – swansong came four days later at Perth, in rather humiliating circumstances, on Saturday 29 April 1939. Panthers scored ten goals past young Macdonald in the 'grove net, without reply. It was a sadly ignominious end to a fine hockey career.

On leaving school, Joe had entered the family clothing manufacturing business, and by 1939 was a director of Collins (Glasgow) Limited, based in the city's High Street. During the summer of 1939 he had volunteered for the Territorial Army, and at the outbreak of war in September 1939 he was transferred to an anti-aircraft unit of the Royal Artillery, as his cousin Gerry remembers:

> Joe was a natural leader, liked by everybody, but he could also hold their respect. He was in the Territorial Army just before the outbreak of war, and he went right through the ranks from Private up to Lieutenant-Colonel, and finished as an Acting Brigadier. That was extremely unusual, particularly in those days, and speaks volumes for his abilities.

As a Second Lieutenant, Royal Artillery, Joe married Ethel Blin, the daughter of a bullion dealer, at Glasgow's Queen's Park Synagogue in December 1941. He subsequently served in Kenya in East Africa, and was awarded an OBE for his military service in the New Year's Honours of January 1946.

His cousin Gerry also served during the Second World War, and recounts a story which illustrates the respect and affection which Joe engendered in his teammates:

> During the war, I was in a Special Service Unit, the Lovat Scouts. We were ski troopers, mountaineers and marksmen, and ended up in the Canadian Rockies for training. We were stationed near Jasper, in Alberta. It's now a ski resort, but then was just one street and two shops. Joe had been really friendly with Bert Forsythe, as they were defensive partners with Kelvingrove, and Bert Forsythe came from near Jasper. I had gone in to Jasper for a skate one day, and got talking to the locals. The next thing, Bert Forsythe's father came down to the rink and asked for this guy Collins (meaning me) because his son spoke so highly of Joe (their hospitality was very generous, and I was on a charge for being late back to base!) We had five months in the Canadian Rockies, and we weren't allowed to play hockey, only allowed to practise! I kicked up hell, and came down from the mountains every six weeks and met Forsythe's father in Jasper.

Bert Forsythe, and his younger brother Jimmy, had joined Wembley Lions in 1934; they subsequently played for Birmingham Maple Leafs, before moving north of the border, where Jimmy joined Perth.

Joe Collins was a generous contributor to many charitable causes in the post-war years, both Jewish and non-Jewish. He became managing director of Collins Juveniles Ltd, employing some 350 staff at a factory in Glasgow's Bridgeton, as Gerry Collins recalls:

Great Britain World Championship team, Dolder rink, Zurich, February 1939. From left to right: Jimmy Foster, Jimmy Kelly, Bob Wyman, Tommy Grace, Gordon Dailley (captain), Pete Halford, Joe Collins, Art Ridley, Billy Fullerton, Tommy McInroy. (*Ice Hockey World* photo)

Gerry Collins (Mohawks and Scotland), younger cousin of Joe Collins, 1947/48. (Gerry Collins archive)

> After the war, Joe was working very hard, and his company, Collins Juveniles Ltd, made children's clothes, and I don't recall him playing hockey after the war. He built up a very substantial business, all his family were in it. He had such a wonderful, wonderful personality; he was loved everywhere he went, by customers all over Britain.
>
> He was even offered a generalship in the Israeli army, but he turned it down because it meant having to move away from his family. [Joe and Ethel had adopted a son and a daughter – Charles and Sharman]
>
> After he married, he and his family lived in a substantial house at Erskine Road in Whitecraigs and, latterly, in a flat at Netherton Court in Newton Mearns, next to Whitecraigs Golf Club.
>
> Ethel, Joe's wife, was a real, real smart cookie. She built up her own business, based at Glasgow Cross, making belts. It was the biggest supplier of belts to Marks & Spencer.
>
> Sadly, Joe's business went down with a very big bust in 1978. We had similar businesses, similar outlets – clothing – and I offered him half my business for nothing, but he wouldn't take it.
>
> Joe was really a most unusual guy. Anywhere he was, on holiday or in any company, everything was 'Joe' within two minutes. Everything was centred round him!

After retiring from his collapsed clothing firm, Joe set up a business importing fashion goods, which led to him travelling extensively in then Communist Eastern Europe and India.

Sadly, Joe Collins passed away on 10 July 1988, at Paisley's Royal Alexandra Infirmary. He had been suffering from Bronchial Carcinoma, and was just two months short of his seventy-third birthday.

Appropriately, during the writing of this chapter, the Great Britain team – for the first time – opposed Israel in an ice hockey international. The game, on 20 April 2006, resulted in an easy 12-0 win for the British. Who, though, could possibly have foreseen such a World Championship match up way back in 1939, when a Jewish homeland did not exist and Joe Collins of Glasgow's Jewish community played ice hockey for Great Britain? Had he still been alive, Joe Collins would, doubtlessly, have smiled approvingly.

Career Record (in World Championships)

	GP	G	A	Pts	PiM
Joe Collins					
Great Britain 1939	4	0	0	0	Unknown

4

The Blairgowrie Project: Tommy McInroy

The venerable building in the Gallatown area of Kirkcaldy may have been restyled as the Fife Ice Arena, but its distinctive Art Deco exterior would have made it instantly recognisable to the elderly gentleman who was to be that evening's honoured guest. He had first known the building as Kirkcaldy Ice Rink almost sixty-five years earlier.

It was Saturday 4 January 2003, and the feted visitor was Tommy McInroy, an original Fife Flyer of 1938 vintage, there to collect an award on behalf of the first Fife Flyers, as their modern-day counterparts celebrated the beginning of the rink's sixty-fifth year with a visit from the Solihull Barons.

Then aged eighty-five, Tommy was one of only two surviving Flyers who had played in the Kirkcaldy rink's opening match back in October 1938, and he received a great reception from the Kirkcaldy crowd.

He was, too, the oldest surviving Great Britain ice hockey internationalist, but few in the old arena that night would have been aware of his short, but eventful, hockey career, which peaked during that inaugural season for the sport in Kirkcaldy back in 1938/39.

McInroy's rise to prominence in the late 1930s was meteoric, and unprecedented; straight out of the pages of *The Victor* or *The Hotspur* – those comics so beloved of British schoolboys of that era. Within the space of only two years, he had gone from a nineteen-year-old novice who had never skated in his life to representing his country in the ice hockey World Championships. And he grabbed a goal in his first world tournament game, for good measure.

He was also the first of a new breed of home-developed players. Before McInroy, the veteran British players were, in the main, wealthy winter sportsmen. Even the younger Scots breaking through in the early 1930s, like Billy Fullerton and Joe Collins, were from relatively affluent backgrounds, which allowed them to participate in what was an expensive pastime. It was also very much a middle class sport at that time in Scotland, reflecting its roots in Glasgow's Scottish Ice Rink at Crossmyloof. Tommy McInroy was to become Scotland's first ice hockey working-class hero.

Thomas Scott McInroy may have been a member of the first Fife Flyers, but his roots were a bit further north, just outside Blairgowrie in rural Perthshire. His father, John McInroy, a farm servant, originally from Forteviot in Perthshire, had wed his mother Williamina Hamilton, a domestic servant from Methven, at Perth, in 1900. He recalled his early years for the author in 2005, only a few short months before his own passing:

> I was born on 3 June 1917, at Rosemount Farm, Blairgowrie, where my father was a Ploughman. I was brought up in Blairgowrie and Rattray, and went to Rattray Public School. We had a good Sports master at the school, and I started playing cricket then for Blairgowrie, I did a bit of batting and bowling.

The original Perth Panthers, 1936/37. From left to right: Mac Ross, Doug Mitchell, Les Lovell, Jim Lightfoot, Les Tapp, Bill Boivin, Tommy McInroy and Jack Stewart. (*Perthshire Advertiser* photo)

We moved to Rosebank Road in Rattray, and my father worked as a Coal Carter. My mother died when I was ten.

When I left school I served my time in the building trade with Willie McLaren in Blairgowrie, and worked in various places in Perth and Dundee. I then left Blairgowrie when I was young and went to Perth. I started playing hockey when the Perth rink opened in 1936.

When the Panthers started they had Canadians like Les Tapp, Bill Boivin and two or three others. They also brought over Art Schumann and a few boys from Germany, who had been playing for Berlin Canadians.

Les Tapp was one of the best; he had a great time in Perth. He was one of the best for learning the young ones.

I was in the building trade, a rough caster and slater, and when the weather was bad, and we couldn't work outside, I spent my time at the ice rink. I learned to skate, I was quite late in starting; I was nineteen. But it was a bad winter in 1936/37, and I went up to the rink most days and got free ice time to learn the game, and got on to the Perth Panthers.

Panthers' coach Les Tapp, a twenty-four-year-old Ottawa native, took the young country boy under his wing. He must have recognised the latent potential of McInroy, allied to his enthusiasm and dedication; the raw materials which, with the input of Tapp's hockey knowledge, could be moulded into a decent hockey player. In essence, McInroy became Tapp's 'Blairgowrie Project'; an experiment in hockey late development.

Tommy was working on the construction of the Muirton housing scheme at the time, behind the new Perth rink and the St Johnstone football ground at Muirton Park. It was therefore convenient for him to apply himself daily to his new sport, under the watchful eye of coach Tapp. Such was his rapid development that he was a regular with the Canadian-dominated Panthers by the end of their first season.

Back in 1936, you could skate at Perth's Central Scotland Ice Rink on Dunkeld Road, from 8p.m. to 10.30p.m. on a Saturday, for one shilling and sixpence. Joe Anderson, the former Perthshire and Scotland cricketer, had opened a branch of his sports shop in the new rink, where the price of gents' skates ranged from 19s *6d* to 25*s*.

Perth went mad for hockey in that first season. By the end of November 1936, a local house league was in full swing at the Perth rink, with St Andrews University, Aerodrome, Black

Hawks and Panther Cubs competing in the Midlands Ice Hockey League. Captain J.T. Grassie, sports master of Perth Academy, had even formed a school ice hockey team, and he himself took up refereeing in the Scottish League.

The senior Panthers attracted sell-out 3,000 crowds and, to cope with demand, the rink would run two senior teams the following season, staffed with mainly Canadian imports. McInroy, however, was not the first local player to establish himself with the Panthers; that honour went to defenceman Douglas Mitchell, who subsequently joined rivals Dundee Tigers in 1938.

Against this backdrop, the first mention of Tommy McInroy in a hockey context appeared in a *Perthshire Advertiser* report of the Panther Cubs 7-5 win over the Black Hawks on 16 December 1936. Les Lovell netted all seven Panther Cub goals, but the nineteen-year-old Tommy McInroy had a hat-trick for the Black Hawks, 'the babes of the league'. While Canadian Lovell was mentoring the Cubs, his compatriot Les Tapp filled the same role for McInroy's Junior Black Hawks.

Tommy didn't have long to wait for his senior debut in the orange and black of the Panthers. With a 'flu epidemic sweeping Perth over the festive period, Panthers travelled to Glasgow on 5 January 1937 minus stricken regulars Burbridge, Lawson and Darling. McInroy was drafted in to a Panthers line-up which included just two defencemen and three forwards, plus T.S. McInroy (substitute). It was to be a one-sided baptism of fire for the Blairgowrie boy, as Mohawks swept aside the Perthshire Panthers 9-1 in a President's Puck match (with Billy Fullerton netting a hat-trick).

By 3 March 1937, the *Perthshire Advertiser* was able to report that 'Tommy McInroy made a huge improvement on his last showing. He was forever in the thick of the fray, and gave Les Tapp a helping hand on many occasions,' as Panthers tied 3-3 with Mohawks at Perth.

Tommy, however, didn't have a rose-tinted view of the hockey he was introduced to in 1936:

> There's no comparison with the game as it was then, it's a lot faster now, and the local players are all pretty good now.
>
> When I first started playing for the Panthers, the only teams we played were all in Glasgow, like Kelvingrove and Mohawks, so you were travelling to Glasgow twice a week.

The Perth rink promoted the junior Black Hawks to senior status for 1937/38, with Les Lovell switching from the Panthers as player-coach, and Tommy moved over to the white and

Tommy McInroy, Perth Black Hawks, 1937/38. (*Perthshire Advertiser* photo)

The first Fife Flyers' team, September 1938. From left to right: Jack Stover, Alec Fullerton, Les Lovell (coach), Norman McQuade, Billy Fullerton, Len McCartney, Tommy Durling, Tommy McInroy, Jimmy Chappell and Chick Kerr. (*Dundee Evening Telegraph* photo)

black uniformed outfit. He appeared in the Perth Black Hawks' opening senior match, a 7-1 victory over Glasgow's Mustangs, at Crossmyloof, on 5 October 1937, as he recalled:

> The following year they started the Black Hawks in Perth, and I played with them. The coach we had, Les Lovell, went down to Kirkcaldy when the rink there opened in 1938, and asked me to go as well and play for the Fife Flyers. Len McCartney, who was a Canadian with the Black Hawks, also joined the Flyers.

The Scottish ice rink boom of the 1930s put paid to the Black Hawks after a single season, making way for the teams operating out of the new rinks opening at Dundee, Kirkcaldy and Falkirk in late 1938.

The demand for players, however, saw Tommy signed by Fife Flyers, and he moved to live in Miller Street, behind the Kirkcaldy rink. He played in Flyers' first ever game, a 5-2 reverse on 30 September 1938 in the inaugural match at Dundee's Kingsway rink; he also iced the following day when Dundee spoiled the Kirkcaldy rink's opening night with a 4-1 victory.

His first Fife goal came at Crossmyloof on 11 October 1938, with a little help from Kelvingrove netminder Cross, as described by the *Ice Hockey World*: '...McInroy scored in rather a peculiar fashion. He sent the puck across meaning Chappell to accept, but Dave Cross was at fault and the puck struck his skate and went in to the net.'

While with Flyers, Tommy's hockey career reached its peak; he represented Great Britain at the World Championships in Zurich during February 1939, where he was Britain's top goalscorer. He was the forerunner of a number of Perth-trained players who went on to appear for Great Britain in subsequent World tournaments: Ian Forbes, brothers Jimmy and Laurie Spence, George Watt, Sam Macdonald and Graeme Farrell.

Tommy, together with fellow Scots Billy Fullerton and Joe Collins, travelled to London for a Great Britain trial on Sunday 15 January 1939. Harringay Racers hammered the British trialists 24-4, as Tommy recalled:

Tommy McInroy (left) and Jimmy Kelly (right), during the Great Britain *v.* Canada match at Zurich, 7 February 1939. (T. McInroy archive)

> We had a trial at Harringay Arena, with Joe Collins, Billy Fullerton and myself down from Scotland. It was actually a waste of time, as we were picked by Percy Nicklin almost right away. Percy Nicklin was a pretty good coach; he was coach at Harringay Arena.

The *Daily Record*'s Sid Montford was obviously pleased with McInroy's elevation to the Great Britain team:

> McInroy has come to the fore with a sensational rush. His selection is something of a romance, when we think that two years ago he couldn't even skate, far less play the world's fastest game. When the Perth rink opened, he applied himself with intense determination and soon gained a place in the Panthers' line-up.
>
> Last season he played with success for Perth Black Hawks, but it was not until he teamed up with the Fife Flyers that he really developed into a first class player.
>
> McInroy has all the necessary attributes. He skates fast, can stickhandle reasonably well, marks his wing, and, unlike the great majority of home bred players, has a powerful and accurate shot. In fact, we might call him a natural in this respect.

He retained fond memories of that tournament, with the Great Britain team travelling by air to a World Championships for the first time, flying out from Croydon to Zurich on the morning of 2 February 1939:

> We flew to Zurich in a DC-3, it was my first flight. I always remember that the pilot flew over all the First World War battlefields, the Somme, and we could see the outline of all the trenches.

Coach Nicklin took his players to watch first opponents Belgium practise during the afternoon of their arrival. The British players had a practice the following day, but were distracted by reports of IRA bombs exploding at the Leicester Square and Tottenham Court Road tube stations back in London.

That notwithstanding, the Championships remained the high point of McInroy's hockey career:

> That was a great time in Switzerland with the Great Britain team in 1939. There was me, Joe Collins from Glasgow, and Billy Fullerton from Kirkcaldy, my linemate. Joe was a good defenceman, I think he got injured a bit. Billy was great, he was right wing, I was left wing. He was a good player, he was really fast. He was the British speed skating champion in the year I started playing hockey. I don't remember what happened to Billy, although I know he was killed during the war.
>
> I think I scored a couple of goals. It was an outdoor rink, the Dolder, in Zurich, and there were big crowds. It was pretty good outdoors, but not what we were used to back in Scotland on indoor rinks. Part of the tournament was played at night; part was played during the day. We were fortunate in that we only played two of our games at night, against Belgium in the opening game and then Canada, as the lighting on the outdoor rink wasn't very good.

Tommy's memory was correct with the goals he scored, as he contributed half of Britain's four goals from their five games. Against Belgium, the British were trailing 0-1 in heavy fog going in to the third period when McInroy grabbed the equaliser after fifty-four minutes, with Kelly and Fullerton securing a late 3-1 win. The next day, he netted against the Hungarians from the opening face-off after just five seconds, being unmarked near the Hungarian goal and converting a Jimmy Kelly pass, to give Britain a 1-0 win to move them forward to the semi-finals against Canada, Germany and Czechoslovakia.

Stewart Macpherson, writing in the *Daily Sketch,* was concerned about the British prospects: 'A tough task indeed, especially as McInroy, one of the stars this trip, is out of action with a badly damaged shoulder.' Tommy played through his injury, however, and appeared in all three semi-final matches, as he recalled:

> Jimmy Foster, the goalie, played well. I remember, though, that Foster broke a skate against Canada; he never recovered and we got beat by quite a few goals. We didn't do as well as we hoped to.
>
> Jimmy Kelly was our centre, with me and Billy Fullerton on the wing. Jimmy was a good player, he played with Wembley Monarchs.
>
> We played Germany, and got beat 1-0, and we had a crowd of 10,000 – which was some crowd in those days. I have a photograph of Jimmy Foster against the Germans.
>
> The Czechs were a good team and beat us 2-0; shortly after, the Germans walked into Czechoslovakia, and I often wondered what happened to those Czech boys.
>
> We went up in to the mountains at Engelberg for a few days after the tournament. We went up on the funicular railway. It was a great couple of days, sat up in the sun and the snow – although I never had the skis on!
>
> We never had much contact after the war. It was pretty good to play in a World Championship; it was a great thing to be in!

With the coming of war in September 1939, the ice hockey season was thrown into initial confusion. Tommy found himself 'allocated' back to Perth Panthers for 1939/40; the opening of which saw him participate in a couple of 'firsts'. On 27 October 1939, McInroy was on target in the opening match at the new Dunfermline Ice Rink, as Perth defeated Dunfermline Vikings 9-5. Jimmy Chappell and Tommy Durling, his linemates with Flyers the previous year, were now members of the new Vikings.

The following night at Perth, Tommy assisted the Panthers to a 9-2 victory over an Ayr Raiders team appearing for the first time. Opposing him was Ayr's Canadian defenceman

Above: Tommy McInroy (right) and Jimmy Kelly (centre) attempt to block Canada's Johnny McCreedy during the Great Britain *v.* Canada match at Zurich, 7 February 1939. (T. McInroy archive)

Right: Tommy McInroy, in the uniform of The Black Watch, Greece, 1945. (T. McInroy archive)

Mickey Shires, as Tommy recalled: 'Mickey Shires of Ayr Raiders was a good player, I remember him quite well.'

His hockey season was to be cut short, however, and his hopes of emigrating and trying his luck in Canadian Senior 'A' hockey were also dashed by the war: 'I was in the army five and a half years. I joined up in 1940, in Perth, and got the Battalion when they came back from Dunkirk.'

Before that, the by-now Private McInroy of The Black Watch had wed Perth girl Ann (Nancy) McFarlane, who worked as a Cardboard Box Stitcher, in February 1940 at Scott Street, Perth. Sadly, the young couple were to experience the pain of the loss of a child that same year, with their new-born son, also Thomas, living only for two days.

Tommy, however, was then to spend most of the next six years overseas on active service, reaching the rank of Sergeant:

> I was then away in the army, in the 6th Battalion of The Black Watch. We did see quite a bit of action through Algeria, Tunisia, Sicily, Italy and Greece. I was a Corporal and Despatch Rider for the CO. When he needed me, his driver would flash a light he had on the side of his staff car.
>
> I came back to Kirkcaldy and joined the junior Flyers, playing against Durham and the other Scottish junior teams. I had been away from the game in the army for five and a half years. It was too long, and I wasn't up to play for the senior Flyers.

Tommy and wife Ann settled in Kirkcaldy's Lorne Street after the war, and their daughter Heather was born there in January 1949.

Alan Murphy was a teammate of his at Kirkcaldy, and remembered those immediate post-war seasons:

> I played in the junior Kirkcaldy Flyers with Tommy McInroy just after the war, all over the country.
>
> We called him 'Mac', and he was some boy, the 'Mac'! I remember he used to wear a trilby on the back of his head, and when we were travelling away he was always quite dapper.
>
> He was that bit older than the rest of us, and he was the only one that was married – so he wasn't chasing the girls like we were! He was a good living fellow, just one of the boys.
>
> He was a fair player, but I don't think he was a star at that time, with all the Canadians, and he had been away from the game for so long during the war. But in the juniors, he wasn't too bad. He didn't get into many fights either. He was a good lad, he wouldn't let you down.

Tommy's last ever hockey match was at Durham Ice Rink on 21 May 1949, when he was a member of the Kirkcaldy Flyers who lost 2–3 to their local rivals, Dunfermline Vikings, in the BIHA Cup final. Tommy and his family moved away from Kirkcaldy later that year, as he remembered:

> After that, I came up to Lossiemouth to work in 1949, liked it, and decided to stay on. I worked for myself for the first five or six years, but carried on in the building trade till I retired.

Tommy's first sporting love back in his home town of Blairgowrie had been cricket, and he would turn out for Elgin Cricket Club in the North of Scotland League until well into the 1960s. His best moments on the cricket field, however, were in the immediate post-war summers, when he would travel to Perth from his Kirkcaldy home to represent Perthshire in the Scottish Counties Championship:

> I played cricket for Perthshire when we got big crowds on the North Inch. After the war, I played with young fellows like Len Dudman, Jimmy Brown, the wicket-keeper, and Wilson, the Yorkshire professional. Before the war I played cricket with Scot Symon, he was one of the good players and he played football for Rangers and Scotland. I enjoyed the cricket, but I didn't really socialise through the cricket, I was too busy with the hockey!
>
> My wife died in 1989, and my daughter died with Motor Neurone Disease in 2002. Since then, I've been on my own, and I'm now eighty-seven. I have grandchildren and great-grandchildren – some in Elgin and some in Blackpool. I still keep in touch with Tommy Durling, who's in Vancouver. He's the only other original Flyer still alive.

Sadly, shortly after sharing the memories of his hockey career with the author, Tommy McInroy passed away suddenly, but peacefully, at Dr Gray's Hospital in Elgin, on 24 July 2005, aged eighty-eight. He had been pre-deceased by his wife Nancy and by his daughter Heather and son Kenneth, but is survived by a grandson and two granddaughters, as well as two great-grandsons and two great-granddaughters.

Career Record (in World Championships)

	GP	G	A	Pts	PiM
Tommy McInroy Great Britain 1939	5	2	0	2	Unknown

5

Coal on Ice: The Brothers Syme

In the first half of the twentieth century, when Britain's reputation as the 'workshop of the world' was underpinned by the power of 'King Coal', the thousands of miners in the British coalfields also provided a rich seam of sporting talent, exemplified by legendary names such as Matt Busby, Bill Shankly, Harold Larwood and Freddie Trueman.

While football and cricket were the prime beneficiaries in attracting those who saw sporting talent as the only means of escape from underground toil, British ice hockey was also to enjoy two major talents who emerged from the Fife mining village of Blairhall sixty years ago: 'Tuck' and 'Tiny' Syme.

At the age of seventy-six, and enjoying retirement in the sunshine of southern California, 'Tuck' was honoured with induction to British ice hockey's Hall of Fame in 2005, while 'Tiny' was similarly commemorated one year later, evoking memories of the sport's post-war golden age in Scotland, when the mining Syme brothers became star players in a league where Canadians were predominant.

The eight-team pro Scottish League encompassed Ayr, Paisley, Falkirk, Edinburgh, Dunfermline, Kirkcaldy, Perth and Dundee, and injected some North American colour and excitement into the grey and austere world that was Scotland in the 1940s and '50s.

The weekly aggregate attendance exceeded 30,000, ensuring that only football was more popular as a spectator sport at the time. With the governing body insisting that a minimum of two slots on each team had to be filled by home-grown players, opportunities were therefore limited for local youngsters hoping to play at the top level.

It did mean, however, that those who managed to break through had to be of a high standard to perform in what was a fiercely competitive circuit, and 'Tuck' Syme of Dunfermline Vikings was one of the League's best defencemen. Indeed, he was the only locally produced player to receive annual end-of-season Scottish League 'All Star' recognition in the period 1946 to 1954; being selected to the 'A' team in both 1950/51 and 1953/54, with a 'B' Team place in 1952/53. Elder brother 'Tiny' also holds a unique record in British ice hockey from that time, as he was the only British born and trained player to be selected to the All Star 'A' team (1955/56) in the six seasons of the Canadian-dominated British National League (1954-1960).

Their abilities were enhanced due to their playing together as a defensive unit, making them a formidable and inspirational pairing for Dunfermline, Paisley and Great Britain.

In March 1953, they were selected for a Scottish Select against the *Ice Hockey World* All Stars, in a televised exhibition from Paisley, with the *Evening Times* noting that the 'Only Scots boys included are the Symes from Dunfermline. There can be little doubt that the Tuck and Tiny are value their recognition. They have been the bulwark of Vikings' defence in post-war hockey, and an example of the players' that Scotland can turn out.' Sadly, injury prevented 'Tuck' from participating, but the selection gives an indication of their standing within the game.

'Tiny' (left) and 'Tuck' (right) after a shift at Blairhall Colliery, 1948. (Tuck Syme archive)

Jimmy Thomson, a former Dunfermline and Scotland winger, played with the brothers from the start of their hockey careers and has remained firm friends with 'Tuck' for nearly sixty years. 'Tuck' was Jimmy's best man at his wedding. Nobody, therefore, is better qualified to offer an assessment of 'Tuck' and 'Tiny':

> They were great players – they were famous – and playing together on defence they were outstanding. These English teams were terrified of them. They were hard, but fair, no quarter given, no quarter asked.
>
> Tuck was just a great, natural hockey player, and when Tuck went up the ice, Tiny was always there, they complemented each other. Tiny was also a good hockey player, and a clever player, too – he thought about the game, and the two of them together was dynamite, you should've seen them! And if anybody did anything to either of them, oh, it was awesome to see their reaction! So, you could imagine the two of them playing together, what like it was.
>
> There was never any kind of rivalry between them, and I never once heard a cross word between them. Tiny was a boy for the dances – and the ladies! Tuck was the opposite. He wasn't into dancing, although the ladies were always round about him! They were different, each was his own man, but there was a real bond between them.

The Symes were giants of the Scottish game, both literally and figuratively. Each stood at 6ft 2in, with 'Tiny' weighing in slightly heavier at 195lbs to 'Tuck's 190. 'Tuck' was a left-hand shot, while 'Tiny' shot right. And 'Tuck', during his season with Paisley in 1953/54, was the highest paid professional sportsman in Scotland.

Thomas Woods Syme was born in Blairhall on 15 May 1928, but he has always been known as 'Tuck':

> When I was a baby, my brother couldn't say 'Tom', and it came out as 'Tuck', and the nickname stuck from then on. Over here in California, my wife and everybody now calls me 'Tom', but when we're back in Scotland she calls me 'Tuck', like everybody else!
>
> When we were growing up, my brother was always James, he never got 'Tiny' till he played hockey. One of the newspapers gave him the nickname 'Tiny' when he started with the Vikings, so they had 'Tuck and Tiny'. The name stuck with him from then on. Now, when I'm back in Blairhall, if someone speaks about 'James', it takes me a while to realise they're talking about 'Tiny'!

Elder brother James Syme was also born at Blairhall, on 1 October 1926, but the family's recent origins were outwith Fife. Blairhall itself was only constructed in the 1900s by the Coltness Iron Company to house the miners and their families attached to its newly sunk

Blairhall Colliery. Thus most of the first occupants of the new mining village were company employees transplanted from Lanarkshire and the Lothians. 'Tuck' and 'Tiny's' parents were both products of this migration.

John (Jock) Syme, a coal miner, and Margaret Woods, both Blairhall residents, had married there in August 1926, under the auspices of the Church of Scotland (although Margaret had been raised in a Roman Catholic family). Jock, however, had been born in West Lothian in 1905, while Margaret, a Domestic Servant, had been born in 1908 at Coatbridge, Lanarkshire.

The Syme family had a strong sporting pedigree, as 'Tuck' recalls:

> My father, Jock, had played professional football with Raith Rovers and his brother, my uncle Robert, played with Manchester City with Matt Busby, and was Busby's best man. My cousin Charlie Fleming – my Auntie's laddie – he played inside forward for East Fife, Sunderland and Scotland.

'Tuck' and 'Tiny', however, spent a brief period in Windsor, Ontario during infancy, but events conspired to ensure that the brothers' Syme exposure to Canadian ice hockey was to be delayed:

> The family moved to Windsor, Ontario in 1929, when I was a year old. My father played soccer, across the river from Windsor, with a team called the Detroit Workers – I remember from photographs that they had a hammer and sickle emblem across their chests, like communists! He had a few medals that I remember playing with as a boy.
>
> The Depression started not long after we'd arrived, and my father couldn't get work. He was mowing lawns for food. My parents decided that if we were going to starve, we might as well go back home and starve among our own people! We moved back to Blairhall when I was two, in 1930. They went back home to the pits, and they were working only three days out of the fortnight – out of the frying pan into the fire.
>
> We moved to Dundee in 1938, and stayed with my grandmother (my mother's mother) for a year. This was to save money so we could get to Canada. My father was working in the pit back in Cowdenbeath. I went to Clepington Road School when we were in Dundee, and 'Tiny' went to Morgan Academy. He moved to Dunfermline High School when we went back to Blairhall.
>
> Then war broke out, and it was only evacuees who could get to Canada, so we went back to Blairhall.
>
> Everybody in that village worked in the coalmines. I went to school at Blairhall, and I left at fourteen, in 1942, and followed my father and brother down the mines.
>
> I remember years ago there was a newspaper article about Blairhall, asking how come there were so many good athletes from this wee village. It was only four streets, and no store! There was Geordie Niven, goalkeeper with the Rangers; Jimmy Walsh played with Celtic, Tommy Wright with Sunderland, and my cousin Charlie Fleming. I was never that great a footballer, and 'Tiny' played football like he played hockey, running through people – he was as bad as me!
>
> I don't know if it was something in the water, but it certainly wasn't the food we got – with rationing then, we were getting one egg per family every seven weeks!
>
> I started skating at Dunfermline when I was fourteen. I remember a couple of years later, I was at the public skating and Johnny Rolland was looking at the best skaters. He came up to me and asked if I wanted to play hockey. Did I want to play hockey? It was like being given the chance to go to the moon! I was sixteen at the time, in 1945. It was just after the war, I was a good skater, and he was looking for good skaters to start with, because some of these kids used the stick as a crutch, take it off them and they would fall.
>
> Johnny's father was a director of the rink, and they wanted to re-form the Dunfermline Royals, the junior team. Johnny Rolland was a true gentleman and a great player. His father was a crook, but he was a gentleman!

Four of Dunfermline's 'locals' take a break at practice, 1947. From left to right: Johnny Rolland, 'Tuck' Syme, Ben Tierney, 'Tiny' Syme, Jimmy Thomson. (Jimmy Thomson archive)

I remember being with him when he told me he had met the girl he wanted to marry. Unfortunately, he took his own life about thirty-five years ago. He couldn't live with her, couldn't live without her. His fourteen-year-old son went out in the garage and found him hanging.

I played my first game of hockey in 1945/46 – and went to the Olympics in the Great Britain team in 1948!

The Royals won the Scottish Championship in 1945/46, and I had a head you couldn't get a hat to fit! We were so conceited, it was pitiful. We each got a leather wallet from Mr Rolland for that – but there was no ten shilling note in it! Johnny Rolland's family were wealthy. I remember we would always get scrambled eggs round at his house after a game, and this was when eggs were rationed. Johnny's Dad, along with Stevenson the furniture man and Jack the lawyer owned the Dunfermline rink.

They brought the Canadians over in 1946. We were Scottish Champions, we challenged them to a practice match one Sunday morning – it was pitiful! We found out that we didn't even know how to play our positions. And then I got taken on by Keith and Herb Kewley.

The *West Fife Annual* for 1946 had already taken note of the Syme brothers' potential: 'More than one of the Royals may take his place in senior hockey before many moons have passed… the hefty, tho' young, Syme brothers had no equal in defence play on the Scottish junior circuit.'

'Tuck' broke into senior hockey, aged eighteen, during season 1946/47 with the Championship-winning Vikings, greatly helped by two of Dunfermline's Canadians, Herb Kewley and Jim Davis, who took to coaching the junior Royals during that season. 'Tuck' attributes his development as a player to his Canadian coach at Dunfermline during 1947/48, Keith Kewley – a fellow inductee to the Hall of Fame in 2005 – brother of defenceman Herb:

> The two Kewley brothers – Keith and Herb – were the best coaches I had ever seen. We played a box defence at that time – it was even new to the Canadians. Keith was a great coach and way ahead of his time.
>
> Keith gave me a chance to play senior hockey and Herb coached me. Without those Kewley brothers, I'd just have been another good skater. They made me a hockey player.
>
> Keith was a good coach. As a matter of fact, he came up with a system in 1947; it was a defensive system when you were a man short. I watched them in Canada, years later, and they had developed it. I asked him, I said: 'Keith, how did you come up with that system?' He said: 'Coming across on the boat took five days, and I was just thinking.' He was a brilliant coach.
>
> He played with Dunfermline originally, and he used to say that wearing glasses was what kept him from going further as a player. I've stayed with his family. There were six brothers, and four of them played in Scotland – Keith, Herb, Hal and Danny – Danny was the goalkeeper.
>
> Herb taught me, and he was a thinking player. If a man's left-handed, and I'm a defenceman, nine times out of ten he would go to my side, my left side – that's the side that I hit with. I was playing with the Vikings against Bob Kelly from Paisley. He'd beat a couple of men, and he'd always just shift the same way. He had a helmet on, and his helmet went over me, and he broke his shoulder! But there was another guy, Scotty Reid of Kirkcaldy, I've knocked him out twice in the one game! And he'd come down the next time and he'd do the same thing.
>
> When I started, 'Scotty' Cameron was coaching the Royals. He had played before the war, but he was totally out of touch by that time. 'Scotty' Cameron was playing pre-war style, and he was going to be player-coach. He'd come down with the puck, and he's dipsy-doodling, Herb Kewley'd probably knock him on his arse. He coached for one year, and that was the end of it. 'Scotty' Cameron told everybody that he coached me to be what I am. Nonsense – he was so out of touch, and the Vikings laughed at him. He was a wee man, and he wasn't that good.
>
> Joe Lay of the Vikings wasn't a good defenceman, but I thought these guys were great when I was just starting. Stan Stewart had to be the worst defenceman. We saw Stan Stewart and he had a little hip-hopper. He played later with Ayr, and I remember coming down the ice, and here's Stan coming across with his ass out, he's going to hit me. And I just stepped inside him and he skated into the boards, looking over his shoulder!
>
> But we used to think these guys were good at first, because we didn't know anything.

Now eighty-one, and retired in St Thomas, Ontario, Keith Kewley remembers starting to develop Dunfermline youngsters, but is typically modest about the extent of his own significant contribution:

> It's hard to say. We started working with the local guys: Johnny Rolland, Tuck and Tiny Syme, probably some others. My involvement was more in team and positional play, schemes we used at face-offs. My brother Herb taught them more of the fundamentals.
>
> I was very much a student of the game. Winning was important. You can go about it one way or another, and I did a lot of pre-season planning. On the boat, coming across to Scotland, I was studying, planning, and drawing diagrams of plays.
>
> I would put Tuck at the top of the Scottish defencemen, skating-wise. He was tough and good in the corners. Johnny Carlyle was a better stickhandler, and Bill Sneddon was a toughie, but Tuck was an excellent team player and very competitive.

> Tuck was green as grass, but always a good skater. Tiny was a slower skater, a labouring, heavy-set type of player. Tuck was a leader on and off the ice. So Tuck was the best all round Scottish player, in my opinion.

Kewley's father, Claude, the sports editor of the *Toronto Globe and Mail*, had selected all the Canadian players in Scotland for 1946/47. He spent some time around the Scottish rinks in January 1947 when he spoke to the *Dunfermline Journal*:

> I think the game in Scotland has a great future. In five years from now, with proper coaching, your young boys will have reached such a pitch that the importation of players from Canada will not be necessary… The Syme brothers and Tommy Walker can take their place in the Vikings. I think they will be really good within the next few seasons.

Prophetic words from Kewley senior and 'Tuck's' senior debut for Dunfermline was to come just a couple of months later, on 14 March 1947, in a 2-5 home loss to Dundee Tigers, as he recalls:

> My first game for the Vikings was a Friday night against Dundee, and Keith Kewley said to me: 'You're playing tonight.' It was tied and I had caused two of the goals, just plain inexperience and stupidity. I said to him: 'Keith, don't put me on, please'; I'd already caused two goals, I didn't want to cause the winner! Sunday morning at practice, he said to me: 'Why don't you do this?' And I reckon that was what I'd done wrong. He never said: 'You screwed up', or anything like that. He was a great coach.

'Tuck' fails to mention, modestly, that he recorded an assist on his debut, setting up Vikings' second goal for Joe Aitken.

A trip to St Moritz for the 1948 Winter Olympics with the Great Britain team was next up for 'Tuck', who was still only nineteen:

> I'd only played hockey for two seasons before the Olympics. I was invited to play in a few trials, and got picked. I remember when I got picked for the Olympics I said I wasn't going to Switzerland, because we [the Vikings] were in the running! And it was Keith Kewley who said to me: 'You're going to the Olympics.'
>
> I said to Keith Kewley: 'Keith, I started playing hockey in '46, and two years later I'm in the Olympics?' To be honest… there wasn't a whole bunch to compete against! Plus, I had two years of good coaching from the Kewleys. There were three of us from Scotland went to the Olympics – Bert Smith, me and Frankie Jardine. I'm now the lone Mohican!

His selection prompted the National Coal Board to make a short film about him, *Coal on Ice*, which was included in the then-weekly *Mining Review* newsreel, as 'Tuck' remembers:

> The Coal Board movie was like propaganda, 'Come and work in the pits, and you get to go to the Olympics!' I could have died laughing when I saw it. Somebody got me a video of it a few years back, and I still laugh every time I watch it. They got me on a train at Dunfermline station, waving farewell to my mother and father and all these well-wishers, meant to be me heading off to the Olympics – and it was a train to Cowdenbeath!
>
> When I went to the Olympics, I just quit the pit and went away for a month. I came back and started working again, and nobody asked any questions! Your ass would be out the door nowadays!

'Tuck' was less than impressed by the British team's management; the patrician Carl Erhadt was coach, with 'Bunny' Ahearne as manager:

'Tuck' Syme of Dunfermline Vikings, *c.*1948. (Tuck Syme archive)

I didn't really rate the coach we had, Carl Erhardt, he was totally out of touch. He would say things like: 'We won't have a practice tomorrow; I'm going skiing!' Erhardt went skiing every day. I never saw him at a game.

And you never met a bigger crook than 'Bunny' Ahearne, the British Ice Hockey Association secretary. He ran European hockey. He was charging for first-class hotels, and we were in hotels with a po' under the bed! You name it, we got screwed. He gave us two Swiss francs for expenses. We went on tour two weeks before the Olympics, playing exhibition games in Switzerland, and we were on wooden benches on the trains and staying in cheap hotels – and Ahearne was charging the Swiss for first-class travel and accommodation!

Archie Stinchcombe, he was a good hockey player; he was the real coach. And I played against Bibi Torriani of Switzerland, who had played in the 1928 Olympics!

The head of the Olympics, Avery Brundage, an American, and he wanted us all to sign a declaration saying we'd never turn professional before we could play in the Games. The man was a billionaire! And yet he was telling us that we couldn't make money from hockey! He didn't even want us to be half-decent comfortable, let alone wealthy.

At the opening ceremony, when all the teams marched in, the Italians were all immaculate in grey-flannel suits, white shirts, blue ties, white hats and gloves – we had no uniform, nothing. We walked in to the stadium with our game sweaters on. And I remember thinking: 'Who won the war?'!

There is an old Pathé newsreel of the British team at the Games' opening ceremony. Sure enough, the British ice hockey team is there as described by 'Tuck', with team jerseys worn over shirts and ties, the antithesis of Italian style. Yet, there is 'Tuck' at the back, with all the confidence of his nineteen years, smiling broadly for the newsreel cameras, the only man sporting a pair of then very trendy sunglasses! Never mind the chic of the Italian team, the boy from Blairhall was the very epitome of cool, 1948-style!

> We got on the outdoor rink at St Moritz for a practice at two o'clock in the morning. That was the only time the ice was hard enough to play on, as it was so mild during the day.

'Tuck's' memory is not an exaggeration. With post-war austerity beginning to bite, the cost of winning the war had left the British impoverished, having to put up their athletes in modest accommodation, imposing similar economies on anything else that had to be paid for in Swiss francs.

Giles, the famous cartoonist of the *Daily Express,* produced a contemporary cartoon depicting the British team under canvas in the snow, beside a five-star hotel, with one of the competitors asking a hotel waiter: 'Garçon, would you mind fetching us a can of water for our cocoa?'

This humorous comment was not wholly divorced from the reality of the British situation, with the American competitors accommodated in the resort's opulent hotels, while their former wartime allies were making do on a pitiful daily allowance. 'Tuck' reflects ruefully on that post-war period of rationing:

> The thing about us, we were all working people. I was working in the pits for eight and six a day, and then my Dad got a contract and it was a wee bit more. And my best friend Jimmy Thomson was an apprentice bricklayer for ten shillings and fourpence – a week!
>
> Jimmy and I have talked about this. In the forties and fifties, there was no food in the country – we got one egg every seven weeks per family! We got twenty-five pence worth of meat, and 18% of that had to be mutton. There was no beef, there was no bacon. Well, if you don't put petrol in the car, it doesn't run any more. Jimmy was working laying brick all day and I'm down the pit. Where did we get the energy?
>
> Herb Kewley and another guy were staying in digs in Dunfermline, and they asked: 'What about meat?' And the landlady threw them out! Hockey has got to be a disease. I mean, you would've crawled through broken glass to play! Blairhall was six miles from town, and I've seen me walk to Dunfermline in the snow, you couldn't get a bus – just to practise!
>
> When I started with the Vikings, I was getting eight shillings and sixpence per day down the pit, and the rink paid me for the days I didn't work because of the hockey. Eventually, I went full-time with the hockey, and went down the pit in the summertime.

Jimmy Thomson remembers the Symes' contribution to the British coal industry:

> Jock, their father, was a development worker in the pits, driving the mine through stone towards the coal. He then went into management in the pits in Fife, and then went into the goldmines in Canada. Tiny was on plant recovery latterly; when a section was finished, he'd remove all the equipment and machinery. He actually worked beside me in Comrie Colliery for a spell.
>
> Tuck left the pit more or less after he got into the Vikings. Mr Stevenson, one of the Dunfermline rink directors, he owned a furniture shop, and Tuck worked for him delivering furniture.

After the Olympics, 'Tuck' shone in a team of young home-bred Scots who tied 5-5 with Czechoslovakia at Paisley on 13 March 1948. The *Daily Record*'s Sid Montford noted that '...the men who deserve the highest compliments were the hard-skating youngsters Syme, two goal Rolland, Smith and Neil. I reckoned that 19-year-old Fife miner Syme was the best on the ice.'

His mentor, Keith Kewley, felt that the young Scot could make a name for himself in the sport's homeland, and recommended him to several Canadian teams. This facilitated 'Tuck' playing with the Ontario Hockey Association's Junior 'A' Guelph Biltmores in 1948/49. In that pre-National Hockey League Draft era, the Biltmores were a farm team of the New York Rangers. So, almost forty years prior to fellow Scot Tony Hand being drafted by the NHL's Edmonton Oilers, 'Tuck' thus became, effectively, the property of the NHL's New York Rangers.

The scale of his achievement, for that time, was considerable. Remember that in 1948 the NHL comprised only the 'Original Six' teams, with no European players and barely a handful of Americans. Such was the Canadian dominance of the hockey world that they could send a Senior 'A' team to the World Championships each year and be confident of a gold medal. For a nineteen-year-old Scottish kid to earn a place on a Canadian Junior 'A' team was unprecedented. His time in Guelph also gave him his first acquaintance with the NHL:

> I also played in an exhibition game against the New York Rangers in 1948, when I had gone over to the Guelph Biltmores. Keith Kewley said to me: 'Why don't you come over [to Canada] and play?' I stayed with the Kewleys at first in Toronto and then I moved to Guelph. Guelph was a nice town, but my mother and father – who had moved over to Canada as well – were way up in Timmins, in northern Ontario, in the gold mines. I was feeling homesick and I wasn't enjoying it. Then I got a call from Bill Creasey, the Dunfermline manager, asking me to come back to the Vikings. Bill Creasey was a true, true gentleman.

In similar fashion to Tony Hand some thirty years later, a homesick 'Tuck' returned to Scotland to become established alongside 'Tiny' as two of the top players in the Scottish National League. Before that, however, they had their swansong with the junior Dunfermline Royals, helping them to the British Championship, on 21 May 1949, at neutral Durham. Their annexation of the BIHA Cup was all the sweeter as they defeated fierce local rivals Kirkcaldy 3-2, as 'Tuck' recalled:

> When we were playing Kirkcaldy in Durham for the British Championship in 1949, I think we had maybe five hockey players on the team. And Kirkcaldy I think paid the referee, because they got my brother and me off for penalties late in the game, but we still won. And some of them in Kirkcaldy were saying that they were British Champions, but Jimmy Thomson put Jackie Dryburgh right on that when Jackie was managing the Kirkcaldy rink, because they even had a banner up in the rink saying they had won it in '49!

'Tuck' and 'Tiny' assisted Vikings to the Canada Cup in 1950/51 and the Autumn Cup in 1952/53, with 'Tuck' earning All Star selection in both seasons.

In 1951/52, Canadian Paddy Ryan was appointed player-coach of the Vikings, and knew the value of the Symes' contribution, as the *Dunfermline Press* noted: 'Backbone of the team again is the Syme brothers, Tuck and Tiny. Ryan's appreciation of their rugged, but effective blocking, is shown by his appointing them captain and vice-captain respectively.'

'Tuck' was paired with brother 'Tiny' on the Great Britain team's first defence line for the 1950 World Championships in London. They were a formidable partnership and their hard-hitting body-checks earned rave reviews, as GB finished a creditable fourth (in the world). He recalls:

> On that team in 1950, 'Tiny' and me were the first defence line, and the other pair were Lawson Neil and Bill Sneddon. Lawson Neil, now there was an honest player. He did not get the recognition that he deserved. Lawson was a very good player, the best that came out of Ayr and Bill Sneddon from Falkirk was another good one.
>
> Bill had some temper, though. I've seen him take off his sweater, his shoulder pads, and went and pick up the goal net and throw it against the end boards! When we played the USA

Dunfermline Vikings at practice, *c.* 1950. 'Tiny' Syme is second right, while 'Tuck' Syme is third from right. (Tuck Syme archive)

in 1950, he picked up a bad penalty, and was going to kill the ref! I was the assistant captain, so I struggled with him and managed to throw him onto the ice. Unfortunately, he sprained his knee badly and was put in hospital. There was an outbreak of scarlet fever in the hospital, and Bill had to stay in quarantine in London!

Bill was an out-and-out Communist. He had come out the army after the war, he was a paratrooper, and we had a mutual agreement not to fight each other whenever Dunfermline played Falkirk. He was a hard, hard man – I wouldn't want to fight Bill Sneddon.

There were kids on that team in 1950, though – English guys – who shouldn't have been there. It was all politics then, too. They didn't want to have too many players from the one team. The most underrated hockey player was Jimmy Thomson from Dunfermline. He was a good player, and better than some who got picked. But there was me, 'Tiny' and Johnny Rolland from Dunfermline, and they didn't want four from the same club. So Jimmy lost out.

Kenny Nicholson was on that team. He was the oldest, and we voted him captain. Kenny got off the train at Newcastle to get beer – with no shoes on! Anyway, the train leaves, and Kenny's still on the platform trying to get his beer. He showed up the next day at the team hotel in London – in his stocking feet! We took a vote to make him the team captain, as he was the oldest. I always remember that he went to the World Championships without a suitcase; he had one blue suit and one white shirt, with seven collars! We called him 'Nick'. If you ever met Kenny, he had a big scar on his face; somebody tried to jump over him and caught him with the skate. He had the longest stick I'd ever seen. It was amazing the length of it. A nice person, but he could drink forty beers! I know he'd been in Canada, because his game, the knowledge he had, he got it in Canada. He was a heavy, slow skater – and a heavy drinker!

Also on that team was Johnny Quales, who was a good hockey player; a natural. He wasn't the cleverest of guys but I think, with good coaching, he could've been a great hockey player. And there wasn't a harder working hockey player than Johnny Carlyle; he would back down from nobody.

It's a very strange game, hockey. You can have good skaters and good hockey players, but without good coaching, you've got nothing. There was a whole bunch of good hockey players in Scotland who didn't get proper coaching.

I remember in 1950, just after the opening face-off against Canada, one of their defencemen flipped the puck some forty feet in the air, from his own blueline. It wasn't really a shot on goal, but Stan Christie, the goalie, instead of tying to catch it, tried to stop it with his pads – and it went through his legs into the net. He never recovered from that start; and Stan was one of the nicest young men I've ever met, it was a shame.

Against the Americans in 1950, me and 'Tiny' just hammered them. One of the Americans, from Detroit, said to me that we wouldn't be able to do that to Howe, Lindsay and Abel of

Above left: A newspaper cartoon of 'Tuck' and 'Tiny' Syme from 1953. Tiny is incorrectly depicted as a left-hand shot! (Tuck Syme archive)

Above right: 'Tuck' Syme, at the start of his last season as a Viking, 1952/53. (*Ice Hockey World* photo)

> the Red Wings. I told him that might be so, but they wouldn't do his team any good, as the three of them were Canadian!

The 1950 World Championships were, incredibly, the last time either Syme brother played for Great Britain, with 'Tiny' aged only twenty-three and 'Tuck' just twenty-one. The British team went to the 1951 tournament in Paris minus their top defencemen, the result of intransigence on the part of the Dunfermline rink, allied to the then-vexed issue of amateur *versus* professional. It had been circulated in the press at the time that 'Tiny' had advised the BIHA that he did not wish to play, but this he strenuously denied in the *Evening Times* of 20 January 1951:

> Says Tiny – 'There was never any question of me refusing to play for Britain. All I know about the matter is that my club has refused to release me. I want to go to Paris, but I can't'... Brother Tuck's cause is a different matter. He was made a senior at the beginning of this season, thus losing his status as an amateur. But Tuck says – 'I'm no better off financially than a lot of other Scots players in this circuit. Yet they are eligible.'
>
> To lose both the Syme brothers is definitely a blow to the British team. Clubs have defencemen who have improved immensely since last year, but none of them has the colour or the calibre of the husky mining brothers from Fife.

These same rules prevented their inclusion in the British team for the 1953 Championships, after which Great Britain went into 'splendid isolation,' in so far as international competition was concerned, until 1961, by which time both brothers were finished with the sport.

'Tuck' now is philosophical about their curtailed international career:

> Maybe it was because they were tired of seeing us, plus the Dunfermline management wouldnae let us go!

Although the Autumn Cup had been won by Dunfermline during 1952/53, the season ended acrimoniously, as 'Tuck' remembered:

> Old man Rolland was a shyster. I remember playing in a Play-Off Championship game against Ayr in 1953, and we asked Rolland for a bonus. He wouldn't pay it, and we said we wouldn't go on the ice. We played eventually, and I won't say we threw the game, but let's say our hearts weren't in it. We played for years for nothing. I was an All Star defenceman, and if I lost a shift at work, I got paid for it, that was it. Old Creasey would give me a fiver.

'Tuck' had received a serious shoulder injury in a match at Falkirk on 4 March 1953, which, on specialist advice, caused him to miss the remainder of the Scottish League programme. This was a massive loss to Dunfermline, as they were pipped for the League title on goal average by Ayr Raiders. He returned for the Play-Offs, though severely hampered, but assisted Vikings through to the two game final with Ayr Raiders. The *Dunfermline Press* noticed that something was amiss in the Play-Off decider that was lost at home to Ayr on 18 April 1953:

> Right from the first face-off it was obvious that there was something seriously wrong. The driving fighting qualities… [were] conspicuous by its absence. Tuck Syme… was not 100 per cent fit, but gone, too, was the inspiring urge of his tremendous team spirit.

None of the players accepted the terms offered by the rink directors for 1953/54, and Vikings folded in the summer of 1953. 'Tuck' and brother 'Tiny' teamed up again with coach Keith Kewley, this time at Paisley Pirates, as 'Tuck' recalls:

> I was in Canada during the summer, when I got a 'phone call to tell me Dunfermline's folded. Now, Bobby Burns was going to be coach of Edinburgh Royals, and I was living right next door to him. I told him that Dunfermline had folded, and he told me: 'Don't sign with anyone.'
>
> Bobby was trying to get Sandy Archer, who was the manager of Edinburgh. The man was a complete idiot. He came over before the war and was playing hockey. Then he turned into an English gentleman, with the camel-hair coat. No rough stuff! But hockey is rough – and he wanted to play it like cricket! And this Archer was in control of the purse at Edinburgh.
>
> Bobby Burns and Sandy Archer wanted me to go to Edinburgh, but Keith Kewley told me: 'Don't call anybody.' Keith was now coach at Paisley, and Bill Creasey, a true gentleman, had left Dunfermline to manage Paisley. They offered 'Tiny' and me money we couldn't refuse to sign for the Pirates.
>
> I was making more money than Geordie Young, the captain of Rangers and Scotland. I got £19 per week from Paisley; Geordie Young got £14 from the Rangers!
>
> Years later, 'Tiny' was moaning to me about the great Gordie Howe turning his back on Detroit Red Wings to move to Houston, in the World Hockey Association, for more money. I laughed, and said to him: 'You can't talk. You went from Dunfermline to Paisley for £4 a week more!'
>
> I enjoyed it at Paisley. I lived in Renfrew and walked every day to the ice rink.

'Tuck' was made captain of the Pirates (a rare honour for a non-Canadian at that time) leading the Paisley side to a treble success of League, Autumn Cup and Canada Cup:

> I remember we beat all the English teams that came up to play challenge matches against Paisley on television – we beat Streatham and Nottingham. Chick Zamick of Nottingham – he was a great hockey player – and I could see he was a little hesitant, because he'd heard about my brother and I; I could see he wasn't playing his game. And I said: 'Chick, we're tough, but we're not dirty, relax. We're not going to cross-check you or slam you into the boards.' (Well, no' unless we get a chance!) I got a great write-up against him; he was a good hockey player.
>
> There was also a Canadian played with Nottingham, Les Strongman; and there was a guy I think who could've gone pro. Oh, he was good.

'Tuck' Syme (Paisley Pirates) (right) checks Ken Perron (Perth Panthers) November 1953. (Tuck Syme archive)

'Tuck' tried his luck again in Canadian hockey, joining the Val d'Or Miners of the minor pro Quebec League in 1954:

> I was unemployed, and was asked to go and play for Val d'Or up in Quebec, about 150 miles north of Quebec City. I was up there in Val d'Or making money to get married. I went up there with a guy who'd played in Scotland called Don Kerwin. They paid around $50 a week, and they asked if I wanted a job as well. I said I'd go down the goldmine, it was 7,200 feet deep. The other guys had got work in stores or as clerks! But mining was all I knew; but I got a lot of respect just for going down the goldmine.
>
> It was a tough place. There was only a dirt road into it, and it was real cold. The record was sixty-eight below zero. I could walk out after a shower and count 'one, two, three, four...' and my hair would be frozen solid!

He remembers playing an exhibition match for Val d'Or against the legendary Montreal Canadiens, facing two ice hockey immortals in 'Rocket' Richard and Jean Béliveau:

> Béliveau, to me, is the greatest hockey player I've ever seen – and a gentleman as well. I was a Toronto Maple Leafs fan, up until I played against Béliveau.
>
> The Montreal Canadiens did a ten-day tour in a break during the season, and came up and trained in Val d'Or. Everybody there supported Montreal, so they played an exhibition match against us. It was the best ever night I had in hockey. My defence partner said to me in the dressing-room: 'Have you got a plan?' I just laughed and told him: 'Relax and enjoy it – you're going to get your ass kicked!' And we did, we lost 12-1.
>
> The next day, one of my teammates told me I had got a good write-up in the paper (I couldn't read it as it was in French). The Montreal coach said he wanted to see me at their

> training camp ten pounds lighter. Jeez, I was only about 185 pounds then, if I'd lost another ten I'd have been skin and bone! But the offer was withdrawn when they found out my age – I was twenty-seven at the time – and they said I was too old.

'Tuck' finished his hockey career with Val d'Or Miners – and it was a fitting end to the boy from Blairhall Colliery's distinguished ice hockey career:

> After I moved to Canada in '54, the whole family eventually moved over. All of them are now gone, killed by lung cancer. I smoke myself, although I never started until I had quit hockey.
>
> My parents had again moved out to Canada – to Timmins, Ontario – in 1948, and then they came back to Blairhall. My father had worked as a superintendent in three pits, but when they decided to move to Canada for good in '54, my father worked as a male nurse in a hospital in London, Ontario.
>
> Susan Marr was the girl I first married. She was born through the wall from me in Blairhall, and I knew her before she could walk! Her family went to Canada and she came home for a holiday, and I was playing with Paisley at the time. I had to go to her uncle's, and then I got attracted. I went over to Canada after, and I was playing up in Val d'Or and I was making all kinds of good money, and I got married to her. She's 'gone Hollywood' now, still going round Los Angeles waiting to be discovered!
>
> After the hockey, I worked for a couple of years as a policeman with Canadian Pacific Railroad, but I wanted to move to somewhere warmer. So, in 1960 we moved to California.
>
> I had gone into the American Embassy in Ottawa to see about moving to the States. I flipped a coin to decide on California or Florida, and California it was! I had an old Jaguar at that time, and I drove from Ottawa to Santa Ana, 3,400 miles.
>
> I was thirty-two then, and I had nothing to offer the labour market – there's not a coalmine within 1,000 miles of Los Angeles! My first job was undercover security in a department store's warehouse. I remember I got a dollar sixty-one an hour. I ended up as a troubleshooter for a 'phone company, and I did that for the next thirty-odd years till I retired.
>
> Dusty, my wife, she saved my life. I've been married to Dusty for twenty years now and she's a beautiful girl. She's sixty-six, and originally from Maine. She's definitely a giver!
>
> See, I was of the old school. We got paid in cash, and you came home and you threw it on the table. And my mother would say: 'There's your pocket money,' and it was shillings!

'Tuck' and second wife Dusty now live in retirement in Palmdale, north of Los Angeles, although they return regularly to Scotland:

> Hockey saved my life. I would have been in the mines all my life if it hadn't been for hockey. I was running once for the bus to go to the pit, and I fell and split my head and needed stitches. I milked that for two weeks – said I couldn't get my helmet on!
>
> It was a great life, coming out of the coalmines. I'm sitting out here in my 'office' – it's the only bit of the garden that's shaded. It's 3p.m. and in the seventies, we're out here in what they call the high desert – all I can see is blue sky and snow-peaked mountains! But I've a dual citizenship, with an American and a British passport. You can take the laddie out of Scotland, but they can't take Scotland out of the laddie!

It's a long way from a West Fife mining village.

The once-dominant Scottish coal industry of 'Tuck's' youth has all but vanished, with its disappearance mirrored in the decline of Scottish ice hockey. The balance of power has swung south, with a plethora of new English ice rinks opened in the past twenty years. The British team is now ranked twenty-fifth in the world standings and barely ten per cent of the players currently representing Great Britain are Scots.

When 'Tuck' and 'Tiny' Syme were the cornerstone of that Great Britain team which was ranked fourth in the world, back in 1950, twelve of the seventeen-strong squad were Scots. When will we see their like again?

Although almost two years younger than 'Tiny', it was 'Tuck' who first made the breakthrough into the senior game, as 'Tuck' recalls:

> 'Tiny' was a late bloomer in hockey, he didn't start playing until maybe a year after me, when he was about nineteen or twenty. Tiny started playing just after me. Well, to be honest, I don't remember him skating with me, because we were brothers, but Jimmy Thomson's closer to me than my brother was.
>
> 'Tiny' was big, and he could skate, but he was kind of like my father. My father was a great ballroom dancer, but he wasn't an athlete. My father was so uncoordinated; I don't know how he played football with Raith Rovers! My father was limber, but he was into ballroom dancing. Now, my aunt was a world champion highland dancer, but my father knew the steps in ballroom dancing. But when you saw my father dance and my aunt dance, he was like a machine and she was just free-flowing. They were in the Scottish Ballroom Dancing Championships, and my aunt and her partner kicked my Dad's ass! He couldn't believe it – he was bronze, silver and gold in ballroom dancing. But he was a machine, he was taught that this foot went this way, this foot followed it.
>
> A lot of folk thought of 'Tiny' as a big, dumbass hockey player. But he went to Morgan Academy and Dunfermline High School, and he could speak French fluently at twelve years old. At schoolwork he was brilliant. I didn't even go to high school and I was down the pit when I was fourteen. 'Tiny' was a very clever man, brainwise, but he had no common sense. He quit high school to get working on a coal delivery truck; because it had a V8 engine and he'd get to drive it! 'Tiny' had a brilliant mind, but he didn't have a wit of common sense. I called him 'Tiny', but people in Blairhall called him James.
>
> 'Tiny' was a smart man, but a lot of hockey players thought he was a big, Neanderthal man. I remember an idiot that played with Kirkcaldy, with a beard, he was a local. He stuck out his chin: 'Hit me!' he says to 'Tiny'. 'Oh jeez,' I said, 'You got to be an idiot; I mean, it's like offering a bun to a bear!'

The elder Syme made his senior debut for the Vikings almost a year after 'Tuck', at Dunfermline on 26 January 1948. Vikings were trailing Falkirk Lions 2-3 with two seconds remaining, when Randy Ellis netted the equaliser to the delight of the 3,000 crowd. The *Dunfermline Press* recorded that 'Jim Syme tried hard, but he found himself a little out of his class.'

'Tiny' appeared eight times for the Great Britain team in 1950, claiming a solitary goal, netting Britain's second twenty-five seconds from the end in a 2-0 win over Norway at Harringay on 15 March 1950. 'Tuck' also found himself once on the scoresheet in that tournament, scoring Britain's second goal in a 5-4 win over Sweden at Empress Hall on 18 March.

Meanwhile, 'Tiny' married clerkess Winifred Mary Sime, of Glasgow, in July 1950, with 'Tuck' as his best man. They had met at Glasgow's Crossmyloof rink when 'Tiny' had played with Dunfermline Royals. Their first child, daughter Rosslyn, was born in Glasgow in April 1951, although the family home was now a council house at 38 John Stuart Gate in Oakley, Fife. It still being the hockey season, 'Tiny's' occupation on his daughter's birth certificate is listed as 'Professional Ice Hockey Player'. Son Thomas arrived in June 1952, also at his maternal grandparents' Glasgow home. It being the hockey close season, 'Tiny' is described as a 'Coal Miner' on the birth certificate!

'Tuck' explains the reasoning behind the naming of 'Tiny's' daughter, Rosslyn:

> He named Rosslyn after Ross Atkins, who played at Dunfermline. He really liked Ross Atkins, and he vowed that if he ever had a child, he would name it after him! His son, Tom,

was a really clever guy and a very successful businessman, with offices in Switzerland and the Bahamas. Tom also died in his forties, like 'Tiny'. [His son, 'Tiny's' grandson, is also called Tom, and is now aged sixteen]

Incidentally, the best Canadian forwards we had at Dunfermline were Ross Atkins and Jimmy Davis.

Jimmy Davis was a brilliant player. I watched Jim Davis score against Kirkcaldy, and it was the play-offs. He broke in from the red line, there was nobody in front of him, and the goalkeeper was getting positioned. He let it go from the blueline and picked the top corner – and the goalkeeper was still waiting on him coming in. He'd already shot the puck. Oh, he was good. He was small and wide, you couldn't knock him down on a bed.

Who are the other Canucks that 'Tuck' remembers from his days with the Vikings?

Randy Ellis was a fantastic skater. Randy was a good player, but he could've been better. I watched him take a penalty shot against Hap Finch of Falkirk. Normally you skate in and you deke. Randy skated in and he was cutting across Finch; and Finch reached down and took the puck off his stick. Randy wasn't as good as Randy thought he was! His son, though, played for the Toronto Maple Leafs. I never saw the kid play, but to have got to the Leafs then meant he must have been a good hockey player.

Randy was the most beautiful skater. I tell you, if he'd been a figure skater, he'd have won a gold medal. And his brother, Mac, played with the Vikings as well, but he was nothing.

Years ago I met Charlie Schultz, of the Snoopy cartoons. He was a big hockey fan, and he brought them from all over Canada and America to an oldtimer tournament he organised up in the California wine country. I met a guy there I had played against on the American team in 1948 at the Olympics. It was funny to see these guys like Randy Ellis and Bobby Burns still wanting to drop the gloves when they were in their late fifties!

'Nebby' Thrasher, he could do without wingers, 'cause he'd never pass the puck! When I was up in Quebec I went over to see Nebby Thrasher in Timmins. It was sad, because he was living like a pauper, and he eventually drank himself to death.

Vinnie Keyes was a good defenceman; and Gar Vasey was the cheapest man you could ever meet! In Scotland, he would cut cards with the bus conductor for a threepenny fare! He was playing in Rhode Island, and his team got a meal allowance for a local diner. He always ordered a cheap omelette, and saved the rest of his allowance. It got to the stage that the other guys would say to the waitress: 'Give me a Gar Vasey!' But he was a good defenceman. He played with Guelph when I was there, and he moved up to the New York Rovers, who were the Rangers farm team.

Of the defencemen 'Tuck' played against, who does he rate most highly?

There were two. Gustavsen of Dundee, he signed for New York Rangers, and they gave him a bonus – and they have never seen him since! See, when all of these kids came over, aged eighteen and nineteen, you couldn't drink in Canada. And within a year a lot of them were alcoholics. And Art Hodgins – there was a great hockey player. And I remember having to put a towel around his neck and pull on it, to help him drink a whiskey. And he didn't drink when he came to Scotland to play with Paisley. A lot of those kids ruined their lives coming to Scotland.

And Gustavsen, he was marvellous. He didn't even think what he was doing; he just did the right thing. And I was in the corner one night with him and this Bill Melville, who ended up playing with the Vikings. Melville says to him: 'Do you think we should clean the kid's clock?' meaning punch me out. 'Nah', says Gustavsen. I've been in the corner with 'Gus' when he was drunk!

Both Gustavsen and Art Hodgins seemed like they'd been programmed. I got in a fight with Art Hodgins at Dunfermline, in the corner. Nobody won!

I got in a fight once with this Archibald. He was about six-four, played with Dundee and Kirkcaldy. He could do everything, and I couldn't figure out how this guy wasn't in the NHL. Then one night he clipped me, accidentally. Now, I dropped the gloves and I hit him. Then I thought: 'Oh, shit!' But, in a stadium you can't back down. And the man lay down on the ice with his hands over his face. I said: 'Now I know why you're not in the NHL!' He'd no heart. But nobody would ever think of challenging this man, he was big, strong and fast.

I was playing against Falkirk, a man by the name of Frankie Davis skates past me. He wasn't a big man, but this was in the days before helmets; he lifts his stick over my head, but not all the way, and he clips me. I said: 'I'll get you, you little bastard.' He was smiling, and I'm thinking: 'He's not even scared of me.'

So, I got a chance, and I dropped the gloves. And Red Thomson, the referee, stopped us. And Red was looking at me kind of funny. So, later, Davis gets in a fight with Art Sullivan, and he splits 'Sully' about four places. I said to Red: 'Who is this guy?' He said: 'That's the middleweight champion of the Canadian Fleet!' So I said to Red: 'Thank you very much!'

At that time 'Tiny' and me had a pretty good name, but he would've cleaned my clock just as easy as he'd cleaned Sullivan's!

Who were the opposition forwards that 'Tuck' most respected?

Ernie Domenico was a good hockey player, a smart hockey player – fast and good. I went to visit him in Timmins – he'd married an Ayr girl – and he said: 'By God, I never thought a Syme would be sleeping in my house!' His friend was another Italian; he played with Ernie, a guy by the name of Ray Dinardo. He died, on the ice, at Burbank, California, at midnight. He was playing hockey, and he took a heart attack. He was sixty-five, for God's sake!

There was a guy by the name of Orville Martini, he played left wing for Ayr and he used to cut in, which was perfect for me. The next season, he'd moved to right wing, which was my weak spot, and I never laid a glove on him – a good hockey player. He ended up in Switzerland, both Andre Girard and Martini, and it was very hard to get Swiss citizenship; and Andre ended up owning a bank!

Jean-Paul Tremblay was a good hockey player. He and I were going to go to Spain together. He got a shoulder injury when he was playing with Ayr, and was told that the arm had to come off. He wanted to go back to Canada to get it looked at, and I was going to Canada and got the call asking if I'd take Jean-Paul's trunk home. So I did, and dropped it off in Quebec City. They told him that the arm had to come off, but he said no. He was back playing a year in Switzerland; then he died – cancer. He was only twenty-four. He was a fine hockey player.

Of the Scots boys, Marshall Key of Dundee was a good centre ice. He was a clever laddie and a nice laddie as well. His father was an invalid, with two walking sticks. He would come to me after a game and say: 'Thanks for going easy on my boy!' But Marshall was a very underrated player; and Jimmy Spence from Perth was a good hockey player.

I've always maintained that there are as many good Scottish kids can play hockey compared to Canadians, but the coaching is where there's the big difference. I was a big idiot, but I could skate. But you can't be a good hockey player without being well coached.

It was bad management. To start with, the Scottish people didn't know hockey. The Royals won the Scottish Cup in 1946. We were playing bad hockey, but these people didn't know. And then they brought the Canadians over. Now, they had to pay their plane fares and everything. We were playing for nothing! The Canadians couldn't put much more in the arena than we were putting. But the hockey was much better with the Canadians.

It was funny. We were a whole bunch of wee, Scottish laddies who played hockey – and it wasn't very good hockey – and we got all these gorgeous women chasing us! We'd go down to Durham with the Royals, and there'd be thirty girls with their weekend cases waiting on the bus. Never knew their names! (Well, I think Jim Thomson and I were the only two that didn't!)

'Tiny' Syme, captain of Paisley Pirates and All Star, 1955/56. (*Ice Hockey World* photo)

'Tiny' stayed on for two seasons with Paisley after 'Tuck's' departure for Canada in 1954. Emerging from the shadow of his more illustrious younger brother, 'Tiny' really blossomed under Keith Kewley at Paisley, captaining the East Lane side in the first two seasons of the new British League, in both 1954/55 and 1955/56. He was honoured with an All Star 'A' team selection in 1956, before quitting British hockey and emigrating to Canada, where he played Senior 'A' in the Ontario Hockey Association, as 'Tuck' recalls:

> 'Tiny' played senior hockey in Ontario, near London, with the Strathroy Rockets. I remember I stayed in Toronto with Bobby Burns, who used to play with Dundee, Falkirk, Kirkcaldy and Edinburgh, and he told me: 'Tiny developed into a very good hockey player after you left.'
>
> When I was playing hockey up in Quebec, I hit this kid a couple of times, and he asked me: 'Is your brother 'Tiny' Syme?' When I told him he was, he said: 'Sacre bleu, I left England to get away from him!'

'Tiny's' daughter, Mrs Lyn Benko, a retired schoolteacher of London, Ontario, describes her father's life after he moved with his young family to Canada:

> I was born in Glasgow in 1951, and we moved to Canada in 1957. We were all over when I was growing up, but mainly in Toronto. My Nana and Papa, my Dad's parents, had moved from Scotland to London, Ontario.

Dad was a very clever, intelligent man. He won a bursary to Dunfermline High School. He quit high school, and didn't tell my Nana, which really upset her, because she felt that he could have gone on with his education.

When we came to Canada at first, we moved to St Thomas, Ontario. Dad was a General Manager at the Vick Chemical plant, where they manufactured vapour rub and other medications. I remember Dad played Senior 'A' hockey at that time. I think it was with St Thomas, because he'd been talking to Keith Kewley, but he may also have played with Strathroy.

My Dad's company moved to Toronto around 1960, when I was nine. He was quite well up the ladder at that time. I would say that when we were in Toronto was one of the happiest times in my parents' lives.

The company was taken over by Richardson-Merrill, which was American, and they started to bring in Americans for the senior positions. Dad didn't get a particular post he felt he should have got, because he didn't have a degree. He was devastated, and he quit. I had finished high school, and we moved back to London, Ontario in 1969, where my grandparents lived.

Dad opened up a bakery in London – that didn't go too well. He then was selling insurance, and then selling cars. My Dad was so kind and wonderful, he did well in everything he did – he just didn't get a break.

I had a wonderful childhood, with really loving parents, but it was really hard at times, hard for my family.

The work responsibilities that my Dad had were so much greater than Uncle Tuck's. Uncle Tuck was like a sort of lineman for the telephone company, up poles and things. Dad's jobs were all about managing and dealing with people, which can be tough.

My Dad died on 22 August 1973 at London, Ontario. It was an aneurism. He was only forty-six. Mum was devastated and never recovered.

I love Uncle Tuck! We talk on the 'phone about five times a week! We were on holiday this summer [2005] with Uncle Tuck and his wife, Dusty, and they showed us round Scotland. It was very bittersweet, as I wished my parents and brother had been there, but both my husband and daughter loved Scotland.

It was the first time I had been back in Scotland in over forty years. We had come over for a month's vacation back in December 1963, when I was thirteen. I remember how warm it seemed, and I remember Dad being asked to play hockey!

My Nana and Papa (Dad and Tuck's parents) were wonderful people. My Papa had mined coal in Scotland, and gold and uranium in Canada. He worked as a male nurse in a hospital in London, Ontario. He was absolutely the most fabulous guy, he taught me how to golf, how to fish.

My younger brother Tom and I both went to university. My brother was personable, an overachiever, who became president of Air Ontario. But he missed so much because we had lost our parents so young. Tom was an Accountant and he moved up through the business. He passed away in 2000, aged only forty-eight. He has a son and daughter, and his daughter gave birth on the weekend [24/25 September 2005].

I am a very private person, as was my Dad. My family situation is bittersweet, I lost my parents and my brother, but I have a wonderful husband.

I was an elementary school teacher, but I'm now retired. We have a daughter who is also a teacher.

My full name is Rosslyn. Dad named me after a hockey player he played with at Dunfermline, Ross Atkins – and do I know this guy? No! Thank you, Daddy! Everyday at school I'd say to the teachers: 'Please don't call me Rosslyn, my name is Lyn!'

As indicated by daughter Lyn, 'Tiny's' farewell appearance to Scottish ice hockey came on Saturday 28 December 1963, when then-thirty-seven-year-old 'Tiny' turned out for Ayr

David Gordon presents 'Tuck' Syme with his British Ice Hockey Hall of Fame certificate, July 2005.

Rangers, helping them to overturn a 0-3 deficit at the end of the second period to defeat the visiting Durham Bees 4-3. He renewed his partnership with former Paisley teammate Joe Brown, the Ayr player-coach, who invited him to turn out. The *Ayrshire Post* noted that "Tiny' Syme had a satisfactory come-back to Scottish hockey. He took time to settle but the more the game progressed the better he became and he finished up one of Ayr's top men.'

Former Vikings' teammate Jimmy Thomson remembers 'Tiny' with great affection:

> 'Tiny's' daughter, Lyn, is a wonderful girl, and her husband, Walter, is a great guy.
>
> 'Tiny' was a really smart, intelligent bloke. He looked just like a big, rough miner, but he'd gone to Dunfermline High School and could speak about three languages; and he'd talk about anything knowledgeably, and you'd say to yourself: 'How did he know about that?' A clever man; he really should've done more with himself.
>
> His wife and my wife were very friendly. They both came from Glasgow and we met them at the skating at Crossmyloof. As a young man, 'Tiny' was just a right happy-go-lucky fellow. It's just a pity that later on he drank too much.

'Tuck' takes an obvious delight in his niece and her family, with a regret that he never had children of his own – or so he thought. He had been engaged to an Edinburgh fashion model in 1950, but the engagement had been broken off through pressure from the girl's family who did not wish her to marry a professional sportsman.

Some thirty years later 'Tuck' met his former fiancée, who indicated to him that she suspected that 'Tuck' was the father of her daughter. In late 2005, after much searching, 'Tuck' discovered that he was, in fact, a great-grandfather, as he relates this happy ending with great joy:

I have a daughter, two grandsons and a granddaughter, and a great granddaughter (with another on the way!).

We got our DNA tested in Liverpool, and it was 99.9 per cent that we were father and daughter. I sent her some photos and cuttings and she knew then there was no doubt! She was just about jumping on the 'plane to come over. She's a nurse, and she takes care of about 500 people at a nuclear plant in Scotland.

Her daughter, my granddaughter, is the youngest. She's a hostess just now at a French ski resort. One of my grandsons is teaching rugby in Florida, and he's coming out to California in March [2006].

Career Records (in Scottish/British Professional Hockey)

	GP	G	A	Pts	PiM
'Tuck' Syme (Dunfermline/Paisley)					
1946-1954	382	46	87	133	596
Great Britain 1948-1950	14	2	1	3	6
'Tiny' Syme (Dunfermline/Paisley)					
1947-1957	562	40	143	183	914
Great Britain 1950	7	1	0	1	27

6

Lionheart: Johnny Carlyle

The eastern outskirts of Falkirk are today dominated by the state-of-the-art Falkirk Community Stadium, the main stand of which has a towering exterior of glass and steel, surrounded by acres of car parking. It's a modern edifice which looks as though it has been transplanted from one of the cathedrals of football in the English Premiership, only to rise up, somewhat incongruously, on the edge of that narrow strip of no-man's land separating Falkirk from neighbouring Grangemouth.

Although only partly completed at the time of writing, it is an impressive structure and, as the new home of Falkirk Football Club, it makes a bold statement about football's pre-eminence in the sporting life of Falkirk.

If, however, you travel a few hundred yards from the new stadium, along Grangemouth Road towards the town centre, a rather forlorn, barn-like structure is set back from the road, dwarfed by the adjoining Falkirk College. The main part of this building is now turned over to an indoor market, with a bingo hall built on to the rear. Yet back in 1938, when newly opened, and with its Art Deco lines pristine, this stadium made a bigger impact on pre-war Falkirk than its modern counterpart, just along the road, has made on the town almost seventy years later.

For this old building was once Falkirk Ice Rink; and, from its opening in November 1938 through until 1956, it was an ice hockey fortress.

No rink in Britain produced as many talented hockey players as were to emerge from Falkirk.

In this period, the game's administrative power base in Scotland also shifted from Glasgow to Falkirk, with the sport being run from the accountancy offices of the arcanely named Mr Festus Moffat, OBE, JP, on Falkirk's High Street. Although sounding like the character from an American TV western of the 1950s, Festus Moffat was secretary of the Scottish Ice Hockey Association as well as being chairman of Falkirk Ice Rink Ltd. His influence was considerable, and he was a champion of local development; his comments in the 1953/54 *Ice Hockey World Annual* bear witness to his support for Scottish players:

> If coaches devote the same time to Scottish players who have been taking part in Scottish Junior Hockey, and at the beginning of the season they coach them and train them as they have had to do with some very indifferent material brought expensively from Canada, the results will be astounding!

Sadly, his vision was not to be realised, and the last ice hockey played in Falkirk was back in 1964, with the building ceasing operations as an ice rink in 1977.

Despite this lost hockey tradition, the name of Johnny Carlyle, arguably the finest of the many talented 'Falkirk Bairns' who received their introduction to ice hockey at their local rink, is still well known in Falkirk, and held in high regard. That this should be the case, more than forty years since a puck was last chased on Falkirk ice, is a testimony to the man's outstanding contribution to his sport, over several decades, as player and coach.

John Cumming Carlyle was born on 31 July 1929, at 7 Baxter's Wynd in Falkirk; the first child of Robert and Evelyn Carlyle (née Cumming). His father was a house painter (a trade that John would also follow):

> I grew up in the east end of Falkirk, in two or three places that we lived in. I had a younger sister, Christina, who died very young. My father, when he left the school, was a miner down the pit. His father and mother, my grandparents, came from Pennsylvania. They came over here, and he dug the coal, and she had a basket on her back and carried it. They came to this country, and he worked down the pit, and they lived at a place called Avonbridge. They lived to a good age. My father was only two years down the pit, and then he became a painter. I went to Comely Park School, and it was used to billet soldiers during the war, so I moved to Victoria Road School, both in Falkirk.
>
> It was the lads down the stair from us who went to the ice rink, and they took me along. I liked it, and a friend of mine sold me a pair of ice hockey skates when I was fourteen. They were two or three sizes too big, 'cause I've a very small foot – a six I take – and I think these were eights.
>
> Thirty bob they cost, which was a lot of money during the war. He said I could pay him up at two and sixpence a week. I thought that was great, so I got the skates, and I hid them in the coal cellar! When I said to my Mum and Dad: 'Can I go to the ice rink the night?' they would give me one and ninepence to hire skates. I did that twice a week, and that money paid for my skates. So that was my first pair of skates, and that lad – to this day – every time he sees me he says: 'I started you off, John!'
>
> Then I saw Canadian Forces teams playing hockey at Falkirk. To get in for nothing, I used to mark the score. I'd sit at one end and put the scores up on a board. It was short ice at that time, as at one end they had a wee dance floor, and I was sat on the dance floor with the scoreboard saying 'Canadian Navy versus Canadian Army' or whatever. That was to get me into the rink for nothing.
>
> I used to lift the curling stones off when they curled – everything was to get you in to the rink for nothing – and that's how I started.
>
> Nelson McCuaig was the coach, and he was starting the Falkirk Cubs, just at the end of the war, when I was about fifteen or sixteen. He came along and he took all the skaters and said: 'Right, round about the rink.' I watched two lads that had played hockey before the war. I said to myself: 'I'll do what they do.' Everybody got picked, and there was only one more to pick – and he hadn't picked me. But, I must admit, he came over and he says: 'Look, you're the best skater here, what's the matter?' I didn't know, but I was holding my stick as a right-hand shot. He took my stick and put it as a left-hand shot. I just picked up the puck and went round, and he said: 'Right, you're in.' If Nelson McCuaig hadn't done that to me, I'd never have played hockey.
>
> After that, George McNeil came down from Dundee to manage the Falkirk rink. Nelson left and George McNeil took over the management of the rink and the coaching.
>
> I went on from there, and had two or three games with the Lions.

Johnny's senior debut came when he was seventeen, on Wednesday 13 November 1946, in a Lions' home loss, 4-7 to Paisley Pirates. The *Falkirk Herald* reported that 'Johnny Carlyle, the Falkirk junior player, deputising for Watts, played a hard, sound game.'

National Service then beckoned:

> I went to the army to do my national service in the Argyll and Sutherland Highlanders. I went in at eighteen on the dot, in 1947. Firstly we went to Germany back and forward, then I went to Trieste in Italy for two years.

The McNair brothers and Johnny Carlyle (right), Falkirk Ice Rink, 1946. (Johnny Carlyle archive)

There were trials for the Olympics in 1948, which were to be held at Falkirk and Crossmyloof, and 'Doc' McCabe of the Scottish Ice Hockey Association wrote a letter to the army requesting that I be allowed to take part. I was in Redford Barracks in Edinburgh at the time, ready to go out, and our CO, Major Snowball – I'll never forget him; he was a gentleman – asked how I was getting to Crossmyloof. I said I didn't know, and he said he would take me. So my CO took me, and I always remember it was an MG with a big belt over the hood. He took me there, and drove me back. Chauffeur-driven by my Commanding Officer because of a letter from 'Doc' McCabe!

When I got demobbed, I started playing hockey again, and I played forward. I was a centre at the start, and I forechecked and elbowed everybody I could! Then George McNeil put me on the left wing and made me a defensive winger, and I wasn't allowed in over the blueline unless I was on a break and it was only me and somebody else. I always had to come back to make sure it was never three against two, always three against three.

Eventually, what turned me into a better hockey player, George McNeil put me on defence, and it went from there. George McNeil didn't make me a hockey player, but he put me on the road. As far as I was concerned, I didn't play good hockey, or great hockey – whatever you want to say – until I went to Harringay.

I'll give you an example. There were quite a few in the Falkirk Lions – I'm not going to mention any names here – good enough, but couldn't fire the puck – and I was one of them.

I went to Harringay in 1956, had a look at the team, and did not unpack my case, as I thought I'd be back home! So, the first practice I was on the point. The puck came out to me, and I fired it in. Bill Glennie, the coach – and I'll never forget it – said to me: 'Hey, John-boy, is your stick broken?' I said: 'No, Bill, that's my bullet drive!' He said: 'One of the cleaners is gonna come down and sweep that in, it's going CCM-blank-CCM-blank!' There were armies of cleaners in Harringay Arena, and they watched us practise, and he said they could sweep in my shot like the curling!

We practised every morning at nine o'clock. Bill Glennie said to me: 'Right, eight thirty tomorrow morning, on the ice, I'll be there.' He got two pucks, and he bolted them together and sunk the bolts. He started me about three feet from the barrier and said: 'Go on, fire it.' After six weeks, I was firing them from the blueline, and during the games they were lifting their ankles out the road. I had a good shot, and I could score goals with it.

The point is, I'd played all that time, and couldn't fire the puck, and nobody had brought that out in me. It was my failing.

Bill Glennie was a very good coach. He could look at players and identify something that would improve their game. There was a Canadian defenceman who played for Ayr, Freddie Hall. He was a big laddie, about six foot three or something. If he was backing up, and he went to turn, it wasn't clean and he wasn't turning correctly, because he was tall and straight. Bill Glennie said: 'Freddie, watch John, and open your legs and bend your knees a little more.' So Freddie bent his knees a bit and it was easier for him to turn, he had more balance and everything.

That was the type of coach Bill Glennie was. And I tried to do that when I was coaching in later years. I used to look at a player, and I had ten points against him. Now, if he had four good points I would say: 'Aye, way to go.' But I would try and find the faults, and make him up to six good points.

That's what Bill Glennie did, and I tried to do the same. And I was quite successful at it. I made a lot of players better. And it went all down to me from Bill Glennie, who, sadly, passed away in March [2005].

It was Nelson McCuaig that changed my stick and got me started. George McNeil for recognising me as a defenceman more than anything else, and Bill Glennie for putting the polish and finish on me.

Senior hockey finished at Falkirk in 1955, and that summer John married Johan Hay, a draper's assistant, in nearby Bo'ness. They celebrated their golden wedding anniversary on 3 June 2005.

During his apprenticeship as a hockey player in Falkirk, Johnny was also learning the trade of painting and decorating in his day job:

It took me a long time to do my five years apprenticeship with Manuel Sinclair in Falkirk, because of the time I was off playing ice hockey. They didn't say to me: 'you can't do it,' that's one thing I must say. The son, Harold, he used to come to the rink and watch the Lions. So, I'd get a cut or something, and I wouldn't be at my work. They never said anything, but at the end of the day, instead of doing five years, I ended up doing about seven – they had docked off all that time that I wasn't there!

Johnny's introduction to World Championship hockey had came with the British team at the London tournament in 1950, aged twenty, as he recalls:

When we got there, we had no coach. They brought in Lou Bates, the hero of Wembley. The toughest game I ever played in was in 1950 against the United States of America – oh was it rough. I took a face-off and ended up in the rigging at the back like a set of underwear!

Johnny netted twice in GB's 4-0 victory over USA in an exhibition game in London on 14 March 1950, a game which replaced Britain's scheduled match against Czechoslovakia, who had withdrawn from the competition.

It was Tuck and Tiny Syme that went over to the bench and said to Lou: 'Right, Tuck and Tiny on defence; Ian Forbes, Johnnie Carlyle and Billy Sneddon on the forward line. That's the line to put out now.' It always ended up that this big American defenceman – he was enormous, must have been six feet four and about seventeen or eighteen stone – carried the puck in. Tiny moved out, he cut in – and Tuck hit him. And the fellow's heels were drumming on the ice; they had to shove a stick in his mouth to stop him swallowing his tongue. Up to then, he was rugged. I always mind Tiny Syme standing over him and saying: 'Dig a hole for this Minnesota cowboy!' Tiny had all the sayings!

That year we played France, and at the end of the first period a French delegation came into our dressing-room. 'Doc' McCabe was there, George McNeil and 'Bunny' Ahearne

Great Britain *v.* USA, Empress Hall, London, 14 March 1950. American goalie Dick Desmond saves from GB winger Johnny Rolland (back to camera, no. 14), while Johnny Carlyle waits for a rebound on the edge of the crease. The other players pictured are GB's Ian Forbes (left) and USA's John Gallagher (right). (Johnny Carlyle archive)

> representing the British Ice Hockey Association. The French wanted to inspect Tuck and Tiny's pants – they said they had planks of wood or something inside their pants, because every time a Frenchman came up he got thumped and carried off! It was the Symes, one went out and the other hit him, whatever way you like. And the stretcher was always on to take a Frenchman off the ice in the first period. So the French delegation said that the Symes were cheating because they had something down their pants. So, they had to take them off!

The match against France, at London's Empress Hall on 13 March 1950, resulted in an emphatic 9-0 tournament opening triumph for the British team; J.C. Carlyle notched a hat-trick.

> And the American team, we actually became great friends with them. They were in the same hotel as us, so you can just imagine what went on there! I must admit, though, we were kind of wild in those days! Although when we went to the Great Britain team in London in 1950, Johnny Rolland took his mother with him! The mind boggles! He was a nice fellow, but he committed suicide.
>
> Any team for Great Britain was poorly organised at that time. It really was terrible. We got dressed and went on the ice at Wembley for a practice – and we didn't have any pucks. We had to practise with a single roll of black tape – the British team, at the World Championships, disgraceful.

I got a bad shoulder injury in Wembley against Norway in 1950. And ten years later, we were playing in Norway, and I was the captain. This reporter asked me if I knew any of the Norwegian team. I said: 'Yes, is Voigt still playing?' So he told me he was, and I said: 'Well, I'm looking for him!' I didn't mean anything by it. (Well, I did if I could've got the chance to!) What happened was, when I went on, he went off; when I came off, he went on! They made a meal of it!

Johnny can vividly recall a conversation he had with 'Tiny' Syme of Dunfermline, on the train heading to the 1950 World tournament in London:

It was Tiny, he used to call me 'Bomber', and he said: 'Listen, Bomber, we've been fighting and battering each other for long enough. We're Scottish ice hockey players, we want to get together and do what we can for ice hockey, to help the British player.' We say 'British', but it was Scottish really, there weren't that many Englishmen coming through at that time.

So, after that, we were friends. But on the ice, if you got checked, you got checked. But there weren't any left hooks or right hooks coming at you! So that was one thing that we did, and I always remember that. I can't remember what I did last night, but I can still see myself sitting on that seat with Tiny!

After a successful season with the amateur Lions in 1956, hockey was discontinued at Falkirk:

There was no hockey here after that. There was a fellow from Fife got an exhibition game on once, but Jack Reid, who came after George McNeil as the rink manager, did not like ice hockey or ice hockey players.

Carlyle headed south and had two enjoyable seasons with Harringay Racers, becoming the first British player to captain Racers in his second season. He led them on a successful tour to Moscow and earned an All Star 'B' team selection:

Johnny Carlyle, Falkirk Lions, 1951/52. (*Ice Hockey World* photo)

The short-lived Murrayfield Royals, September 1958. From left to right, back row: Jimmy Mitchell, Vern Pachal, Doug Orvis, Ted McCaskill, 'Red' Imrie, Marshall Key, Johnny Carlyle. Front row: Joe Kreklewetz, George Lamb, Jim Mattson, Jackie Dryburgh, Vic Kreklewetz (player-coach). Carlyle, Key, Mitchell, Dryburgh and Imrie were all Scots; Mattson was an American; the remaining six were Canadian. (Johnny Carlyle archive)

> I remember that Barry Davies, the BBC television football commentator, started as a boy as the *Ice Hockey World* Harringay correspondent. He was always hanging about looking for stories, and the Canadians used to kick his arse out the dressing-room door at Harringay! But he was a good lad!

Sadly, North London's Harringay Arena closed in 1958, and Johnny headed back north to Murrayfield:

> Harringay folded, and Vic Kreklewetz – who had played at Harringay in my first year there – said that he wanted Marshall Key and me at Edinburgh, or he wouldn't take the job as coach. So, we went to Edinburgh, and they brought in other Canadians, not the Harringay team. But halfway through the season, at Christmas, old Mr Kerr decided: 'No; finished.' And Kreklewetz went to Wembley, and I went to Nottingham with a fellow called Vern Pachal Marshall Key went to Paisley with a fellow who was in the film *Slapshot*, I can't remember his name.

Johnny spent 1959/60, the last year of the British League, with Brighton Tigers, before returning north for a successful stint as player-coach of the amateur Edinburgh Royals, leading them to a British Championship in 1961. He would return to the South Coast, however:

> The Brighton Tigers were popular; you couldn't get a seat; it was packed. If I wanted to get somebody in to see a game, a commissionaire had to go and get a chair and go to one end above the time clock, which was just a balcony, and he'd squeeze that chair in there.

Johnny Carlyle of Brighton Tigers, 1959/60. (Johnny Carlyle archive)

The crowd were at the side of the pad, there was no glass in those days, and when you passed they used to spit at you and hit you with handbags and things like that. But when I went back to play for them, everything was alright! Upstairs it was real good, because the crowd was right over you, and it was a small rink. I played alongside big Red Kurz when I went to Brighton. He was six foot three or something like that, with a big, long reach, so defence was a very easy position to play in Brighton because of the size of the rink.

They used to come in and say that they were doing an advert for soap powder or something. Eventually they did a big one, for Timex watches. I had a watch attached to my skate, and I would skate about and come off the ice, and they would wipe the watch and show that it was still going. It took a couple of days to do at the rink. It so happens that it was Les Lovell's twenty-first birthday – and that was a mistake, because instead of lunch we were on the champagne! Those cameramen were ducking and diving! I had to go in between two defencemen and score. Once I got to the two defencemen, instead of them making me deke, and letting me through – bang! They hit me! So, all you heard was: 'Cut! Try that again.' We'd done it about a dozen times; I had to tell them that they were dropped if they didn't let me through!

That was great, and we got paid for it! Down there you got the opportunities to do these sorts of things. When we were in Brighton, we won every game. But the 'threat' was Altrincham. They had two boys from Durham played for them, and they had 'Eenos' Forbes, Spence and Macdonald. That was the team. If any team could have beaten us, it would have been them. They had a good team, and a nice wee rink, too.

Roy Shepherd made his name in Wembley against the Russians when they came here. He had a body-check, he was a solid lad. He played for me in Brighton. But he was always playing with good players. The English side of the hockey, Canadian-wise, if you know what I mean, was better than Scotland. They paid more money and could get better quality Canadians. I'll give you an example, my wife used to sit in a seat at Falkirk in the second row that cost 3*s* 6*d* and I had to nearly beg McNeil for that ticket. Whereas 3*s* 6*d* at Harringay, you were away up at the back, and the front row seats were for film stars and VIPs. So Harringay could afford the big wages (no' that I ever got any!)

The year I went south, there weren't any football players making more than £20 a week. I got a fiver when I started with Falkirk Lions – £3 for the away game and £2 for the home game. Then, when I went for more money, they wouldn't give me it. That's when I was out the game for six weeks.

The top Canadians in Scotland were on £20 or under, because that's what the football players were making. But at Harringay they were above that, but not a lot. George McNeil's biggest failure, as far as I was concerned, was that he was the manager and the coach. So, as coach, he'd like to get a certain player, but as manager wouldn't want to spend the money.

George McNeil wouldn't sign me one year at Falkirk, because I wanted more money, and I was out for six weeks. Andre Girard 'phoned me from Milan, wanting me to go and play for the Diavoli Rosso Neri. My job was to be to pass the puck up to him, because he had to come back to get it, and it was killing him! I had to go to McNeil and Festus Moffat to get permission. Festus Moffat says to me: 'You're injured.' I said: 'No, he won't give me more money.' So Moffat said to McNeil: 'Give him his money, and give him a pair of skates.' I had an old pair of skates, and I got my first pair of CCM Tacks for nothing from the team. Festus Moffat was alright, he was good for it.

Then I was supposed to go to Bologna in Italy, but I couldn't agree the contract!

Not only an All Star as a player, John was also an All Star coach, and had a successful spell leading the all-conquering Murayfield Racers of the early 1970s, as well as an association with the London Lions short-lived incarnation at Wembley in 1973/74 as a Detroit farm team:

Detroit 'phoned me from the Munich Olympic Games in 1972 saying they wanted me to set up the Detroit team, asking me for my answer sharpish. I said 'Yes' after about two seconds! I took them down to Paisley, Fife and Falkirk. Everybody that I 'phoned and made appointments with, they were there to meet me and John Ziegler. When we came to Falkirk, there was big Peter the ice man, who sorted the rinks for the curling! That man Jack Reid didn't even come.

We were sitting in Edinburgh Airport, and I asked John Ziegler: 'Where would you like to go?' He said: 'Falkirk – the catchment area, Glasgow and Edinburgh, Cumbernauld.' He knew it all. They wanted to come here, before they even thought about Wembley. He had heard about this rivalry in football between Scotland and England, and he wanted to develop that. They made a mess of it.

Carlyle had been player-coach of the Great Britain team which won the Pool 'B' silver medal at the 1961 World Championships, and later bench coached British teams at Pool 'C' level in 1971 and 1973:

A thing I don't like, and have never liked, is Canadians being here for three years and playing for Great Britain. That, for me, is a no-no, definitely. I've opened my mouth about it, and some people have not been too happy, but it's a no-no. We went to World Championships, had a couple of good years, had a couple of bad ones, dropped down. But at least we were all British. If a fellow comes into the juniors, then gets into the seniors, the next step for him is into the Great Britain team – it's something to aim for, and that all stopped. When you look at the British players now, they're not there, you couldn't make a team.

We had a couple of lads from the north of England, Terry and Kenny Matthews, when we went to the Championships in Holland in 1971. We beat Holland, and there was an interview after the game with myself and big John Milne, the manager. They said to me: 'Very good result; where's your training camp?' Well, I said that Terry and Kenny Matthews, and another one from down there, they came up on a Friday to Murrayfield and we had a couple of hours. So they laughed, and said: 'You joke, you joke!' Well, it got that bad, they just wouldn't believe me, but that was the truth. So, I told them: 'Well, I must admit, we've been in training camp in Aviemore for three months!' They believed that, and wrote it – it was a lie! We could never get that, or have afforded it.

Which Canadian players impressed Johnny over his long career?

Well, I would go with Bobby Burns; Jerry Hudson, I had a lot of time for him; and a fellow called Frank Davis, that was at the start.

At my very start in ice hockey with the Lions, the Canadians didn't talk to me when I got a game, and I had to fight at a practice. But this Frank Davis, I was skating, and he joined me and said: 'They think you're doing a Canadian out of a place.'

So, there was Frank Davis at Falkirk and, I've got to say, Bill Glennie at Harringay; and Don Johnson at Harringay, a big, strong player.

The likes of 'Nebby' Thrasher and company, they were good wee players, but the only reason they were over here was that they'd have got slaughtered in North America. We had George Sinfield at Falkirk; my wife was bigger than him! And 'Nebby' Thrasher was the same. Good wee stickhandlers, and good for the crowd. But, if you go into the meat of things, they had a player in Dundee, Norm Gustavsen, now he went to the NHL. But he broke out of training camp and came back with a case of beer over his shoulder, and that was him bombed out!

I liked Jerry Hudson's style of play (and I was at his funeral, too). He was the type of lad who could stickhandle, set you up, all the rest of it. If we were a man short we gave Jerry Hudson the puck, because they couldn't get it off him.

One of the best hockey players I played with was Bobby Burns, who played with Dundee, Kirkcaldy and Falkirk. I only got two real checks in my lifetime: one was Lawson Neil sneaked up on me at Ayr, I can see it yet, I had cut in – bang! Where did he come from? And the other was Bobby Burns. I said: 'Hey Bobby, how did you do that? He said, 'you were a potential puck-carrier!"

I remember that line of Andre Girard, Domenico and Martini with Ayr; they were good. I played against them later for Edinburgh, opening the rink in Geneva. I got injured!

Who were the best of British remembered by Johnny?

They say now that Tony Hand's the best British ice hockey player ever. He's a great hockey player, but he's a great forward. I've saw him trying to play defence, and he hasn't a clue. I always think they should differentiate between defencemen and forwards.

To me, 'Tuck' Syme was a great defenceman. He could break up a play and move, and when he came back, the reach he had, being a big boy. Again, it's a matter of opinion. I always admired 'Tuck'; I thought 'Tuck' Syme was the best British defenceman ever. And when 'Tuck' went away to Canada, 'Tiny' still played with Paisley. They were two different people, the two Syme brothers.

The line of Spence, Forbes and Macdonald, at both Altrincham and Kirkcaldy, was, to me, the best British forward line. Ian Forbes was the man. Jimmy Spence was a good hockey player; Sammy Macdonald, not as good as the other two, but fitted the line perfectly. The combination of the three of them was good.

Marshall Key from Dundee was a damned good hockey player. As far as I was concerned, he was the best centre-iceman in Britain. He went to Harringay with me, the same year. He had signed for a Swiss team, and couldn't get out the contract. So Bill Glennie let him go and play in Switzerland, because the Racers were going on their eight-week tour and Marshall would only miss a couple of weeks, because the Swiss season was a short one.

'Red' Imrie and I played with Falkirk, and then I went to Harringay. 'Red' Stapleford from Streatham wrote me a letter saying I had been very successful at Harringay, and asking if there were any more in Scotland like me. First of all I went to Glennie, and showed him the letter. I told him I could recommend a player – a good player – and asked if he wanted him. He said he couldn't, he already had two (meaning me and Marshall Key). So, I gave Stapleford 'Red' Imrie's name. He went down, and played well in Streatham. Then, when it folded, and I went to Brighton, they told me that they weren't putting any Canadians in the team – it'll be all-British, that's our gimmick. So I got 'Red' [Imrie], he was still up in Streatham (he got married up there), and him and I played as a defensive team together.

When I was quitting Brighton, they asked me who I thought should take over from me as coach. I said: 'Give it to 'Red' Imrie, he's got a good hockey brain.'

I was a salesman, and I would never knock the opposition's product! There's a lot I could say, but it's only your opinion! Johnny Quales played on that British team in 1950, and if you had opened the doors he would have been out through them into the car park! To me, if Johnny Quayles had another brain it would've rattled! An ice hockey brain I'm talking about. He could skate, but if he got going, you could have opened the doors and went right round the car park and back again, he was that type.

Big Geordie Watt, from Perth, we used to call him 'Quarter-to-three feet', if you got past his feet, you were in!

We went to Switzerland in 1961 with Great Britain, and Joe Brown, rather than write in scrap merchant when he filled in his passport, he wrote in ice hockey player against his profession. And they nicked him for it, but we got it all sorted out in the end. That was the year that Ian Forbes had peritonitis, we went into his hotel room and he was lying on the floor; his appendix had burst. Do you know, they wouldn't sort him, or operate on him, until they got the insurance details, which we couldn't find. Alan Weekes wrote a cheque there and then to have him attended to.

There were players when I was coaching Great Britain who were good; of the two Brennans, Billy was the better hockey player, as far as I was concerned; he had it up here. Alastair, for a start, was too wee. But the London Lions wanted two British players to bring in, to work out with them; and I put Alastair Brennan's name forward – I don't know if he ever knew this – and the other name I put forward was Kenny Matthews, from the north of England. They never got there, because it folded. Kenny was a hard, wee player. I used to ask him to rough it up a bit, and he'd come off aching all over; he couldn't sit down!

Andy Williams was my apprentice painter with Sinclair. The best game that Andy Williams and Joe McIntosh had, and I tell Joe every time I see him, was our last game with Edinburgh when we went down and had to play Brighton. We had beaten Southampton on the Saturday, and we had to beat Brighton on the Sunday for a clean sweep. 'Red' Imrie and me was one defensive pair, and Joe McIntosh and Andy Williams was the other. They weren't big, those two laddies, and they were playing against Jack McDonald, Lorne Trottier, Bob Bragagnola, Bob McNeil – these were all good Canadians back from the continent – top men. Well, we beat them. We were winning 6-5 and they drew their goaltender. We got the puck and scored on the empty net to win it 7-5. But those two were playing against hockey players who were streets ahead of them, and they beat them. It was the best game they had. And wee Andy died there, three or four years back.

When we played in Paris at the 1951 World Championships, they were putting down eight-course meals on the table for us, and bottles of wine; that was fatal in those days! Tommy Paton was quoted by an English reporter as saying he'd have preferred tatties and mince!

Two of John's Falkirk and Great Britain team-mates hold a special place in his affections, Bill Sneddon and Kenny Nicholson:

Johnny Carlyle (Edinburgh Royals) receives the BIHA Cup from Sussex and England cricketer Ted Dexter, Sports Stadium, Brighton, 1961. (Johnny Carlyle archive)

Bill Sneddon was a very good player, there's no doubt about it. You could always depend on him for 100 per cent commitment. But, a character! When you played as a unit on defence, in my day, one's the boss. One says: 'I've got him,' or 'On you go.' That means he goes out, and if he comes here – bang! If I've got him, and he comes inside, the other fellow hits him – bang! Now, I've said to Billy: 'on you go', and looked, and he's no' there! He's up six rows, eight rows, fighting in the crowd! That was him!

At Ayr, he drew a right and hit Andre Girard. Oh my god, it was a riot! I was in it, too, and they were fighting and battering in the crowd. You know at Ayr, you sat on the bench, then there was a walkway, and the seats just went up. The crowd came down, and that was it, Billy got the jail that night. McNeil got put off the bench, and the next time we were there he was sitting away up sending wee notes down to the bench. But I can always remember there was a fight at Ayr, and McNeil threw us on to the ice. Somebody had George Sinfield over the wee, low barrier and the people sitting in there were hitting him! So, McNeil said: 'over you go.' I can always remember that Ken McMurtrie of Ayr came up to me and said: 'Johnny, come oot o' there,' and bang – Bobby Burns hit him! And Ken was just trying to get me out of the fracas!

Billy went to Canada, and played for Chatham Maroons. He was doing the same there. They brought him back as a 'Canadian', and he brought two players with him from Chatham: Earl Towers and Nobby Campbell (Wee Towers was alright, Campbell wasn't that great).

We were in Edinburgh playing the Royals. Billy did something, and Bert Gemmell, who was the referee, put him off to the dressing-room. We were sitting on the bench, and Billy used to stay with me occasionally at my mother and father's house, and I was his pal. So, McNeil says to me: 'John, off you go; get into that dressing-room with Billy.' When I went in, he'd had his shower and was getting dressed. Billy was very soft-spoken and he says: 'John, are you coming up for a meal?' I said that I'd just be up and asked him if he was waiting for me. He said no, so I asked him to order me tomato soup and a piece of fish! So, he goes away and I got dressed, and I go up to the rink restaurant. He's sitting at a table; I went over and says: 'Alright, Bill?' He said: 'Yes, I've ordered you something.'

But before my meal was served, two policemen came into the restaurant and came across. One says: 'You're under arrest, for assault' and they're looking at me! One of them said: 'William Sneddon?' I said, pointing at Billy, 'that's William Sneddon, no' me!'

Falkirk's Scottish defensive unit: Johnny Carlyle (left) and Bill Sneddon (right) *c.*1951. (Johnny Carlyle archive)

What Billy did say was that Bert Gemmell put him off, and when Bill was on his way to the restaurant he saw that the game had finished. So he went round to the referee's room and knocked at the door. Bert Gemmell had a stutter, and he answered the door, saying: 'Hello Bill, what's the matter?' Billy said: 'Well, you were a big man on the ice, are you a big man now?' Bert said: 'Oh, Billy, come on…' Bang! I think Billy broke his jaw, and then just shut the door. And went up to the restaurant and had his tomato soup!

Oh, the things he did!

Half the team in Brighton wouldn't go on a tour, so I asked Billy to come with us, along with Willie Clark, Glen Reilly and Gordie Ross from Edinburgh. We were in Innsbruck, in Austria, and they had this Canadian that they'd flown over for this game. He was a centre-ice, and he was doing his stuff, So, Billy says: 'I'll take centre.' Billy went for the face-off, and it was like a bayonet fight for a second or two! Of course, the referee whistled, and put Willie off. And he's saying: 'Me?' and appealing to the crowd. Then he starts giving Nazi salutes to the Austrians, you could have heard a pin drop!

When I was with Harringay Racers, the Moscow State Circus came in for six to eight weeks. We played three games a week before that, and then three games a week after it left. But the two months it was there, we went away on tour. Czechoslovakia first; then Russia, Sweden, Norway, Poland, Germany, Belgium; always finishing up in Holland. And Billy was always asking me about Russia; what did I think?

Billy's biggest failing was he couldn't control his temper. His other saying was: 'I was a paratrooper; I had to hold my breath for ten minutes – come on!' But he was a good, good player.

He was in the Pathfinders in India during the war, and he was a great friend of William Franklyn, the actor. When Franklyn was on *This Is Your Life* on TV, Billy's voice came over saying something like: 'Attention, hands out your pockets!' Bill Franklyn called him 'Jock'.

Bill died in a swimming pool on holiday; he was dead before he hit the water, because there was no water in his lungs. There were a lot of hockey players at Bill's funeral, and I was the leader of them, if you like. There was no minister at the service; just this man preaching communism. When I went out after the service, Kit (Bill's wife) had gone to a car, and this man was standing, but I never shook hands with him, and neither did any of the other hockey players. Do you know what he said about Billy's hockey career? 'He was also an ice hockey player.' That's all he said about one of the finest players produced in this country. He spoke plenty about Billy sitting in at the pit at Bo'ness, stopping a big ship in the Forth, getting the jail for striking an official; but that's all he said about his hockey. It was terrible.

Billy listened to the crowd, as we've all done. But he'd be up three or four rows, or challenging them to come down and outside and everything. He turned a few faces white, I can tell you!

The story about Kenny Nicholson was that he spoke a mixture of Canadian and Scots; kind of half and half! Saying things like: 'Goddammit, I've broken mah pincil [my pencil]'; things like that! He married a girl from Cowdenbeath in Fife, and when he finished the hockey he went down the mines. He had an accident, and had one leg shorter than the other. He was a good friend of mine, although he was a good bit older than me. He looked older, even when he was in his early twenties. And he died quite young.

That was 'Nick', but a good hockey player. He didn't look great as a skater, but if he got in front of you, you couldn't get past him. And when he went in on a goalkeeper, which you don't see now, it was four down and three across – that's where he'd put the puck. It's a slapshot now. Oh aye, 'Nick' was good.

As I say, he never looked fast, and if he got in front of you, you were trailing at his back, you couldn't get round him. But he was a good hockey player. He was a clever player; he was more brains than robust. He didn't go flying about and charging like me. A good, brainy hockey player, he could set you up.

'Nick' had been brought up in Toronto, but his parents were from one of the Scottish islands. He'd played hockey at Crossmyloof and Paisley with Jim Kenny ('The Fox') and Don 'Schoolboy' Cumming. He'd been in the Navy during the war and came to Falkirk from Glasgow and got a job working with Aitken's Brewery. Then he went as a relief manager for them in their different pubs, eventually getting the tenancy of one in Bo'ness, before moving over to Fife to go into the mines.

Johnny returned to Falkirk before the Brighton rink closed in 1965:

When I finished with the hockey, I came back to Falkirk and, let's face it, going back to £11 or £12 a week as a painter, who are you kidding? So I became a Hoover rep. I had a friend who worked for them who put my name down, so they took me to Nottingham for six weeks, and my wife had to show me how to wire a three-pin plug before I went!

I became a supervisor with them, and my boss there went away to Parnall washing machines. He approached me and said I'd get a car, £20-odd a week (a lot of money then), and an expense account that didn't require receipts! They gave me the job, and I was there until I went to Rank Bush Murphy, selling colour televisions to shops all over Scotland. I got fed up with that, finished, told them it wasn't for me.

I came back and put an advert in the local paper, and became a self-employed painter and decorator for a while. Then I bought a shop in Falkirk that sold everything – wallpaper, pails, bicycle clips, everything! I then made it a fruit shop; then I had another fruit shop; then I had a café, The Penny Farthing, in Falkirk.

But then my wife took ill, it was too much work. Her health was more important to me, so I threw it all in and thought: 'What do I do now?' My son, Garry, was working with a computer firm which had folded, and he couldn't get a job. So, we got help for a year from one of these enterprise schemes, and we started up a painting and decorating business again. He runs it now; it's been going all that time. He doesn't advertise; it's all word of mouth.

Johnny Carlyle, when coaching Murrayfield and Great Britain. (Johnny Carlyle archive)

Johnny and his wife now live in retirement in a flat in their native Falkirk, doting on their young grandson. A well-known and respected individual in Falkirk and district, he still retains a keen interest in his first sporting love of ice hockey.

He is dismayed by the current state of the sport, particularly in Scotland. What really saddens this legend of British ice hockey, however, as he looks back over his 'Life with the Lions', is that the sport which was his passion has been torpid in his hometown of Falkirk for over forty years and will never return.

This knowledge is somehow all the more unsettling to those, like Johnny, who remember when Falkirk was the epicentre of the sport in Scotland. The building that was Falkirk Ice Rink still stands on Grangemouth Road; a cruel daily reminder of what has been lost.

Career Record

	GP	G	A	Pts	PiM
Johnny Carlyle (Falkirk/Harringay/Edinburgh/Nottingham/Brighton/Murrayfield) 1946-1965	572	118	215	333	560
(Records unavailable for 1960-1962.)					
Great Britain 1950-1961	16	9	3	12	8

7

Red Lion: Bill Sneddon

The many accolades bestowed upon Bill Sneddon at the time of his sadly premature death in 1990 are indicative of his abilities as one of the best ever British defencemen. The *Falkirk Herald* said that:

> Bill Sneddon was a legend – and will remain so wherever ice hockey is played or talked about… As a defenceman he had few equals… In the years after the war, when ice hockey caught the imagination of the nation, the name of Bill Sneddon stood out like a beacon.

Yet, there was also a great dichotomy at work, because the same Bill Sneddon had twice been suspended *sine die* by the Scottish Ice Hockey Association. This Latin legalese, which translates as 'without day/date', was much favoured by the middle-class accountants and doctors who administered Scottish ice hockey in the post-war era.

Usually mispronounced as 'Sin Dye', it was wrongly assumed to mean a life ban, but was formulated to allow the hockey authorities to circumvent any restraint of trade claims that such a ban could possibly invoke. Like the 'retain and transfer' system employed by their football counterparts at the time, it ensured that the governing bodies and clubs held all the aces.

That Bill Sneddon received two such bans in his career in part reflects his rugged, no-nonsense style of play, but it also brings into stark relief a darker side of his fierce competitive spirit and will to win. Conversely, it is, too, indicative of the more rounded personality of a complex man who railed against authority for much of his life, be it referees within the narrower confines of ice hockey, or social injustice in a much wider context. Thus the tributes he received at the time of his passing were more than just ice hockey related, as the *Falkirk and Grangemouth Advertiser* noted:

> …his efforts were always aimed at improving local conditions in the workplace and in the community… He will be remembered for the work he achieved, for the tasks he attempted and for the inspiration and encouragement that he gave to so many others.

William Sneddon was born on 13 July 1925 in the family home at 3 Kerse View, Dalgrain Road, Grangemouth. Kerse View is an Edwardian sandstone terrace, comprising four houses. Sneddon was born in one of the two mid-terrace houses which, at the time of his birth, overlooked the Forth and Clyde Canal (this part of the canal is now, sadly, filled in and a dual carriageway runs along its length).

He was the third son of Samuel Sneddon and Jeanie Savoy, who had married on Boxing Day, 1911, at The United Free Church Manse, Laurieston, Falkirk. His father, a former spirit dealer, was employed as a ship checker in the Grangemouth docks at the time of Bill's birth.

Bill Sneddon, on the ice at Falkirk Ice Rink, 1948/49. (*Ice Hockey World* photo)

Bill received his primary education in Grangemouth at Dundas School, before moving on to Grangemouth High School. His widow, Kit, recalls that he was still at school when the nearby Falkirk Ice Rink opened:

> Bill started going to the skating at Falkirk when the rink opened in 1938, when he was aged thirteen. He started playing hockey with the Falkirk Cubs, the junior team. I think it would have been Nelson McCuaig that would have started him off with the hockey, as he used to talk about him. He also had a great deal of respect for George McNeil as a coach.
>
> After he left school, Bill was an apprentice electrician in the docks at Grangemouth. As a boy, he was greatly involved in something to do with the Navy, the Sea Cadets, I think. They wanted him to go into the Fleet Air Arm, but Bill went into the Air Force and trained as a pilot.
>
> Bill had two sisters and two brothers (one of his sisters, Sheena, is still living in London). He was desperate to get in, as he had lost his two elder brothers in the war. Jim was in the army and died in a Japanese POW camp; Sam was in the Merchant Navy and had been blown up on a tanker.

The loss of Jim, a signalman, was particularly hard for Bill and his family, as he left a little daughter who was aged only two when last seen by her father:

> He went in about two and a half years before the end of the war. I think you were called up at eighteen, but you could volunteer at seventeen – Bill volunteered.

Bill did his pilot training with Bill Franklyn, who became a very successful actor after the war. After their training they found themselves in a Holding Section. They were both desperate to get into action, so they both volunteered for the Paratroopers. They then did their paratroop training together at Ringway, in Manchester.

They were split up after their training, Bill went to India, where he was a Pathfinder, and lost touch with Bill Franklyn, who always called Bill 'Jock'.

Franklyn was to achieve nationwide television recognition in the 1960s as the star of the 'Schh...you know who' Schweppes advertising campaign. Bill was to make a television appearance with his wartime friend, as Kit describes:

Years later, William Franklyn was featured on *This Is Your Life*, and the researchers tracked down Bill at a conference he was attending in Aberdeen. It took quite a bit of talking to get him to agree to do it, as that sort of thing just wasn't Bill. They flew him down to London, and he came on as one of the guests.

Kit remembers that Bill Sneddon was also a keen amateur boxer and fine junior footballer, and he might have made a name for himself in that sport, but hockey was his love:

He played football in his younger days. When he was in the Pathfinders, they were delayed in getting to a match in India or Burma, and Bill had a photograph of them getting off the 'plane in their football strips, and straight onto the field for the game!

Bill's wartime service in the Far East was with the military elite as the role of the Pathfinder required men of the very highest calibre, both physically and psychologically. Arriving at a drop zone in advance of the main body of airborne troops, they had to secure the immediate area from enemy interference, as well as setting up beacons to identify the dropping areas.

After his demobilisation from the Forces at the end of the war, Sneddon resumed his hockey at the Falkirk rink. His senior debut for Falkirk Lions came on 22 October 1947, when he helped Lions to a 9-2 Autumn Cup win over Dundee Tigers at Grangemouth Road. The *Falkirk Mail* noted that, 'Junior player Sneddon played with confidence when on the ice.' That may be interpreted as a veiled criticism of his six minutes of penalties on his debut! He would, however, play just another three Scottish National League games for Lions that season.

Sneddon first represented Scotland some six weeks later, playing in an Olympic trial on his home rink. The Scots lost 2-4, with the *Falkirk Mail* reporting that: 'The Scots' main strength lay in defence, and Sneddon of Falkirk and T Syme of Dunfermline, attracted the interest of the British selectors present by their clever position-play, smart poke-checking and constant vigilance.'

Unfortunately for Sneddon, he didn't receive the call to the 1948 Winter Olympics; but, for a player too often associated with the more physical aspects of the game, it is also interesting to note a local press report on the junior Falkirk Cubs' 4-2 win at Glasgow over Mustangs on 6 January 1948: 'W Sneddon, the Cubs' captain, was outstanding for his stick-handling and easy skating style.'

The *Falkirk Mail* of 17 September 1948 reported that:

Last season's juniors Bill Sneddon and Ken Nicholson have shown up very well in the early training. Both should hold their own in the match play. The former has greatly increased in speed and finish, while Nick has that good aptitude at the net.

The *Mail*'s words were prophetic, as 1948/49 was his breakthrough season with the Lions when, at the age of twenty-three, he played in 63 games, scoring 8 goals and recording 22 assists for 30 points, accumulating 63 penalty minutes.

Great Britain *v.* USA, Empress Hall, London, 14 March 1950. Bill Sneddon (left) challenges the USA's Prince Johnson. (Stan Christie archive)

Given the backing of coach George McNeil, Bill Sneddon became the mainstay of defence during a very successful Canadian-dominated post-war period for Falkirk Lions; assisting them to successive Play-Off Championships and Canada Cups in 1948/49 and 1949/50, with the Scottish Cup also secured during 1948/49 and a further Canada Cup in 1951/52.

In January 1950, Sneddon impressed for Falkirk against touring Edmonton Mercurys, who would represent Canada at the World Championships in March. The *Falkirk Mail* commented that:

> Finch is still the best keeper in Scotland. And comparable with him was Billy Sneddon. His defence work and occasional rushes were excellent and the Mercurys had some more than complimentary remarks to say about his play after the game. Billy if he keeps up that form will be a star in the championships in London.

Sneddon and Ayr's Lawson Neil provided Great Britain's second defensive unit in the 1950 World Championships, in which the British finished fourth. Like the Syme brothers, this was to be Bill's only World Championship. His subsequent 'senior' status with the Lions meant he was deemed a professional and unable to be selected for World tournaments in the rules then prevailing (he would have gone with the British team to the Swedish World Championships in 1963; work commitments, however, precluded this).

Ayr goaltender Stan Christie backstopped the British team in 1950 and he was a great admirer of Sneddon, as he explains:

> Bill was a great player, but he was a Jekyll and Hyde character. If a goal was scored against his team, he always blamed himself. Bill was the nicest chap you could wish to meet – off the ice. He just got heated up with the hockey, but you're the best of pals off the ice.

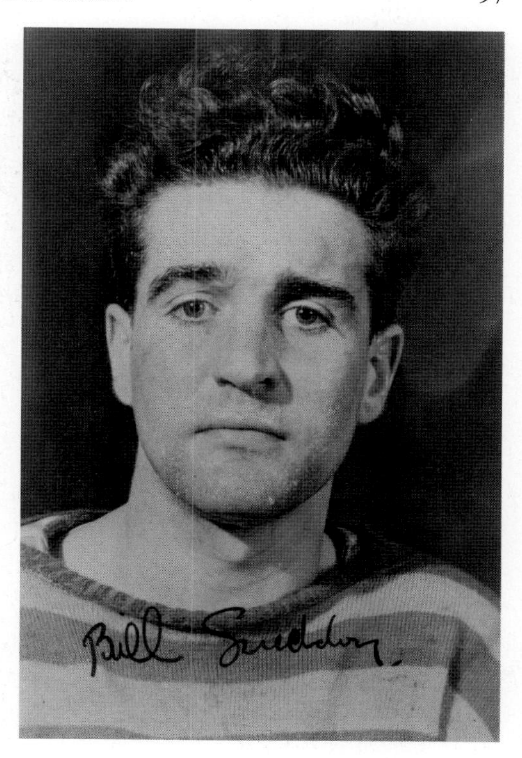

Bill Sneddon, Falkirk Lions, 1950/51. (*Ice Hockey World* photo)

Sneddon found the net on his GB debut, a 9-0 rout of France on 13 March 1950, with Sid Montford noting in the *Daily Record* that: '...Sneddon, with his sharp interceptions and powerful rushes was another who claimed attention.' Sneddon's second goal of that tournament was much more important, coming as it did only two seconds from the end against Norway four days later, when his high shot into the corner from the blueline gave Britain a 4-3 win at Wembley.

Bill received a knee injury at the 1950 tournament in unusual circumstances, during a 2-3 defeat by the USA at Wembley, as Sid Montford of the Glasgow *Evening News* related:

> Bill Sneddon... was picked up then held forcibly on the ice by fellow Scot 'Tuck' Syme during the Britain *v.* America match at Wembley... Syme 'iced' Sneddon when the latter was protesting violently to the Swiss referee against a penalty given to one of his colleagues. Sneddon attempted to get at the official, but Syme, deputy captain of the team, jumped on him and forced him to the ice still struggling.

Sneddon struggled to assist the injury-depleted British team in the next match against Canada at Harringay, but his painful knee ended his participation early in the second period. Subsequently, the *Falkirk Mail* reported that Sneddon '...had an operation to his knee in the Falkirk and District Royal Infirmary on Monday [27 March 1950]. A torn cartilage was the trouble, and lack of proper attention in London aggravated matters...'

The injury would have quite unexpected, and pleasant, consequences, as Kit explains:

> I first met Bill at Ayr Ice Rink one summer. He had had a cartilage operation and was trying to strengthen up his knee. He was looking for some ice to start skating again, and had gone down to Blackpool, but there was an ice show or something on there. So, he came up to Ayr, where there was summer skating every day.

Bill wed Catherine [Kit] Reid Ewing a year later, on 7 May 1951, at The High Kirk Manse, Catrine, Ayrshire. Kit was then a twenty-four-year-old cashier at Ayr Ice Rink, residing at her parents' home, Beechgrove, Sorn, Ayrshire, where her father was a wood contractor. As it was the hockey close season, Bill's occupation was listed as 'Electrician.'

Their first daughter, Katerina, arrived on Boxing Day 1951, at Beechgrove, Sorn, and her birth certificate describes her father's occupation as 'Ice Hockey Player'. A second daughter, Wilma, was born on 5 March 1954, at the then family home at 483 King Street, Stenhousemuir.

The newlyweds could have gone to Canada in 1951. Bill had received a good offer from ex-Lions' defenceman Johnny Callanan that summer. Callanan would have fixed up a job for him and a place on a Canadian team, but Sneddon turned down the offer as he had already signed for another year with Falkirk. It was to be a regrettable decision and subsequent events in the 1951/52 season precipitated a move to Canada.

During a match at Ayr on 25 January 1952, between the local Raiders and Falkirk, Sneddon was assessed a minor penalty for cross-checking Ayr's Girard after twenty-six minutes; Girard at the same time was penalised for high sticking. Sneddon then hit Girard as he lay on the ice and was thus awarded a further five minutes for fighting and a match misconduct penalty. According to the *Ayr Advertiser*, 'He crossed the ice towards the visitors box, with his hands outstretched and laughed in derision at the crowd who were enraged at his behaviour.' He then became involved in an altercation with a spectator, whom he struck with his stick on the forearm.

He was arrested by police, and led from the stadium in his hockey uniform. An appearance at Ayr Burgh Court followed the next morning. The *Evening Times* reported that:

> On his own behalf Sneddon said that during the game Girard... had cross-checked him across the neck... Accused said he skated towards his own bench. He was not using obscene language. Some of the spectators pushed down to the team bench and one of them, he said, 'made a grab for him. I took my stick and struck one of them on the arm.'

He was fined a total of £10 on two charges; one of assault and another of breach of the peace, and given fourteen days to pay, with an alternative of twenty days' imprisonment.

Bill sent a letter of resignation to the Scottish Ice Hockey Association, and told the *Evening Times*:

> ...that he would go on the first available boat, but if no berths were available meantime, he would travel to Canada with the Canadian players when they return home at the end of the season... Falkirk are certainly going to miss Sneddon. He has been their best defenceman since the war.

The SIHA announced the following week that he had been banned from playing hockey in Scotland, 'for the part he took in an incident at the Ayr rink'. Festus Moffat of the SIHA clarified the nature of the ban for the *Evening Times*:

> The Sneddon suspension is not in any sense intended as a life sentence as some supporters seem to think... So far as the Association were concerned... they were dealing solely with the referee's report on the match misconduct penalty imposed on Sneddon during the match at Ayr... Any suggestion of imposing a life suspension on an international basis just could not be entertained... Only a maiming offence is considered by the International Association [for a life suspension]. Whatever may have been true about Bill Sneddon, he never was a fellow likely to maim any player in the course of a game. News that he goes to Canada with a complete release of Association and his club will be welcomed by all concerned in the game here.

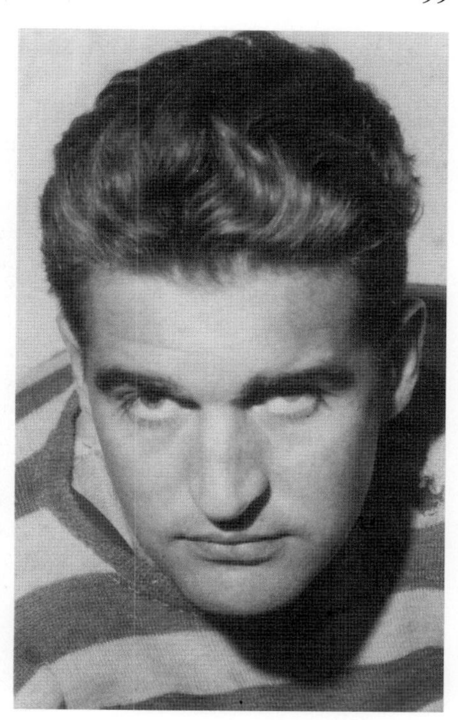

Bill Sneddon, Falkirk Lions, 1951/52. (*Ice Hockey World* photo)

Sneddon then spent eighteen months in Chatham, Ontario, as Kit remembers:

After his first *sine die* suspension, he went to Canada for two seasons. He played so much with Canadians, some of the fellows spoke to Bernie Gold, who owned the Chatham Maroons.

The hockey in Canada was rougher – much rougher – it suited Bill great! We said that the referee blew his whistle to start the game, and didn't blow it again until the end of the game!

Bill gave his all in everything; he went on the ice to win. One of his proudest possessions was a letter he had from the Detroit Red Wings of the NHL, inviting him for a trial, during the time we were in Canada. He kept that letter for a long while.

Bill actually worked part-time with Libby's, the fruit juice people, at their canning factory in Chatham. They were doing a conversion, changing the voltage to the American way of electricity, and Bill worked on that. The Chatham Maroons did practise a lot, and had a lot of away games, so he got as much time off work as he needed. The Maroons were like local celebrities in Chatham. He would come home with cans of tomato juice, orange juice from the factory.

His suspension was lifted by the SIHA in March 1953, as reported by Bill Stewart of the *Evening Times*:

Sneddon, one of the best defencemen that Scotland has produced, was suspended towards the end of last season… He went to Canada and has been playing there this season. But, although Bill was holding his own in Canadian hockey, he wanted back to this side of the Atlantic. Recently he wrote to the Scottish Association asking if his suspension could be raised so that he could play on the continent. That the association have gone one better and left him free to play again in the Scottish circuit will, I'm sure, be good news to Scottish fans.

Falkirk Lions 1953/54. From left to right: Canadian Bob Campbell and Scots Bill Sneddon, Joe McIntosh, Johnny Carlyle and Tommy Paton. (Johnny Carlyle archive)

Kit remembers that their return to Scotland was not as clear cut, however:

> He got word from Scotland that the *sine die* suspension had been lifted. They tried hard to get him to stay in Canada; I remember Detroit wanted him to go out west to play in Calgary. But he got a lot of letters from Falkirk fans pleading with him to return. He swithered a bit, but I don't think it was a difficult decision for him to go back home to the Lions.

On returning to Falkirk, Bill brought over two of his former teammates from Chatham, Earl Towers and Nobby Clark, to play for the Lions.

His return to the Lions was to be shortlived, however. Falkirk were coasting to an emphatic 5-0 win over Edinburgh Royals at Murrayfield on 8 February 1954, when Sneddon was given a two-minute penalty for holding late in the game. He argued with referee Gemmell and was then given another two minutes for showing dissent. He went to the penalty box, where he was given a misconduct penalty, but then came back on to the ice and was assessed a match misconduct.

The aftermath of this incident, when he assaulted referee Gemmell, is described elsewhere in this book by Bill's teammate Johnny Carlyle. As a result, the Referees' Committee of the SIHA met at Crossmyloof the following week and imposed another *sine die* suspension on Sneddon. Ironically, the loss of Bill Sneddon allowed Falkirk coach George McNeil to introduce youngster 'Red' Imrie as a replacement, and he in turn would have a long and successful career in British ice hockey.

Kit recalls that Bill's second suspension was to have a much longer duration:

> His second *sine die* suspension wasn't lifted for a long, long time. I think that's when he went to work for Alexander's Coachbuilders at Drip Road in Stirling. I remember that Sid

Montford, the sportswriter (and father of Arthur Montford) stuck up for Bill through thick and thin. Bill was Sid Montford's blue-eyed boy!

Bill's personality off the ice was somewhat different to the image of him held by the average hockey supporter, as Kit explains:

> He was a quiet fellow; you would only find out things that you asked him, he wouldn't volunteer information.
>
> He was very quiet, unassuming off the ice. As soon as he put the skates on, he was an extrovert. He very much believed that if you do it, you do it right and you do it to win.
>
> I remember he was particularly unpopular with the crowd at Ayr, which was quite ironic as I worked in the office at Ayr Ice Rink! They were throwing coins onto the ice at Ayr, and I can remember Bill going round waltzing and curtseying, picking up the coins and thanking them for their money! Off the ice, you could not imagine him behaving like that.
>
> If he ever got a penalty playing at Durham with the Falkirk Cubs, old 'Icy' Smith (who owned the Durham rink) would demand that the referee put Bill back on the ice because the fans wanted to see him!

He inspired his Falkirk teammates by his own selfless example, bringing out that little bit extra in everyone. He would rally the team with his battle cry, which employed a local saying used in the Falkirk district: 'Come on, lads, let's give them ten minutes of Dunipace!' Bill's tough, uncompromising, competitive style ensured he was idolised by the Falkirk fans, and his fitness was legendary, as Kit relates:

> He was a tremendous keep-fit person, did exercises all the time and watched what he ate. I remember during one hockey close season, he cycled up one coast of Scotland, along the north, and back down the opposite coast. That was the start of his keep-fit exercise regime for the season in earnest! He did that a few summers, sometimes going up the east coast and back down the west, and vice versa, and he always met the same chap halfway each year who was doing it the opposite way!
>
> Bill would never admit to being ill. He would come in from the hockey stitched, walking with a limp or whatever. But he would always manage to be up and able to walk to the car the next morning.
>
> I remember a televised game from Wembley, when the girls were quite young. We were all settled down at home in front of the television, ready to watch Bill, and the first thing the cameras zoomed in on was Bill on the bench being stitched!
>
> It was like that back then, he was always getting teeth knocked out, dislocated shoulders. You'd get a 'phone call at home from the police to say that he'd been taken to the hospital after the game to get fixed up!
>
> Bill wasn't one who would ever knock anybody. He liked everybody who played ice hockey with him. Johnny Carlyle was the name he mentioned most of the Falkirk boys and he also had a lot of respect for Ken Nicholson. He was also fond of the Syme brothers of Dunfermline; he would speak a lot about them.

After a seven-year absence from the sport, Bill returned to hockey with the amateur Falkirk Lions during 1961/62, at the age of thirty-six. He captained Murrayfield Royals in 1962/63, when he was an All Star 'B' team defenceman.

In 1963/64, Sneddon teamed up with Fife Flyers, who were spearheaded by player-coach Ian Forbes and Jimmy Spence, both from Perth. The Kirkcaldy side swept all before them in winning the Scottish League and play-offs, and lifted the televised BBC *Grandstand* trophy. It was a personal triumph, too, for Bill Sneddon, as he was voted on to a defensive berth on the All Star 'A' team.

Sneddon was an All Star 'B' defenceman with Flyers in 1964/65, and was a stalwart at Kirkcaldy the following season (when no All Star selections were made).

At the age of forty-one, he harboured no thoughts of hanging up his skates, and teamed up again at Murrayfield with the newly-formed Racers for the inaugural Northern League in 1966/67. Returning to Fife for 1967/68, he picked up another All Star 'B' team nomination, and was similarly honoured the following season when back at Murrayfield, assisting Racers to the Spring Cup play-offs title, just short of his forty-fourth birthday.

His surprising longevity in top-level hockey finally ended with Dundee Rockets, in 1971/72, under coach Ian Forbes, a former teammate from the Great Britain team back in 1950, as Kit remembers:

> He played hockey into his forties, but he got his skates on again for an Oldtimers tournament in Kirkcaldy in 1980, when he was fifty-five. Two of the players died during the tournament. One of them had been changing over with Bill, who thought the chap had tripped and fell, but he had actually collapsed and died on the ice. That made him decide that enough was enough.
>
> We would still have the odd skate together after that, but Bill never played hockey again. His other main interest was hillwalking and rockclimbing. He did all the 'Munroes' in Scotland, and went to Austria and Italy to climb.
>
> He was also a great trade unionist, but politics were never discussed. I would never know that he had been to get coal for old people or whatever – he'd never talk about it, he played it down. He was quite a secretive person; he didn't talk much about these things.
>
> All his talk was of golf. I didn't do the hills with him – he was too quick – but we golfed together. He never felt he was good enough for the golf. He played off eighteen, but would never enter any tournaments; his competitiveness meant he would have needed to have been a scratch player before entering.
>
> When he left Alexanders, Bill went to work as an Electrical Engineer at Kincardine Power Station, and then for the Coal Board at Kinneil Colliery in Bo'ness.
>
> When they wanted to close Kinneil, a decision was taken by the unions to go underground for a sit-in protest. Bill was the Shop Steward for the tradesmen and it was originally the National Union of Mineworkers Steward who was to go down. Something happened, however, and this man couldn't go, so Bill volunteered to take his place.
>
> They were down for quite a few days. I would go down to the pit each evening and speak to him on the telephone.
>
> The treatment the coal industry got at that time [1984-1985] was dreadful – Bill was very strong about that. He was very involved with the picketing of the Longannet power station at the time.

As can be seen, ice hockey was only one of many other facets of Bill's full and interesting life. A widely-read and well-informed man, he was a member of the Communist Party of Great Britain all his adult life. Kit remembers a visit Bill made behind the then-Iron Curtain in the late 1950s:

> I remember that Bill went out to the former Soviet Union for some union conference one time, I can't recall where. He hadn't over enjoyed the food, and the only thing he told me was that he had gone out one evening for a walk, and passed a man digging his garden. Bill spoke to him in English, and this chap rushed into the house to bring out his wife, who turned out to be an English teacher. The first thing she asked him was: 'Do you think Princess Margaret will marry Group Captain Townsend?' Bill was amazed at this, particularly as he was the last person to have an opinion on it, or to be remotely interested!

This incident must have sorely stretched Bill's faith in the 'Dictatorship of the Proletariat'!

Appropriately, Bill last spoke in public in April 1990, shortly before his passing. The venue was Falkirk Town Hall at a campaign meeting to retain services at Falkirk Royal Infirmary. He spoke on behalf of the local trades council to express support for the campaign but, typically, took the opportunity to place the issue in a wider social and political context. He was a much respected figure in the Falkirk area, as Kit describes: 'I know people remember him. Older people from Falkirk will say to me, when they hear my surname: "Are you connected to Bill Sneddon?" He was very well known.'

At the time of his untimely death, Bill and Kit were having a short holiday on Jersey in the Channel Islands. Bill, as secretary of the Falkirk and District Trades Council, was due to attend the Scottish Trades Union Congress on his return. He died on 14 April 1990, aged sixty-four, as Kit remembers:

> Bill had been retired for a couple of years, when we had gone to Jersey in April 1990 with the company I worked for. We stayed at the Grand Hotel on the seafront at St Helier. Bill enjoyed playing golf with the company reps and they had talked him into going down to play golf one morning.
>
> He was to meet them for a swim at 8 o'clock. Bill, being Bill, was tremendously punctual, and would have been down before eight. He was found in the hotel swimming pool. He had taken a heart attack and fallen into the pool. He had died immediately, as there was no water found in his lungs.

Bill is survived by his widow, Kit, and his two daughters:

> When the girls were younger, we would take them skating at Falkirk, but neither of them were all that keen. Our eldest daughter, Katerina, now lives down in Ayrshire at Perceton, near Irvine. She's a lecturer in English at James Watt College in Kilwinning. Our younger daughter, Wilma, is in Glasgow. She was a college administrator in Glasgow, but has now started her own business and has bought a house in Callander.

Kit moved from their home in Larbert's Pembroke Street and is now living in retirement in the Stirlingshire village of Callander. She retains in her flat an unusual and appropriate reminder of her late husband:

> I still have the metal bar over the kitchen door that Bill used every day for his exercises.

Career Record in British Hockey

	GP	G	A	Pts	PiM
Bill Sneddon (Falkirk/Fife/Murrayfield/Dundee) 1947-1972 (Records unavailable for 1960-1963;1965-1967)	358	55	122	177	578
Great Britain 1950	6	2	1	3	14

8

First Line of Defence: Lawson Neil

The late Jack Siemon first arrived in Scotland in September 1950. A twenty-three-year-old goaltender out of Kitchener, Ontario, he was to build an outstanding reputation over his subsequent ten seasons of British hockey; firstly with Perth, then with Nottingham. A successful coaching career in Sweden and Italy was to follow, and he and his Perth-born wife, Barbara, enjoyed a happy retirement back in her native city until his death in late 2006.

Having played with or against all the great players from British hockey's pro era of the 1950s, together with his coach's eye for judging talent, his opinion on a player is one that should be noted.

His thoughts on Lawson Neil, probably the most underrated of the top British players of that era, are particularly apt, as Siemon played against him when Neil was with Ayr and Wembley, and then had him as a teammate on Nottingham's defence for four seasons:

> He was great; he was as good as the Canadians. Back then, we normally had ten Canadians and two spare Scots or English guys. Lawson wasn't one of those spares; he played regular all the time at Nottingham. He did his job.
>
> Some of the British defencemen at that time, like the Syme brothers and Bill Sneddon, these guys had a reputation for being rough. Lawson was never like that. He wasn't a body-checker; he never went out of his way to cause trouble. He never went into the corners using the butt-end. Lawson was a straight up and down hockey player; an intelligent player with a great hip-check; nice and clean.

Lawson Neil was born in Ayr, at 22 Princes Street, on 24 March 1930. He was the younger of two sons born to Robert Neil, a Motor Mechanic, and Jessie Lawson (who had married at Ayr, in 1928, after the forms of the United Free Church of Scotland).

He was educated at nearby Russell Street School, from the ages of five to fourteen, in a part of Ayr that is now unrecognisable from the area where Lawson grew up. Princes Street and the neighbouring district, including his former school, were swept away in late 1960s redevelopment.

Lawson's former teammate on the junior Ayr Spitfires, Jimmy Agnew, was brought up in nearby Wellington Street and also attended Russell Street School, although he was five years Lawson's junior, as he recalls:

> Lawson was brought up in Princes Street. His uncle had the dairy there. His Dad worked as a mechanic for McGill & Smith, the seed merchants. It was the 'posh' bit of Princes Street, not the tenements! There were wee, terraced bungalows next to the dairy, where the Neils lived. His mum and dad moved to a nice house in St Andrews Street in Ayr, after the war, which was just five minutes walk from the rink. The dairy got sold, and everything in that area got demolished.

Great Britain team, World Championships, March 1950. From left to right, back row: Ray Hammond, 'Tiny' Syme, Johnny Carlyle, Bill Sneddon, Jock Muldoon (trainer), 'Tuck' Syme. Middle row: Dr J.O. McCabe (manager), Roy Harnett, Ian Forbes, Bert Smith, Ken Nicholson (captain). Front row: Lou Bates (coach), Johnny Murray, Johnny Quales, Stan Christie, Lawson Neil, Johnny Rolland. (*Ice Hockey World* photo)

The new Ayr Ice Rink on Beresford Terrace opened on 13 March 1939. It was Scotland's largest, with a capacity of 4,614, and a 200ft x 100ft ice pad. It immediately became a Mecca for local youth, including Lawson and his elder brother Bert.

Some sixteen years later, when Lawson was an established Ayr Raiders and Great Britain defenceman, the *Ayrshire Post* published a sports profile of him in January 1955, referring to his connection with the Ayr rink right from the start:

> When Ayr Ice Rink opened its portals in 1939 one of its first skating patrons on opening day was nine-years-old local boy Lawson Neil... Ice Hockey has always been Lawson's chief sporting interest and during immediate post-war seasons he was one of the outstanding juniors of the Scottish circuit with the Ayr Spitfires...

His introduction to ice hockey came shortly after the Ayr rink's opening, as his younger son Vernon Neil recalls: 'I know he started when he was young. My son James started when he was five, and my mother thinks dad started when he was about nine.'

The Pee Wees at Ayr during the war were coached by the rink's then-Canadian icemaster, Les Saultrey, and it was under his tutelage that Lawson developed his basic hockey skills, progressing to the junior Ayr Spitfires when barely into his teens, as the *Ayrshire Post* of 4 December 1947 noted that: 'Defenceman Neil, who is only 17 years of age, is employed as a motor mechanic with Messrs McGill and Smith, Ayr, and has been with Spitfires for more than three years.' The term 'junior', in the context of Scottish ice hockey at that time, did not indicate any age demarcation as it would today. Basically, each rink's junior team was in effect the reserve team of the senior squad, with no upper age restriction. Each senior Scottish team in the immediate post-war years had to ice ten Canadians and two 'juniors', with the configuration changing to eight and four from 1953. Lawson would, therefore, have been playing with and against men from the age of thirteen or fourteen.

In this respect, 'junior' was interchangeable with 'Scottish-trained'. Thus the *Ayrshire Post* was able to note in January 1955 that Lawson, having reached the age of twenty-five, and, 'although recognised as one of the soundest defencemen in the circuit, is still officially a junior. Opposing forwards have found to their cost, however, that there is nothing sub-standard about his play.'

Stan Christie, five years older than Lawson, played behind him as goaltender for the junior Ayr Spitfires and senior Ayr Raiders and with Great Britain at two World Championships (1950 and 1951). He remembers him fondly:

> Lawson was a Pee Wee when we were playing during the war. When I came back from the army, he was all grown up.
>
> He was a good, solid player; a terrific defenceman. In fact, sometimes Lawson was on the ice all the time with the Spitfires when his usual partner on defence was George 'Rusty' Spence.
>
> I've never seen any Canadian who could hip-check like Lawson. He was the best hip-checker I've ever seen. Tuck Syme of Dunfermline hit them hard, but Lawson could get right underneath them and lift them up in the air – a great hip-checker.
>
> He was an attacking defenceman, too, particularly with the Spitfires; he could carry the puck, too. He was really good, and a solid, good skater.
>
> Lawson wasn't tall, about 5ft 9in or 5ft 10in, but solid built (his elder brother, Bert, was taller and slimmer).
>
> He just got better and better once he started playing with the Raiders, playing with and against better players.
>
> He was underestimated. If you hit Lawson, he bounced back up with a smile on his face. I never saw him lose his temper. In fact, I never remember him being in a fight, and he never boarded anybody. He could look after himself, though; he just waited and got them with a great hip-check.
>
> Lawson was always smiling; a great character; liked by everybody. You never knew what Lawson was up to. He liked a wee gamble on the horses, and you'd find him rolling in money one day, and with nothing the next, but it never seemed to bother him.
>
> Lawson's father was in charge of all the vehicles at McGill & Smith, the seed merchants in Ayr, and Lawson started in there as an apprentice motor mechanic. They were good to him, as they gave him as much time off as he needed for the hockey. Then he eventually went full-time with the hockey.

Lawson first came to prominence during 1946/47. He was actually two months short of his seventeenth birthday when, in January 1947, he took part in Great Britain team trials, along with Hugo Hamilton and Bill Nicol from Ayr. Lawson was named along with Johnny Carlyle as one of two reserves for the Great Britain team, due to compete in that year's World Championships in Czechoslovakia (Dr J.O. McCabe of the SIHA had contacted the International Association and requested that Scotland be represented in Prague. This was rejected, however, with the British Association deciding, in the end, not to enter a team that year).

The following season, he was the dominant force on the Spitfires, with the *Ayrshire Post* recording that 'Lawson Neil... found himself unmarked twice and from near the centre line, sent home two power drives that had the goaltender beaten all the way.' His two long-range goals helped Spitfires to a 3-2 win over Mohawks at Crossmyloof on 18 November 1947.

Spitfires defeated Glasgow Mustangs 9-5 at Ayr on 1 December 1947, with the *Ayr Advertiser* reporting that 'Olympic trialist Lawson Neil was outstanding in the home team...' The

Olympic reference was in respect of his selection, along with fellow Spitfire Bill Nicol, to play for Scotland against England in two matches in mid-December 1947, which would be used to pick the Great Britain Olympic team of 1948. Both Ayr boys, however, were out of luck on this occasion.

Lawson's introduction to senior hockey came on Friday 5 December 1947, when he took the place of the injured Bob Leckie in the Raiders' line-up to play the visiting Dundee Tigers. It was to be a tough baptism for the seventeen-year-old Neil, the only local in the home line-up, as Dundee led 6-5 until Doug Free netted Ayr's equaliser with ten seconds on the clock.

The game was rough and intensely contested, as evidenced by the following from the *Ayrshire Post*: 'Dundee 'keeper Kovac, incensed about a goal decision, discarded cap, gloves and stick and vaulted the barrier in the direction of the young goal judge.'

Lawson saw plenty of action, however, as Raiders only iced three defencemen: Jack Clancy and Jack Leckie being his blueline colleagues, backstopped by the nineteen-year-old Ken Johnson, who would precede Neil in later serving Nottingham Panthers (it was a youthful defensive unit, as Jack Leckie was just a month older than Lawson Neil, and Jack Clancy was only in his early twenties).

His first appearance for Great Britain came during the 1950 World Championships, held at the three major London arenas, in March 1950, as his son Vernon recalls:

> I remember him saying that they turned up the night before and went out and had a few beers! But they came up with the goods. I don't think he kept in touch with the guys on that team, don't think he mentioned them.

Lawson marked his World Championship debut with a goal in Britain's 9-0 demolition of France in the tournament opener. He also netted GB's second goal in a 4-3 win over Norway at Wembley, firing home a great shot from a Bill Sneddon pass.

The British finished a very creditable fourth, behind Canada, the USA and Switzerland, defeating Sweden, France and Norway (twice) along the way. His Ayr colleague Stan Christie was the British goaltender:

> He played with Bill Sneddon on defence with the Great Britain team in the World Championships in 1950. He got on well with Sneddon, and Bill and Lawson were exactly the same type of player, although Bill had a temper. It was the same with Lawson and Joe Brown of Paisley. They had a great rivalry on the ice, but they were great pals off it.
>
> Lawson, myself and Davie [McCrae] were the Ayr players who went to Paris in 1951 for the World Championships. I remember that the Americans, Canadians and ourselves all stayed at the same big hotel, and there was always a bus laid on to take us wherever we wanted to go in Paris. Lawson had the idea of us all going to see the Folies Bergere one night and we all went there on this bus. Lawson was sitting in an aisle seat during the show, and the head girl came from the stage and picked Lawson and Doug Wilson, of Wembley, to go up on to the stage to dance with the girls! He got a wee bottle of cognac for that!

Neil's National Service was delayed until he was twenty, to allow him to complete his motor mechanic apprenticeship, but he entered the Royal Air Force for two years just after the World Championships in March 1950. Although his hockey would be disrupted over the next two years, it was not as bad as it might have been, as he was posted to a base less than sixty miles from Ayr, at West Freuch near Stranraer, as Jimmy Agnew recalls:

> Lawson was in the RAF, posted to Stranraer, I think it was when the Sunderland flying boats were based there. He was one of the home-based 'Brylcreem Boys'; but a hard 'Brylcreem Boy'! He had a car as well, which was unusual for that time, so he was up and down the road to Stranraer for games.

Lawson Neil, Ayr Raiders, 1952/53. (*Ice Hockey World* photo)

The *Evening Times* noted in January 1952 that:

> Lawson… is still in the forces. He has been pretty well out of hockey this season. Recent injuries to Raiders, however, have had coach Keith Kewley calling around for help. With Gordie Lewis out for a month with a cracked fibula Keith had to play Mack Clement in attack this week. That left him a defenceman short. So, when Lawson intimated that he could get leave to play, Keith got down to the business of getting him in shape. Here again there were snags. The Ayr ice pad this week has been taken up by a big curling bonspiel, and Raiders could get no practice time.
>
> So coach Kewley tackled the job of working 10 or 12lbs of superfluous weight off Lawson in the dressing-room. And Lawson did it by skipping, punching the bag, and stickhandling round the room with a golf ball.

Curiously, during this spell of leave, Lawson iced for Raiders in a 6-5 home win over Nottingham Panthers in a friendly, on 7 January 1952. It was the first time he'd faced the team from the city which he'd come to call home.

Keith Kewley, Raiders' Canadian coach, does not accept any praise for Lawson's development as a player, although he certainly added improvements to his hockey knowledge. From his home in St Thomas, Ontario, he recalled that: 'Lawson Neil developed nicely on defence; he and Dave McCrae were pretty much ready for hockey by the time I got there.'

Lawson, however, learned a lot from playing and practising alongside some fine Canadian defencemen who played in Ayr; notably Jack Clancy, Bob Leckie, Gar Vasey and, the cream of the crop, Herb Kewley (brother of Keith).

A calm, collected and smooth-skating defenceman, he was not one to pick up needless penalties. An intelligent player, with excellent positional sense, he saw the ice very well and was adept at delivering a telling pass to set up an offensive play, as Jimmy Agnew remembers:

> As a player, he was first class. These guys – like Lawson, the Symes, Bill Sneddon and Johnny Carlyle – would've made it in Canada, easily.
>
> Lawson had the height for it as well, he was about 5ft 10in, and very solid built. He was a nice chap; he wasn't big-headed with it. He had time for everybody. When you played with him, he kept you on the right road; you learned a lot from him.
>
> Lawson was also a bit of a wild boy; he liked a wee gamble! We used to call him 'Sport' Neil when they played poker at the back of the bus going to away games with the Spitfires. I've seen him win £7 on the way up, and lose £15 coming back down! He took his beatings well; that's why they called him 'Sport'! I remember that Lawson and the other poker players would always shout at the driver every time the bus hit a bump in the road, as all this money would get knocked off the table!
>
> He was always dressed immaculate. I remember going with him to Miller's the outfitters on Beresford Terrace in Ayr, across the road from the rink. He bought a big Burberry overcoat; £34 it cost him, which was a lot of money in the 1950s.

Off the ice in the early 1950s, Lawson's entrepreneurial spirit, which would see him operate several successful businesses in later life, was already apparent to Jimmy Agnew:

> Lawson even sold ice cream down the shore on a Sunday in the summer. He had an old bicycle with the ice cream at the front – that's how he supplemented his hockey wages during the close-season! At the latter end of his time with the Raiders, he was a full-time hockey player. He packed in his work – or they packed him in! One or the other, as the hockey was taking up too much time.

Early in the 1953/54 season Lawson was involved in an incident with Canadian Gus Galbraith, a newly-arrived import with Paisley. Galbraith broke his leg as a result of a clean check from Lawson; unfortunately, his leg required amputation, as Jimmy Agnew remembers: 'He was unfortunate when he body-checked the guy Galbraith in Paisley; it was a clean hit.'

Two benefit games, at Paisley and Ayr, involving Scotland playing a Canadian Select (of Canucks attached to Scottish clubs), were arranged for Galbraith in November 1953 and the *Evening Times* noted that:

> The Scottish defence for the Paisley game is Tuck and Tiny Syme, along with their clubmate Joe Brown and Jimmy Mitchell for Kirkcaldy. And, for the Ayr game, Bill Sneddon of Falkirk and Lawson Neil of Ayr come in for Brown and Mitchell. These defences are as good as any Canadian in the circuit.

What a tragedy that these gifted players had such limited international opportunities at their playing peak through no fault of their own.

Lawson was a stalwart on the Raiders' defence through to the folding of the senior team in April 1955, with the *Ayrshire Post* commenting on his '...solid defence work and cool generalship...' His standing with his Canadian teammates can be gauged from the following snippet in the *Post* of 11 September 1953: 'Herb Kewley is again the captain of the side and it was a nice gesture by the players to nominate Lawson Neil as vice-captain.'

A couple of months later and the *Ayrshire Post* was suggesting to Raiders' coach Andre Girard that Neil was the answer to the team's offensive shortcomings: 'Neil has the build, speed and "go" to ginger up the attack and his example on the ice might prove to be better medicine than dressing-room harangues.'

Raiders were expected to do well in the inaugural British League season of 1954/55 under coach Stan Obodiac. Things started to unravel, however, amidst a spate of injuries, indiscipline and recriminations, which saw Ayr consigned to the British League cellar. Tommy Gordon, the

Lawson Neil (left) and Jean Tremblay, Ayr Raiders, September 1953. (Frank Dempster archive)

Ice Hockey World's Ayr correspondent, absolved Neil of blame, however, noting that 'Not all the players were guilty men... Scots defenceman Lawson Neil skated himself into the ice.'

Unfortunately, his final game in a Raiders' sweater, on 29 April 1955, although resulting in a 12-4 home win for Ayr over Perth, was not a personal success for him, despite recording an assist, as the *Post* noted that: 'The disappointing feature of the game was the failure of Lawson Neil to recapture his form of earlier in the season that made him one of the most consistent defencemen on the circuit.'

Although the inaugural British League had comprised twelve teams at the start of 1954/55, it had contracted dramatically by the onset of the following season to just five teams: Paisley, Nottingham, Wembley, Harringay and Brighton. With such a reduction in employment opportunities for hockey players, it is a creditable reflection of Lawson's abilities that he was still in demand.

He had been offered a slot with Brighton, but had gone down for discussions with Harringay at the end of September 1955. On 29 September, he played for the *Ice Hockey World* All Stars who defeated Paisley 4-1 at Ayr. The following week, the *Ayrshire Post* reported that '...he came to terms with Wembley Lions', who had snatched him from their North London rivals as a defensive partner for Sonny Rost (Les Anning, a Canadian teammate from Raiders, also joined Lions at the same time).

His Wembley debut came in a defeat at Paisley on 7 October 1955. His fans in Ayr had the chance to see him on television the following month, playing against the Czechoslovakian national team.

Wembley also hosted the Soviet Union, on 1 December 1955. The Russians won 3-2, but the match is best remembered for Londoner Roy Shepherd's legal body-checks, which removed two Soviet forwards from the game, with much persuasion needed to ensure that the Russians continued the game. Lawson Neil, however, had also delivered several of his textbook hip- and body-checks earlier in the game. It was, therefore, a curious paradox that the Russians had come to Britain to gain exposure to Canadian-style hockey, only for an Englishman and a Scotsman to demonstrate to them the art of body-checking.

That latter period of 1955 saw Lawson wed Barbara Christison, at Willesden in North London, as Stan Christie recalls:

> Lawson married Barbara, or 'Babs', who was a chorus girl at the Gaiety Theatre, in Ayr. Barbara was a lovely girl, and my wife and I went down to visit them in Nottingham two or three times once they had moved there.

Barbara was originally from Hull on Humberside, as she remembers:

> I'd left Hull when the war finished and went to the Beverley Stage School in Yorkshire. I'd been with the Tillers for two years on tour, and in cabaret; I came to work at the Gaiety in Ayr when I was nineteen; that's when I met Lawson.
>
> There were sixteen girls in the dance group; Lawson was one of the quite well-off young men who used to come into the show. They used to come and meet us at the stage door; we'd go out dancing to the Bobby Jones Ballroom in Ayr and then go to Prestwick Airport for breakfast; we were young and enjoying ourselves!
>
> Lawson had been engaged to a very lovely Ayr girl before I met him. He broke off the engagement and she married someone else in the theatre.
>
> I stayed nearly three years in Ayr with the Gaiety; I lived in a boarding house in Ayr and went to work with Samuel the Jewellers, but I didn't watch much hockey then.

Lawson Neil, Wembley Lions, 1955/56.
(*Ice Hockey World* photo)

Lawson Neil, Nottingham Panthers, 1958/59. (*Ice Hockey World* photo)

> Lawson was a really, really super bloke; you couldn't have met a nicer man. He was very well respected and well liked.

After one season with Wembley, Lawson moved to Nottingham Panthers in 1956 for four seasons, going into the bookmakers business with, firstly, Jack Siemon and latterly with another Panthers' teammate, Lorne Smith. Son Vernon takes up the story:

> He did Wembley for a season, and then moved to Nottingham. It was touch and go whether he came to Nottingham. He had been approached by Andre Girard to go to Switzerland. He had played with Girard in Ayr, and we were out in Switzerland a few times visiting Girard – I always remember he had a big, beautiful house overlooking a golf course.
>
> But Chick Zamick came in and asked him to go to Nottingham, so that was that. Zamick and Les Strongman at Nottingham were the two players he rated most highly.
>
> My elder brother, Dale, was born in Nottingham in 1959, and I was born there in 1962. Dale's in London now, where he has pubs and restaurants.
>
> The old man had a bookies' in Ilkeston, and then he went into the pub game in Nottingham, then the nightclub game in Boston, Lincolnshire. Then he had a café in Nottingham.

After the Panthers folded in 1960, Lawson concentrated solely on his business interests, until persuaded to return to the ice with Altrincham Aces in 1963, where he played for several seasons alongside Keith Machin, a director of Notts County Football Club.

His sons Vernon and Dale followed him into hockey, although somewhat belatedly, once the sport was reintroduced to Nottingham in 1980, as Vernon remembers:

> My Dad used to take my brother and me down to the rink in Nottingham. I remember he came back home once with two pairs of skates for us; old brown leather things.
>
> We played for the Nottingham Trojans, the second team, when hockey started back up at the Ice Stadium in 1980. Dad did a little bit of coaching. And I remember he played a game for the Panthers against the Sheffield team in the second season they had hockey back, so he must have been fifty-one then.
>
> Things got a little busy then, and though he came to the odd Panthers' game, he never got back into the hockey.
>
> He never went to the Wembley finals in the 1980s. I went every year and would always invite him, but he never wanted to go.
>
> He died in 1990. It was cancer, of the lymph glands. It was pretty sudden; I would say six to seven months from start to finish. He didn't do himself any favours with his cigarettes. I remember he told me that when he was playing he used to come out the dressing-room between periods for a smoke.

A third generation of the Neil family is now playing ice hockey in the form of Vernon's son, James Neil, who looks as though he has the makings of a player to rank alongside his grandfather, as father Vernon explains:

> James was born February 1990 and I've got a photo of my Dad holding James as a baby.
>
> James started playing when he was about five. He's played all the different teams: he plays for the Under-16s, plays up for the Under-19s, and plays up for the English Premier League team, as well as being in his second year with the Panthers.
>
> He's represented the country many a time, winning the Quebec tournament three years ago. He went for a week to a hockey camp for the Norwegian national team. He'd be off to North America like a shot if the chance came, but we need to consider his education as well, as hockey is a very short career.
>
> He was diagnosed as diabetic, which came as quite a shock, but has made him even more determined. He's been contacted by Sir Steve Redgrave, the rower, who is also diabetic, which has been a big help for him, and James keeps in touch with him regularly.
>
> My daughter, Kelly, is eleven, but she's not a skater. She's a horse-riding fanatic, and we spend a lot of time taking her to gymkhanas and things.

Vernon Neil was closely involved in the successful development of the sport in Nottingham, being manager of the Nottingham Ice Stadium:

> I worked for twenty-four years at the Nottingham rink. I worked my way up; helping out in the skate hire shop, working in the bar. I was made general manager, and went all the way through to the rink's closure. I did two years project work on the new arena, and then managed that for three years.
>
> I left to go into consultancy. A new chief executive had been appointed, and there was always so much politics to deal with, whereas I had always been used to working for a private company at the old rink.
>
> I now work as a consultant for a company which puts up temporary ice rinks. We have ten projects on the go at present, including the one at Somerset House in London.

Lawson died in Nottingham on 2 June 1990, aged just sixty. His widow Barbara, since remarried, regrets his early passing:

> It was sad that he went so quickly. He only saw one grandchild, James; now he has seven grandchildren. I still get people that I've known for over forty years coming up to me and telling me that they remember Lawson and what a lovely man he was.

His two old Ayr teammates, Jimmy Agnew and Stan Christie, still maintain he was the finest ever British defenceman, as Jimmy explains:

> Lawson Neil wasn't a dirty player; Lawson was a good, heads-up player who gave you more time on the ice – these other guys were taking penalties and their team was getting penalised. Lawson was a 'stay-at-home' defenceman, but he could hit. It was nice and neat how he did it; down and up – he was really first class. Lawson Neil was the Daddy of them all.
>
> The last time I spoke to Lawson was at Ayr Races, about three or four years before he died. He was wearing a shiny suit, like an American gangster!

As a Great Britain teammate of Lawson's at two World Championships it is appropriate that Stan Christie has the last word:

> Lawson always had a cut on the nose, or somewhere else on his face through the hockey, but he was always smiling and laughing. That was the type he was. I'll always remember him as smiling, with those half-closed, laughing eyes.

Career Record

	GP	G	A	Pts	PiM
Lawson Neil (Ayr/Wembley/Nottingham/Altrincham/Glasgow/Sheffield) 1947-1976 (Records unavailable for 1960-1963;1965-1975)	536	29	93	122	197
Great Britain 1950-1951	15	3	2	5	4

9

Paisley Pattern: The Brennan Brothers

It was wet and windy in the west of Scotland on Wednesday 22 March 1939. The newspaper headlines that day reported on the Nazi annexation of the German-speaking Lithuanian city of Memel the day before, which followed on from Hitler's march into Czechoslovakia a week earlier. The thought of impending war was now more than a nagging worry for the British public. Having witnessed the failure of Prime Minister Neville Chamberlain's policy of appeasing Nazi Germany, and viewed the cinema newsreel footage of the horrors of air raids in the Spanish Civil War over the past three years, it was an anxious time for the British people.

On that same day in Paisley, however, a father and his young son had more pleasant thoughts in mind. They set off on the thirty-odd mile journey from Paisley to Ayr in the early evening, on a London Midland and Scottish steam train, to see their first ice hockey match.

It was also to be the first ice hockey match staged at the new Ayr Ice Rink, and the pair had a particular family interest, as the father's Canadian cousin, Mickey Brennan, would be playing for the Trail Smoke Eaters, who had just retained the World Championship for Canada the previous month.

It was an entertaining and exciting game as Trail defeated a Scottish Select by four goals to two. Bill Brennan senior, a packer in Paisley's Anchor Thread Mill, took his five-year-old son in to the Trail dressing-room to meet his cousin. For his son, also Bill, it was to be a first acquaintance with a hockey dressing-room; an environment with which he was destined to become very familiar. Twelve years later, he would be playing in senior hockey in this same Ayr rink, go on to captain and coach the Great Britain senior side, and earn a deserved induction to British ice hockey's Hall of Fame. The GB captaincy and Hall of Fame membership were honours that would also be earned by his, as yet unborn, younger brother, Alastair.

Sixty-six years later, Bill Brennan recalled that visit to see the Trail Smoke Eaters:

> My father's cousin, Mickey Brennan, played with Trail Smoke Eaters. In those days, they used to send a Senior 'A' team to represent Canada in the World Championships – and pick up the trophy! I think it was automatic that the previous year's Allan Cup winners went, and I think Trail were the Allan Cup holders.
>
> I don't know how my father got to know about it. My father was big into sports anyway; he followed most things, especially football; a true St Mirren supporter.
>
> But he discovered that Trail were playing at Ayr in the opening game at this new rink. I suppose there must have been talk at that time, Paisley Ice Rink would have been in the throes of being built, and we ended up down at Ayr and in the dressing-room. This was a cousin; he knew that some of the family had gone out to that area of Canada on the west coast. So, that was the first; that was the start.
>
> I remember it very vaguely, but you begin to wonder! I've an action picture of Mickey Brennan, and is it that I remember, or can I actually remember it? It was unusual; he had a

Billy Brennan, Paisley Pirates, 1953/54. (Bill Brennan archive)

baseball cap with the skip turned up. And, of course, the wee shorts and the long, long sticks; they all had these low lying sticks, lie three and lie four sticks, then. No slapshooting at that time!

So, that was the start.

William Patrick Brennan was born in Paisley's Barshaw Hospital on 13 January 1934; the first child of William Brennan and Helen Deveney, who had married in Paisley in August 1930. He developed his skating and hockey skills at the old Paisley Ice Rink at East Lane:

I started skating when I was about ten or eleven and, to my horror, my mother bought me a pair of figure skates! My big cousin, Barbara McGuinness, was of an age to go skating, and she worked in the office of a company in Paisley called Lyon's Leather Company at that time. One of the directors of Paisley Ice Rink was called Lyon, who owned this leather company, and Barbara later became his secretary. She took me skating, and I learned how to skate. She used to take me on to the ice and hope that a guy would take my other hand, skate about, and hope that she'd get a lumber for the night!

Then I got a pair of hockey skates from Canada; but the boots were like speed skating boots, with no toe-cap on them. That was my first pair of hockey skates.

I saw a lot of hockey during the war. My father, before he went into the forces, used to take me to see Scottish Select games at Paisley with guys like Billy Bodnar, Dave Cross, Tommy Lauder, Don Cumming, Kenny Nicholson and Mickey Shires. I was taken to these games and that started my interest.

I was brought up in the West End of Paisley, a wee street called Arthur Street. It was funny, because there were quite a few folk involved with the hockey all within a couple of streets of each other in that area – Johnny Quales lived two streets away in Clavering Street, and Malcolm Beaton was round the corner in Underwood Road.

Just after war broke out in 1939, my grandmother and family had got a new house in the Ferguslie Park area of Paisley. With my father away during the war, and my mother working, it was easier for us all to move in with my grandmother, although my parents still kept the house at 5 Arthur Street. After the war, and with the arrival of Alastair giving my parents four kids, we ended up in a council house in Renfrew Road, in the Gallowhill area of Paisley.

I went to St Mary's Primary School, in Queen Street, which was near to our flat in Arthur Street. I had been getting good marks at school, in the eleven-plus, and my mother had delusions of grandeur! Somebody had convinced her that St Mungo's Academy in Glasgow was a better school than St Mirin's in Paisley, so I got sent to St Mungo's. I used to take the train from St James Station in Paisley to Glasgow Central every day, starting as an eleven-year-old.

By the time I was fourteen, I was going to the rink on a Saturday morning myself, and it's a progression. If you wanted to get a hockey stick you waited to get a broken one! Malcolm Beaton was the leading light of the Wildcats, the Paisley junior team. He decided to start a Pee Wee team and word got round fast and fifty or sixty boys turned up.

We were coached by Roy McKean and Eddie Noble, who played with the Wildcats; they gave up their time to coach the youngsters. The first Canadian coach that got involved with the juniors was Les Tapp. He had a florist shop down in Richmond, in London, and the season that Paisley had two senior teams – the Paisley Pirates and the Glasgow Bruins – he came up to coach the Bruins; he stayed on for one or two years to coach the Pirates. He was the first Canadian to coach us, which he did very much as a pastime for a while – he didn't travel to games.

Billy's hockey ran in tandem with his football for several years:

I played a lot of football from when I was twelve until about sixteen. I even played at Hampden Park in a schools final for St Mungo's (we lost 1-0 to Govan High).

I had pneumonia when I was fifteen, and it cost me a year at school. I was playing football for St John's Boys' Guild, a Barrhead team. It was a really wet and wild day, on an old ash pitch, and I got absolutely soaked. We were changing in an old corrugated iron hut, with the wind blowing through it, and no showers. I foolishly went to the pictures that night, and I couldn't stop shivering. I was whipped into hospital, and they kept me in for four weeks, as there was a big worry about it developing into TB in those days.

So, after that, I concentrated on playing hockey – indoors!

When the Wildcats lost their ice time at Paisley, Billy joined the junior Glasgow Mohawks at nearby Crossmyloof:

Dorry Boyle and I started out with the Pee Wees at the same time; we were starting to get games for the Wildcats when I fell out with Malcolm. I was a stupid wee boy! I moved to Crossmyloof shortly after that, mainly because Paisley stopped running a junior team. I don't know why, because the cost was minimal; whether it was supplying the sticks, or the cost of ice time. It was certainly short-sighted. The sticks and equipment were just hand-me-downs from the senior team. The outfits we had, it was thick, heavy wool that had gone matted over the years. The Wildcats had a yellow top and green bottom, with a big wildcat figure on the front. It wasn't a case of a new set every year; they had to last for years. Was it the cost of transport to away games? It seemed to be just a case of we've given up.

We were lucky at Paisley, in that we could move to Crossmyloof, and they formed the Mohawks and the Mustangs, which was harping back to a previous era. It was a bit of

> a windfall for them, because they could pick the best of two teams and make that the Mohawks. The youngsters, like myself, and a few of the older heads that were maybe getting past it were the Mustangs. We took some terrible hammerings which, in hindsight, was a good thing, as we learned to lose before we started to win.
>
> Crossmyloof was very 'true blue' amateur. It was a different social class with quite a few of the guys there; certainly different from us hooligans! There was no skate hire at Crossmyloof in those days – if you hadn't your own skates, you couldn't skate there! Frank Jardine, who captained the Mohawks, was from money; and Milne, the chairman of the ice rink, had a cold storage company in Glasgow.

A precocious talent, he made his debut, on defence for Ayr Raiders, in the Canadian-dominated pro Scottish National League as a seventeen-year-old schoolboy – on 21 November 1951. Raiders were hit by injuries, and their Canadian coach, Keith Kewley, called up the young Brennan to stand in for Gar Vasey, as Billy remembers:

> I was invited down to Ayr for a Sunday morning workout with the Raiders. It was difficult getting from Paisley to Ayr by public transport on a Sunday back then. By the time I got down, the workout was nearly finished. But Herb Kewley stayed on, as did Girard, Martini and Domenico. I was quite surprised that these guys stayed on, but Keith Kewley had asked them to. He taught me more tricks in an hour that morning than I had learned in four years. I couldn't wait to get back to Crossmyloof that night and get my skates on, to be able to talk to people about what I'd learned. It was a different level of coaching.

Brennan's first game was on the rink where he learnt to skate, against his home town Paisley Pirates and he played ten games for Raiders during 1951/52, collecting one assist and one minor penalty. He was in good company, as Raiders won the Scottish National League and Autumn Cup that season. His debut game was actually broadcast live on the wireless on the BBC's Scottish Service, and young Brennan missed a penalty shot!

'Ah kent his faither' is a pejorative Scots term, but it could have been applied in its literal sense some fifty-two years later when the author had the honour of advising Billy that he had been inducted to Britain's Hall of Fame. His first question was: 'Is your father Tommy Gordon who wrote for the *Ice Hockey World*?' Your scribe confirmed this was the case, and Billy recalled that Gordon senior had written some kind comments on his Raiders' debut back in 1951.

The 'true blue' amateurs who ran Crossmyloof were determined, however, that Bill would obtain no financial advantage from his spell assisting Ayr, as he recalls:

> It was Ross Low, the Ayr manager, who came into the dressing-room and said to me that he couldn't pay me, he could use me, but he told me: 'I'm not allowed to give you any money.' At that time, the Paisley juniors that were playing with the senior Pirates, the likes of Johnny Quales and Joe Brown, were getting £3 for an away game and £2 for a home game. A fiver a week was quite a lot of money in those days. The pair of skates I had then were falling apart, and I was the eldest of four and still at school; we were living in a two-room tenement flat, my father was a labourer in a thread mill and my mother was out working as a school dinner lady, so money was at a premium. There was no way I could ask them to buy me new skates. So, I asked Ross Low if they had any used skates; old skates. He said: 'No, I'm warned off.' He told me that he had to buy raffle tickets for Crossmyloof's annual Christmas raffle, using the money that he would have paid to me for the games I played for Ayr!
>
> I'm saying to myself: 'What the heck is this?' I ended up in Mr Milne's office at Crossmyloof on a Saturday morning to plead a case. It was a huge office with fancy old furniture, and I'm sitting there quaking, trying to explain the Brennan family circumstances! But I got no joy. I was 'Brennan', not 'Billy' or 'Bill', and was told that he didn't believe in that sort of thing, they were strictly amateur.

It finished up that I got the chance to move to Paisley for the end of the season, which I did. That didn't go down well with Crossmyloof. I had to go back up there to collect those old skates – it was the only pair I had!

I left school at seventeen with one 'higher' and two 'lowers', and didn't know what I wanted to do. My mother, again, knew somebody in Babcock's, so I left school on the Friday and started at Babcock's on the Monday as an apprentice draughtsman.

I remember the old boy that taught hockey at Crossmyloof was Jim Kenny. He was a Canadian, and he was the icemaster for both the big rink and the two curling rinks that they eventually had. He taught the hockey – I don't know if he got a retainer for that.

We used to laugh, because he'd wear a brown duster coat, which was his normal work wear, over a pair of dungarees. He'd put that on coming on the ice to coach, and he used to be flying down the ice with a stick – no gloves on – and this coat trailing out behind him! To me, he seemed old then, but you learned a lot.

Jim Kenny taught us a lot of things, but when it came to actual hard hockey, it was Keith Kewley. Guys like Jim Kenny were from a different era. They were still using low-lying sticks, and a big sweep shot. By the time the likes of Girard were playing, he was using a lie 7, which made you more upright on the ice, and that was being copied by youngsters. The whole concept of hockey had changed from before the war.

The Syme brothers, 'Tuck' and 'Tiny', joined Paisley for 1953/54, and Pirates would do a clean sweep of all the honours in Scotland that season. Billy rates the brothers highly, both on and off the ice:

Basically, Tuck was the better hockey player; he could do things. Tiny, for a big, big guy didn't have much of a shot. Tuck played himself, but Tiny was the guy that looked after the likes of me, but he'd have a go at me.

I always remember Bob McNeil played at Brighton; him and I had a wee thing going with each other. As luck would have it, we had a go at each other on a Friday night at Paisley, and our next game was at Brighton on the Sunday night. It went from a niggle to something more serious. We had a skirmish in a corner and the gloves and sticks were gone. When they had separated us, I bent down to pick up my gloves and Bob McNeil appeared from my back somewhere and dealt me an upper cut! Tiny had been trying to act as peacemaker, and as he turned, he saw this happening, and he brought his stick across like a whiplash. It missed Bob McNeil by that much.

It was just at the interval, and we were in the dressing-room and he had a go at me: 'I could've been up for murder ya stupid wee…!' he said. He told me to look after myself, not to pick up sticks and gloves, the other guys will do that. He looked after you, but let you know what you should've been doing.

He did that, in fact, more than Joe [Brown]. Joe was always there, if necessary. The two of them, I suppose, were fearsome playing, but they didn't play together on defence.

Tiny had a mate, Ray Boucher, a wee fellow who came across from Canada; they played defence together after Tuck went to Canada. Joe played with Gerry Corriveau for years.

Tiny and Joe Brown were great mates. Joe Brown's family were always in scrap. They used to break down the old bakelite switches to get tiny pieces of brass, in the days when brass and copper were at a premium. Joe broke away from the family business, and set himself up. Tiny worked for him when he moved to Paisley. Joe had an old washhouse, through a close, somewhere at Paisley Road Toll, handy for the docks and the shipyards; they used to get guys coming in dumping loads of stuff stolen out the yards.

Some guy came in and said: 'I've got a load of stuff.' Tiny was working with Joe at the time, and Tiny said: 'Bring it in.' But the guy said that it was too heavy to carry and that they would need to go and help him. At that time they had an old truck that they used to run up and down between the rink and Paisley Road Toll, and this is where Tiny's lack of common sense, or streetwise, came into it. Tiny took off in the lorry with the guy, went into a close and down into the 'dunny', as they say in Glasgow. And on the way back up, struggling with this load, the police were waiting at the top of the stair! This was about a week before the season started.

Tiny was duly in clink! Joe was sending him in cigarettes and said all you could hear coming from the cells was Tiny shouting: 'Get me out of here, stuff your so-and-so cigarettes!' He was trying to emigrate to Canada at the end of that season, and, of course, with a criminal record, you were screwed. Joe got him out, through his contacts, I suppose, without any charges.

Joe was tearing a strip off him in the dressing-room, saying: 'Why do you think we keep all these hangers-on about the place, a fiver here, a fiver there? That's what they do, they take the chances – we don't take the chances.'

But Tuck was the best of the two, there's no doubt about that. He had a few contemporaries, Lawson Neil and Bill Sneddon, but Tuck had the edge as far as being an all-round guy. Tuck had the aggression that big Bill Sneddon had, but Bill couldn't keep a grip of his temper. Lawson was more sedate; clever. But Tuck had just about everything you were looking for. He'd drag a team through by his own efforts. Tuck was immense.

The two of them were real hard; Tuck could really charge up the ice, while Tiny was the more defensive of the two. Like Bill Sneddon, if Tiny put in a shift, everybody had to put in a shift. You got your money's worth out of them.

Their father, Jock, was a big guy, too, and you'd think it was three brothers, rather than a father and sons. But Tiny was definitely the boss of the family.

Tiny used to sing 'Les Marseilleses', word perfect in French, for the French-Canadians in the team; he learnt all the words at Morgan Academy. Him and Joe Brown also used to sing 'The Sash' in the dressing-room at Sunday morning practices, for the benefit of the Catholics like me!

I remember on New Year's Day 1954, I had taken Tuck down to my mother's on Renfrew Road in Paisley to sober him up. He was singing this song, 'Oh Mine Papa', which was in the charts at the time; we couldn't get him to stop singing it!

Years later, when my brother, Ian, was based in Southern California, my mother was out on holiday visiting. Ian 'phoned up Tuck, who lived in the area, and explained who he was and that my mother wanted to say hello to him. As soon as my mother spoke to him, Tuck burst into 'Oh Mine Papa' down the telephone!

'Tuck' always told me that he hated working down the mines so much that he walked to work in the middle of the road, hoping he'd get knocked down by a bus!

Dundee was the farthest away game in those days, and we called it going to Siberia as it was so cold.

'Tuck' filled a wash-hand basin with hot water in the dressing-room at Dundee. He stepped into the sink with his skates on, to heat up his feet. As he lifted himself in, the backside fell out of it and he had the rim of this wash-hand basin hanging around his hips!

Coach Keith Kewley converted Billy into a checking right winger during his time in charge at Paisley, as Billy recounts:

I don't know the amount of backchecking that went on pre-war; I was too young to realise what was going on in that sense. But Kewley definitely had a game plan before you went out on the ice, everybody had a function.

He used Bill Crawford and me as penalty killers. There was another wee altercation (I must have been a big-headed little so and so without realising). It was a Sunday morning practice and we were playing Nottingham on the Monday or Tuesday night. I always had the job against Nottingham of marking Les Strongman. I got the funniest jobs for somebody my size – Les Strongman, Bill Glennie, Red Kurz – big guys! I used to put them out the game, that's

Four of Paisley's Scottish players, happy after lifting the 1953/54 Autumn Cup. From left to right, back row: 'Tuck' Syme, Billy Brennan, 'Tiny' Syme. Front row: Joe Brown, and Canadians Hal Schooley and Ed Lochhead. (*Ice Hockey World* photo)

what I was instructed to do. Bug them! This Sunday morning, I don't know what was going on. It must have been well over half an hour had passed before I got shouted to come on – and I'd been sitting reading the *Sunday Mail* on the bench! Whatever I was doing, I wasn't doing it deliberately, but I wasn't performing. The result was I didn't play in the game against Nottingham. As the team went out the door and onto the ice that night, Kewley shouted at me. I used to sit in the corner, and he started to lay it off to me about how I had let him down and let the team down. Irrespective of what had happened on the Sunday, I was earmarked to do that job. He knew that he wanted me to mark Strongman, and he'd other things in mind that were more important than my role, that was already decided.

He told me that this was my job, and that I couldn't keep up with the Canadians in terms of stickhandling, because they'd grown up on that. But he said I had attributes that he could use, killing penalties, my backchecking, and always getting the odd goals, or whatever. He told me: 'You're sensible; you're clever enough to know what you're up to out there. So, that's it – take it or leave it.'

I think Bill [Crawford] used to get a bit annoyed at times with Kewley. I could understand, because I was probably the same about Simpell later. Bill was used by Simpell, whereas I was dumped by Simpell – for having a big mouth! Well, that was my version!

There was one game down at Wembley, and Tiny had left for Canada by this time. Creasey, the manager, had told me that I was playing in Tiny's place, number 4 instead of number 14. Which didn't go down well with me, actually, because I liked the fourteen, it was unique! Teams went up to twelve in those days; I liked it different!

We were playing a double-header – Wembley Saturday, Brighton Sunday – Joe Brown was ladling in to Les Anning of Wembley. At one point, the crowd are literally screaming, and it suddenly dawned on us – Anning was stretched out behind our goal at the other end of the rink, not a soul near him! To this day, I don't know what happened, but obviously Joe caught him unawares and laid him out. Anning – when they got him revived – said something to Joe, and Joe demanded retribution! They had several dressing-rooms at Wembley, in a row under the seats, but had a communal shower room, which both teams had to use. I was always last to get my gear off, and by the time I got to the shower room I could hear the shouting before I got in! Les Anning's standing under a shower and Joe's out in the middle of the room, shouting at him in Glaswegian terms: 'Come here till we sort this out!' Roy Shepherd of Wembley was trying to calm Joe down (Roy was an aggressive player, but he was never hot-headed). Roy's trying to get to Joe to calm him down; Ian Forbes is saying to Roy: 'You and I!' Roy's saying: 'I don't want any trouble!' Then Joe managed to get a grip of Anning and had him out. I was in between them, and you can just imagine the scene: three naked bodies, covered in soap, all sliding about!

Eventually it was all sorted out, and we got back to the dressing-room. Simpell was reading the riot act, and he's telling Joe and Ian that they were suspended from the game the following night. Of course, idiot here, all I could see was that they would be in trouble anyway with the Association, and told Simpell he was setting them up for the Association by admitting it before the fact. I was arguing with him – which was a big, big mistake! I was trying to argue a case for them, who were old soldiers, and they belted up! So, from then on, I knew my days were numbered.

I lost form, anyway. It was at least a year before I discovered what had gone wrong with my hockey. It was Creasey, he used to watch everything that was going on; he was a great hockey fan. He'd drive us to games when the team bus had left too early for us to get off work. He said to me one night, out the blue: 'Do you know your problem?' I said no, if I knew I'd do something about it! He said: 'If the puck comes to you, you stand still.' Of course, if you stand still in any sport like that, you're dead; you've lost possession. I'm saying to myself, how could Simpell not have spotted that? Was he interested in clearing that up, or did he just want me out the door?

He never spoke to me, and there was an article in one of the papers castigating him. It was the last game of the season, a nothing game, and I sat on the bench for the sixty minutes, never appeared on the ice. The *Paisley Pictorial* did a scathing article on Simpell for benching me most of the season.

Billy had the opportunity to guest with Wembley Lions in the former Soviet Union over the Christmas and New Year period of 1958/59:

There was a Canadian playing for Wembley that year in the Canadian Air Force, based in London. Wembley were going abroad for their normal Christmas and New Year tour, when they had the big ice show at Wembley. This Canadian couldn't go, so I was duly invited to go with them.

While I was away, Gerry Corriveau broke his leg, and Paisley brought in Red Imrie.

After three games in Finland, with Billy netting in a 6-3 win over Helsinki All Stars, the Lions spent Christmas in Moscow. Their three matches on outdoor rinks were all lost: 1-6 to a Moscow junior select; 2-6 to the senior Soviet national team; and 2-7 to the Air Force team, Wings of the Soviets. They played several matches in Stockholm over the New Year before returning to London.

My wife, Jeanette, was a figure skater at Crossmyloof and I remember we got married in Glasgow on 19 of November 1956, a Monday. Jeanette and I went on honeymoon to London, and the next game was in London, either Harringay or Wembley, on the Saturday night. I had to appear; play – or no pay. Tommy Forgie was the coach at that time, ex-Perth, and he brought in Ian Forbes from Perth, and I lost out playing right wing for a while.

The old amateur Mohawks had moved from Crossmyloof to Paisley in 1958, and Billy took charge as player-coach the following year, having fallen out of favour with Pirates' Canadian coach, Bill Simpell. He could, however, have been a Panther or a Tiger at one point:

When I was younger, I got the chance to go to Nottingham. I was still working in Babcock's, but I was waiting for National Service at that time (which I eventually failed the medical for, anyway, but that's another story). I had to write back to Zamick at Nottingham explaining that I couldn't leave my job in Renfrew because I still had this National Service hanging over me. So, that was the opportunity to play at Nottingham gone.

When I had this thing with Simpell at Paisley, and wasn't playing, Brighton were chasing all over Paisley and Glasgow looking for me one year; I might have finished up at Brighton.

By this time Bill Creasey was Managing Director of the Paisley rink. I remember that I'd got a telegram at the office from George Edwards, the Brighton coach, asking me to come down to Ayr, bring my gear, would I play for him that night in a friendly at Ayr for Brighton against Paisley? They must have been short. I went in to the rink to get my gear and Creasey hailed me. He must've been watching for me coming, and he had the big chief engineer as a witness; this was in the corridor, not even in his office. He said to me: 'I'll let you play tonight, but no way are you going to play for Brighton in here. I am not going to be embarrassed.' I told him that he knew what I was capable of, but that he wasn't going to argue with Simpell about not playing me; he took a back seat, but wouldn't let me play for somebody else. He told me that if I played for Brighton in Paisley, I was finished in so far as practice time in Paisley. This was him referring to my coaching of the Mohawks at that time. I wasn't playing with them then, but I was running their practices at Paisley. It was that word 'embarrassed' that he used, which was a back-handed compliment, I suppose.

The Pirates, along with the rest of professional hockey in Britain, collapsed in 1960. Billy and the Mohawks kept hockey alive on an amateur basis, but the residue of resentment at the financial consideration given to Canadian players continued to rankle, as Billy explains:

The British players were viewed as a form of cheap labour, and that carried on after the British League folded. One of the biggest riots that we got involved in was at Brighton, and it was through that situation. By then, Joe Brown, Bill Crawford, myself, Dorrie Boyle, Robert Stevenson, and all the youngsters like Alastair, were playing for the Mohawks. One night we went down to play Brighton, and I don't know if they were in danger of losing their own tournament, but there was something going on. They brought in a lot of Canadians on their way back from the continent. The likes of Joe, me and Bill Crawford had a bit of needle with these guys, who could wander back and forth, picking up money when we were playing for the fun at that time.

Young Billy Miller went into the corner and this big Canadian defenceman said something to him. Joe Brown was watching like a hawk, and at the interval he said to Miller: 'What did he say to you in the corner?' Billy said: 'He told me that if I went back in there he was going to break my leg.' So, Joe replied: 'Well, you've got a choice, you either go back in and break his leg, or I break yours!' That set the tone!

So, a fight broke out between Joe and this Canadian, right in front of the bench. It got serious, because Crawford was out there, and he'd lost the place completely, he was wandering about kicking Canadians! The only Mohawk that didn't go on the ice was John Milne. I wasn't bothering about that, I didn't hold it against him, because it kept the line to Ahearne open – I was looking beyond the row on the ice!

I remember there was a wee Brighton bookie, who was a pal of Benny Lee, the Brighton rink manager, who used to always turn up with his dark brown suit, collar and tie, and brown suede shoes. He saw Crawford, and he jumped on the ice amongst all these flashing skates and punching – the two goaltenders were having a go as well (Jim Black was in goal for us) – with Joe and this Canadian rolling about on the ice. I had a grip of the wee bookie, holding him back, but trying to keep an eye on what was going on. A photograph was taken, and it looks as though I've got a grip of this bookie by the throat! Fortunately, it didn't say in the local paper that it was Bill Brennan, it just said something like: 'A Mohawk punching lumps out of a spectator.' Shows you how the camera can lie!

The game was abandoned; Benny Lee had jumped on to the ice and told the referees that he wasn't having this. The crowd was going berserk, and they drew the bus up so we stepped through a back door right onto the bus, and the crowd was battering the bus. Malcolm Beaton was at the game, in an unofficial capacity. Malcolm says: 'I have never left a rink by

Great Britain team, World Championships, Colorado Springs, USA, 1962. From left to right, back row: Johnny Murray (in coat), Tony Whitehead, Terry Matthews, Bert Smith, John Cook. Middle row: Harry Pearson, Dave Lammin, Red Devereaux, Roy Shepherd, Billy Brennan. Front row: Rupe Fresher, Ray Partridge, Red Imrie, Sammy MacDonald, Ian Forbes. Missing from photo – Joe Brown, Derek Metcalfe, John Milne. (Bill Brennan archive)

the back door in my life, and I am not going to start now!' So we told him: 'Cheerio, you're on your own, pal!'

On the Monday morning, we were all deeply in trouble, with all sorts of suspensions and severe warnings if it were ever to happen again. That was all caused, initially, by this needle between us and the Canadians, because they rode roughshod over us as far as money was concerned.

Some of the Canadians used to only play when they wanted to. I remember that Bert Oig at Paisley always seemed to be carrying some sort of wrist injury that kept him from functioning, or practising. Suddenly, in the last month of the season, when the management were thinking about who they would be retaining, Bert's wrist didn't seem to bother him at all!

At Paisley, you used to get these young Canadians coming in, and some of them were quite gullible. There must be dozens of Canadians that played at Paisley that think Hogganfield Loch is Loch Lomond! We used to pass it every time we were on an away trip to Falkirk, Kirkcaldy, Dunfermline, Perth or Dundee, and we'd tell them it was Loch Lomond!

Billy's international career had begun aged seventeen in 1951 when he assisted Scotland's Juniors to a convincing victory over their English equivalents at Richmond. He also recalls a bench-clearing brawl in this match, much to the chagrin of Dr J.O. McCabe, the Scottish manager! Billy's first outing with the senior Great Britain came in Basel and Zurich at the 1953 Pool 'B' World Championships aged nineteen. He would play in a further four World tournaments in the 1960s: in 1961 they were Pool 'B' silver medallists in Switzerland; in 1962 Billy captained GB in the Pool 'A' tournament in the USA; and he was player-coach of the British side in both the 1965 and 1966 Pool 'B' tournaments, in Finland and Yugoslavia respectively: 'I remember shaking hands with Marshall Tito as he moved down the line when we played in Zagreb, Yugoslavia in 1966.'

Billy finally came out of retirement to play in the 1971 Pool 'C' championships in Holland, when with Glasgow Dynamos. Billy played on the wing in the 1953 and 1971 World Championships, but was on defence for his other four tournaments:

John Carlyle was coaching the Great Britain team in Switzerland in 1961; John Murray was the player-manager. I got to know John Murray in 1953, when he was in charge of the British team. John Murray was never a great player, but a nice guy and a good manager.

We had a great team, 1961 in Switzerland; we had too many fighting for too few places. I remember I started out playing the exhibition games on left wing, and I scored two or three goals. Carlyle was putting the line together, and John Murray got left out; so there was a bit of an argument between the manager and the coach. But give John Carlyle his due, he picked his team.

We were playing a game one morning in that Championship, on an open-air rink. Red Imrie was playing defence, and they were winding up and going down, and Red was carrying the puck from behind the net. Instead of getting the puck in, he was trying to dipsy-doodle; it happened several times. We were all racing up, and then the brakes had to go on at the blueline. I was getting a bit short-tempered and, the third or fourth time it happened, I'm screaming at him: 'Pass the f—ing puck!' This was echoing round this empty, outdoor stadium! John Carlyle says to me after the game: 'You hurt the boy's feelings!' I said: 'John, I hope I got the message through to him.' But he thought it was a bit over the top. I told him maybe it was, but we were better for it, knowing what we needed to do.

We had a good team that year. Willie Clark let in the slider that cost us the Championship. God help him, but the puck slid from the centre circle back to him; he put his stick down to stop it – it wasn't even a shot – and it slid under his stick into the goal!

That happened, and then Rupe Fesher got a ten-minute penalty. Ahearne had us lined up for the Fair Play Trophy; he must have figured that was the only one we could win! It was Rolex watches that were handed out to the winners of that trophy, so we were all a bit miffed and Ahearne was not pleased with Rupe! We were grateful that it was one of the English boys that had done it, one of his own, rather than one of the Scots!

Ian Forbes had an ulcer that burst in Switzerland. We finished joint top of Pool 'B' at that time. We had been drinking a lot of wine, and we all went out to watch the last game of the tournament on the Sunday night. We all went out, and one guy that Ian had got friendly with had turned up at the hotel and asked for him. The guy on the desk 'phoned up to his room and couldn't get an answer.

Eventually, he got the guy to go up and check on the room, and here was Ian, collapsed. They got him to hospital but they had to contact Ahearne at the rink to find out what class of operation he wanted done, first class or second class!

Ian had that stomach operation for his ulcer in March, and he was back playing hockey again in a couple of months, gritting his teeth, and away he'd go! Ian was a hard grafter for a guy that suffered a serious ulcer complaint; a good guy to have on your team.

Ahearne used to invite the British team up to his suite for drinks – soft drinks! That was the big moment of the fortnight of the tournament, it was the only time you ever saw him. When we were in Colorado Springs in '62, Ahearne had met us in the foyer of the Broadmoor Hotel. The hotel had a big facility, with outdoor swimming pools and an indoor rink. We were all in apartments under the rink; it was nice, a big deal for us. Joe [Brown], big John [Milne] and myself were sharing a room. Joe had got injured and they'd put a plastercast on his wrist. Joe said to us 'I cannae play with this. I can't grip a stick with this bit across my palm.' We needed Joe, so the hacksaw came out!

Ahearne had talked sweetly to the Broadmoor management, and he met us in the foyer of this big hotel, and we were all in our best bib and tucker. That was the year that the East Germans had been barred because of the Berlin Wall being built, and the rest of the east European countries withdrew in protest. So we got bumped into Pool 'A', which was great, I suppose.

Although the British defeated Finland 7-5, an unexpected 3-6 loss to the Swiss saw Great Britain consigned to last place, receiving some heavy defeats on the way: 2-12 to Canada, 5-12 to the USA, 2-12 to Norway, 0-9 to West Germany, and 0-17 to champions Sweden, as skipper Brennan recalls:

But Sweden were running riot, I think they won it that year, but as the tournament went on the Swedish public began to scream, because there was no television coverage. The television companies, who'd turned down the deal because of the upset with the east Europeans, were now running to Ahearne's door. He was left to negotiate on behalf of the International Association.

This guy approached him in the foyer and said: 'Can I have a word, Mr Ahearne?' In typical Ahearne style, he said: 'No, no, you know my price', waving him away with his hand, but winking at me at the same time! He told me: 'They know my price, and I'm not going any cheaper – I've got them over a barrel.' Which he had, because they came up with the money at the end of the day.

Up to that point, all the World Championship games were held in the one location; Pool 'A', Pool 'B', whatever. This meant that TV could cherrypick the games they wanted. He told me what he wanted was to have Pool 'A' in one city, Pool 'B' in another city, and at different times. He wanted all sport, not just hockey, barred from television for a year, as he felt that would bring the television companies to heel, and they'd realise how much they got for how little. He'd have loved to be the sole negotiator for sport against the TV companies. He was away ahead of his time, when you see the money being bandied about now for TV rights.

Billy, and Alastair, are rightly aggrieved that their full contribution to the British cause in international competition has been lost to posterity, as only scoring details of World Championship games have been retained, as Billy explains:

Alastair played over 100 games for Great Britain, but only the details from 47 of them are recorded. I played in a lot more games than the 36 I'm credited with. For example, on the day in April 1961 that England beat Scotland 9-3 at Wembley [at football], Great Britain beat the Canadian Forces at the Empire Pool in the evening; yet that game doesn't count in the records. When we went to the USA in March 1962 for the World Championships, we played tough warm-up games, in Muskegon and Des Moines, against minor pro teams, and against the University of Denver; none of these are included, but we were all very conscious of representing Britain when we played in them.

I remember a game against France, in Paris, in 1964, that was televised live – and that was just a World Championship qualifier. I remember that Dorry Boyle stiffened one of the French players, knocking his teeth out. One of France's leading dental surgeons was watching the game on TV, and he rushed round to the rink to assist this guy!

Who were the players that stood out for Billy in the course of his career?

Playing against Zamick of Nottingham; he was such a bouncy, wee individual. He looked after himself. He was a bit remote; I don't think he was ever really one of the boys; did his playing, and that was him.

But when we were eventually going down to play at Wembley with the Mohawks, they brought Zamick back, and they had Art Hodgins playing. I've said that 'Tuck' Syme was the best British-born defenceman, but big Art Hodgins was probably the best defenceman that ever came from Canada. You never saw him lose his temper, but he could hit you. It was all done in the best of spirit!

But Wembley had Hodgins playing, and Roy Shepherd and all the locals down there as well, and then they brought Zamick back. I had warned our crowd – I didn't need to tell Joe or Crawford, they knew all about him – but I told the youngsters, like Alastair, that they were up against something totally different in Zamick. For a start, they saw him going into the shower room, where they had bars across, and he was doing a warm-up series of exercises. They came back and told me this, and I said to them again: 'I told you, this is something completely different.'

That night, he got the puck in front of our net, about ten feet out, and he fired it. It hit the post, and came straight back to him – and before the goalkeeper had moved, he'd hit the other post, just his speed of thought and speed of action. He was unbelievable.

There were a lot of players who could've played what was recognised as Senior 'A' hockey back in Canada at that time.

Johnny Quales from Paisley was a great skater, and a powerful guy. He worked as a wagon repairer on the railway, so he was very strong, like a pocket battleship. He played for Dundee for a spell, and then he went down to Brighton, and then just disappeared, went out of circulation. A few years later, once we had the Mohawks as a good going team at Paisley in the early sixties, Johnny and Gus Munro turned up at a practice, looking for a game. But they were in their thirties then, so I said to them: 'I've got a good, young team doing helluva well, why should I disrupt that just to accommodate you guys?'

We also had a lot of workers, grafters which, I suppose, playing for Kewley you had to be a worker.

Some of these Scottish guys, especially from Falkirk, fell by the wayside, either because they lost interest or because they weren't encouraged at Falkirk because the rink there closed down too quickly. When you talk about Falkirk, you tend to think about Bill Sneddon, John Carlyle, Red Imrie. But you had virtually a full team of locals there – Tommy Paton, Alex Ormond, Mike Smith, Andy Williams. But there were so many of them left. Tommy Paton came back for a couple of years – I think it was John [Carlyle] that managed to coax him to play – but that was it, he had to be coaxed to play.

Obviously, when the senior team folded, there was nowhere for them to go. Other than travelling up and down the country to get a game, the way the Perth guys did, like Jimmy Spence and Ian Forbes.

Jimmy Spence proved himself playing at Nottingham. Marshall [Key] went to Harringay with John Carlyle. Marshall was, like Bert Smith, probably one of the best stickhandlers in the league – from a Scots point of view – but was a wee bit short on aggression. You could bounce him out a game, and he would complain bitterly, but you knew you never were going to get any reaction behind the net or in the corner. He'd try, but you knew it was kind of half-hearted.

Jimmy Spence was different; you knew that if you messed with Jimmy, you were going to get something back!

Bert Smith, as I say, had so much natural ability, but loved the good life shall we say! His pal from Kirkcaldy, Jimmy Mitchell, was a good defenceman.

Bill Sneddon was a great defenceman, a great competitor and a fitness fanatic. He was a fervent Communist, and he fell out with all sorts of authority – he'd been *sine die*d from amateur boxing and junior football I believe.

I remember playing for the Mohawks against Fife up at Kirkcaldy, and Bill was playing for the Flyers at the time. I was taking a face-off with Bill, and my stick caught him. He stepped back and said: 'You wee Fenian bastard, Brennan.' An obvious reference to me being a Catholic. He came into our dressing-room after the game, and he was looking for me. He came over to me, and I was worried! But he had tears in his eyes, and he wanted to apologise to me for his remark! He said: 'You know me, Bill, I believe that we're all Jock Tamson's bairns.' I was much relieved, and breathed a big sigh of relief! But that was the kind of man he was. Bill Sneddon was a great player, and I'm surprised that he's not been inducted to the British Hall of Fame. His disciplinary record shouldn't be held against him, because he was such a tremendous competitor, and a superb defenceman.

Robert Stevenson was quite young at the time and something had happened, because Robert had backed off. Jimmy Mitchell was having a dig at him in the dressing-room at the interval, and I got a bit embarrassed at this. I said to Robert: 'Don't you realise, son, if you want to play ice hockey, you're going to get hurt? Either by somebody stiffening you, or you stiffening them, and they react; but, one way or another, there's no doubt you're going to get hurt. You're as well getting your retaliation in first, get with it.' And it turned him like that. In fact, he took one of my teeth out later on when he played in Crossmyloof!

I actually got an email from Robert in Australia recently. He said that he had only had

Great Britain team, World Championships, Finland, March 1965. From left to right: John Milne, Hep Tindale, Mike Jordan, Terry Matthews, Glen Reilly, Graeme Farrell, Willie Clark, Marshall Key, Derek Metcalfe, Dorry Boyle, Billy Miller, Billy Brennan, Joe McIntosh, Robert Stevenson, Alastair Brennan. Missing from photo – Bill Crawford, Sam MacDonald. (Bill Brennan archive)

> two coaches in his hockey career: Jim Kenny at Crossmyloof had taught him stickhandling and suchlike, and I got the credit for teaching him not to shit it from anybody, to get that aggression, which had stood him in good stead!
>
> A bit later, more Alastair's era, I remember Derek Reilly of Murrayfield had all the ability. Derek flew up the wing this time, and I'm waiting, and went to meet him; something you should never do, I suppose, because he could step back. But by the time he reached me, he was on his hands and knees sliding, he was just going down, and down, and down! I'm saying, 'Derek, son, get that wee bit aggression into your game.'

Coaching was something that Bill had started in his mid-twenties with the Mohawks, whom he moulded into the grand slam-winning dominant force of British hockey in the late 1960s. An innovative coach, he introduced a varied off-ice fitness programme for his players, allowing maximum use of ice time for skills and tactical development.

He also arranged for his Paisley team to undertake short European tours, matching them against Canadian Air Force teams and helping their development by playing quality opposition. A number of the Paisley players he developed went on to achieve international recognition with Great Britain – including his younger brother, Alastair, Billy Miller, the late Jackson McBride and Alistair McRae:

> Jim Kenny taught us a lot, but Keith Kewley introduced a more professional approach, like taking people into the corners and keeping them there; don't let your man back out, that sort of thing.
>
> Thinking about tactics, I laugh when I watch overlapping full-backs in football; Kewley was doing that in hockey before he left Ayr, and nobody realised it. If it was a powerplay, he had the centre carrying the puck, as usual, and the winger was screaming for a pass while cutting into the middle, and Herb Kewley, the defenceman, was going up on the outside – and the pass was always going to Herb; it was never going to the guy making all the noise and attracting attention. That's all that was, an overlapping full-back. So, Kewley was ahead of his time in things like that.
>
> Kewley was picking up his ideas from a Canadian book called *The Hockey Handbook*, written by Ace Percival. He was involved in some sort of Institute of Sport, and Percival had guys all over Canada, and further afield, doing statistics and writing in drills and so on. This book must have come out in the early fifties, and I had got an aunt in America to send me a

copy of it. Kewley used to laugh, because when he was making a point, he'd turn to me and say: 'What was his name?' And I'd reply so and so, or whatever, and Kewley would say: 'There you are, and he's never been to Canada!' He'd always turn to me to supply the punchline, because he knew I had read this coaching book!

I used that book for years as a grounding. Percival was way ahead of his time. He was talking about 'miracle foods', like yoghurt, and this was the early fifties. He'd taken everything into consideration, different body types, endorphins, diet and how different personalities were best suited to different types of coaching – you name it. It was a great book for any sport, really, but it was mainly for hockey; way ahead of its time.

So, that's what started me on coaching, mainly through Kewley; I became interested in how things should be done, like shooting the puck. If you're a right-hand shot, you should be standing on your left foot, because you can still get your body through, and that leg going through into the next stride, that sort of thing.

Tiny Syme, for example, was shooting off his wrong foot; he was a right-hand shot and would shoot off his right foot. And doing that, you're throwing your body back. And if somebody steps into you when you're throwing your body back, you're away – you're balance has gone; you're lying on your back.

Teaching kids things like that, I remember when Alastair started playing, and the youngsters all wanted to slap a puck. I told them that they were like a joiner going to do a job on a cabinet with a big hammer. There are so many different ways of shooting – snapshots, slapshots, sweepshots, flipshots – but they all want to slap a puck because of the big effect. Plus, they can do it with the sticks now; the older sticks wouldn't stand up to continual slapping.

It's like a golf shot, it's all a matter of balance – you don't need to be a big guy to have a good shot.

I used to go on the ice on a Sunday morning – even if there was no practice, I'd still be on the ice – going from end to end, shooting. I had read in this book about getting the balance right; switching your weight from one foot to the other when taking a shot – like a golf shot. One of the ways of doing it for a right hand shot was to cut across, and as you got to the left-hand blueline, you swung yourself back and let a shot go. I'd been doing that on a Sunday morning for weeks, but not with the idea that I must do this in a game. I always remember playing against Ayr, and 'Doc' Holliday was in the goals, and there was a quiet spell in the game and I had come up the ice with the puck, and this happened just to work out as I had practised. I happened to let a shot go, and it hit the bar behind him, and bounced up into the seats somewhere. There was a wee guy at Paisley then called Benny Robbie, who did various jobs like timekeeper, stickboy, whatever, and I always remember Benny screaming: 'He's been daein' that oan a Sunday fur weeks!'

Again, of course, Percival's book talked about fitness, exercises, running and so on. When I was coaching the Mohawks, we were only on the ice once a week and I thought: this is a waste of bloody time, you can't get them fit and work on the technical aspect – you can't do both in the time available and at midnight players aren't very receptive!

It was interesting, plus I was enthusiastic enough to enjoy what I was doing, and seeing the results happening.

After I had quit coaching the Mohawks, you wonder to yourself if you could've done it again. But when Aberdeen came along, things had changed socially.

Billy and his family had moved to Aberdeen in 1975 when he joined a Norwegian engineering company as Sales and Projects Manager, retiring as their UK Managing Director in 1999. Billy's hockey involvement resumed in 1992 with the opening of an ice rink in Aberdeen, and he was invited to assist with the setting-up of its hockey programme:

It might just have been the crop that was there at Aberdeen, but they didn't seem to want to do things on a repetitive basis, which they had to do to learn how to do them. They just seemed to want to go racing in and slap the puck, or else slap it against the boards and somebody else had to race in and get it. There was no thought to it.

When I came back to coach at Aberdeen they didn't want to learn and seemed not interested. They brought in a young Canadian coach from the continent, with his rink diagram, and they just couldn't follow his drills. I told him: 'I don't know what you're trying to achieve, so how are these kids meant to follow it?'

For example, Kewley used the one defensive system all the time we were at Paisley. At face-offs in your own end, he had a defenceman taking the face-offs, against the opposing centre, normally. Our centre was against the back boards, and the two wingers were at the side of the face-off circle. The winger that was furthest out had one of two choices as soon as the puck was dropped. If we lost possession, he went out and covered the defenceman. If we got possession, the defenceman who took the face-off would take the opposing centre out, and our centre picked up the puck – and always, always went behind the net, to give him time to see what was happening. And he didn't try to carry the puck from behind the net; he'd fire the puck out to the winger who'd moved across against the boards. That was it, cleared, because everybody else was moving up by that time. You still see that defensive play that Kewley used being set up in the NHL games today.

This Canadian at Aberdeen wanted to take all the face-offs, because he was a centre. I tried to explain to him about having a defenceman take the face-off in his own end; what good was he to the team as a centre, being tied up in his own end? His reply was that he was good at face-offs and won more than fifty per cent of them. I said that even if he won fifty per cent of face-offs in his own end, he was still likely to be tied up and unable to set up any break-out play. But he just wouldn't accept this.

If you're not getting a reaction when you're coaching, you don't feel the same enthusiasm. That's what I felt at Aberdeen, and I just walked away.

Playing in Russia in 1959, there was not a lot I picked up in terms of coaching, but just playing against Russian teams was an education. We used to argue with the Canadian players at Paisley that these Russian guys were going to take over the sport, but the Canadians just laughed; they thought their hockey would always be the best!

We had a lot of success at Paisley in the sixties, but it was helped by the fact that players like myself, Joe Brown and Billy Crawford had all played together with the Pirates for so long and knew the right things to do. I had a good crop of youngsters who came through, who had ability and wanted to learn: like Joe Conway, Jackson McBride, Billy Miller, Tom Reid, Alistair McRae and my younger brother, Alastair.

I came in for a practice, early in the 1969/70 season, and there were only a couple of guys in the dressing-room, and a couple out on the ice. And we had also lost the nucleus of the team: Bill Crawford had emigrated; Jackson McBride went to Ayr; Joe Brown had retired; Robert Stevenson had gone back to Crossmyloof. I just picked up my skates and walked out; my heart wasn't in it anymore.

At the same time, my working life took a different direction. A new product group was formed, within Babcock's, to come up with ideas for new business, and I got whipped on to that. Suddenly, the world was my oyster; I got a company car, and went into what was effectively a semi-sales job. Coming off a drawing board, where I had worked for twenty years, into this type of environment was great.

So, I didn't really have much time for hockey. But Great Britain was going to re-enter the World Championships in 1971, for the first time in five years, and I was persuaded to come back for that. Paisley had closed, and Sam Stevenson asked me to go to Crossmyloof and play with Glasgow Dynamos. I played there on the wing for one season, with Robert Stevenson and young guys like Martin Shields and John Hester. I went to Holland with the British team, and retired at the end of the season, as I felt that my fitness wasn't what I'd like it to have been.

I spent 1973 to 1975 living in Stourport on Severn in Worcestershire, working in Birmingham with Babcock's. Life was ideal in Stourport, as you were away from the hassle.

Billy Brennan accepts his mentor Keith Kewley's British Ice Hockey Hall of Fame certificate from committee member David Gordon, 12 December 2005.

Then I got a call telling me the Norwegians wanted to interview me! That's how I ended up in Aberdeen in '75.

My children all got their secondary education in Aberdeen. My eldest daughter, Barbara, she and her husband live more or less round the corner from us. They have two daughters, and her husband works off-shore. My younger daughter, Leigh, is in Houston, Texas. Her husband works for Bristow Helicopters (he's vice-president of Global Business Development). They have two boys.

My son, Mark, had an interest in hockey, but never had the opportunity to play – although he watches a lot of NHL on TV. He got two HNDs and then two degrees; he's still in Aberdeen.

My other brother, Ian, retired as a Colonel in the US Marines. He lives in Pensacola in Florida. Ian played a bit when the Mohawks moved to Paisley; he was friendly with Jimmy Allen. Ian started as an apprentice turner, and we had an aunt and uncle in the USA who had a machine shop, so they sponsored him to go there. But he got caught up in the draft, and went into the Marine Corps.

Billy and wife Jeanette now live in retirement in Bridge of Don, Aberdeen, where his sporting activity is now confined to the golf course, and he is a former captain of Murcar Golf Club in Aberdeen.

Like his elder brother, Alastair Brennan was born in Paisley's Barshaw Hospital on 17 February 1945; the fourth – and youngest – of the Brennan children. And, unsurprisingly, it was elder brother Billy – then an established Paisley Pirate – who introduced nine-year-old Alastair to skating:

The first pair of skates I ever wore was a pair of figure skates, but don't put that in your book! I was seven when we moved to 168 Renfrew Road in Paisley. I went to St Catherine's Primary School then to St Mirin's High School in Paisley. Across from my parents' house in Renfrew Road in Paisley, there was a bit where we used to go sledging. It wasn't a park as such; just a wilderness. Over a period of time, the rain used to run down onto this ground, and there was a railway line went through it from Paisley to Babcock's with a wall alongside it, so the water used to gather there, and freeze solid – it was huge.

Everybody went skating on it, so Jeanette, Billy's wife, said to him, or vice versa, about taking me over to see if I was interested in skating. I was about nine at the time. Jeanette got me a pair of black figure skates that were in the ice rink; it was the only thing wee enough to fit me.

They put them on in my Mum's house, and Billy carried me across the road and down to this field, which is now a retail park. That was me on skates for the first time. There was a name I'll never forget; he played with the Pirates: Hal Schooley. They called him 'Smiler', and he was always banging into barriers and things. The way I was trying to get my balance, I said to Billy: 'I look like that Hal Schooley!'

My Dad used to take me to watch Billy with the Pirates, but I'd never skated at that point. I really learned to skate on roller skates, and I could go roller skates better than I could ice skates. I used to fly up and down the pavement outside my Mum's house with a stick that Billy got me and a tennis ball; the neighbours used to sit at their windows and watch me!

At the weekends, we'd go and play in the school playgrounds – just along where Chivas Regal is now – there were three schools there in the 1950s. There were quite a crowd of us from that scheme [Gallowhill] who went and played there; we used to form wee teams.

Billy went away to Sweden on a trip with the Pirates and he brought me back a pair of skates – hockey boots. I was in bed when they came home that night, and he came in with this pair of hockey skates. That was me, started going to the skating.

Billy never, ever took me to the skating, or forced me into it. My mates from the roller skating, one or two of them went to the Sunday morning practices at Paisley Ice Rink. One Sunday morning, Billy had taken me for a Coke in the Sherwood Café. We were walking back to where he and Jeanette lived at the time, round the back of Paisley Grammar School, when he said to me: 'Do you fancy going to the practices on a Sunday morning?' I said: 'I don't know.' Billy says: 'I thought a couple of your pals went, do you want to go?' I said okay, but that I didn't have the money! You had to pay two shillings to Walter Munn, the wee guy that did the ice.

Billy took me back up home to Renfrew Road. The Czech national team had played against the Pirates and left a load of sticks, and Billy had brought a couple home. One of the sticks was red on the front, so Billy cut it, gave it to me. I went away on my own to Paisley Ice Rink, and that wee Walter – he was a cheeky so and so – he's sitting at the cash desk. He knew who I was and I said that I was here for the practice; there's my two shillings. He says to me: 'Where do you think you're going with that stick? Where did you get it?' I said: 'My big brother gave me it.' He tells me: 'You'll need to leave it in here; we supply sticks.' That was my introduction to hockey! I was eleven when Billy brought me those skates, so I'd be about eleven or twelve when I went to the first practice, 1956/57.

I just took to it. Some of the Pirates, who used to practise on a Sunday morning at that time, used to stay on the ice for the junior practice. One of them that Billy was friendly with, Gerry Corriveau, used to play defence; he'd stay on and show me things like if you're playing on defence and if the puck goes into that corner, you go over to that side, but if it comes over here, just go to halfway, you know? That's your domain on that blueline, not that I was playing on defence or anything.

Sometimes the Pirates, depending on when their games were, had a practice on a Saturday morning before the public session. Billy and some of the others were watching the general skating, and I had learned to skate a bit by then. But, when I was skating round at that time, I had an awful habit of jumping round corners. During the week, Billy was in my Mum's, and he says to me: 'I'm going to tell you something. See this jumping round corners, don't do it.' I said that you see them all doing it, and Billy says: 'They're losing time, skate round corners.' And that was the only thing Billy ever said to me about skating.

Then you just progressed at Sunday morning practices. If you were getting any better, sometimes you got into the Mohawks practice on a Sunday night. I remember a wee guy called Roy Collins, who lives in Canada now, telling me that he'd got us in for a practice with the Mohawks on a Sunday night, half-past-six; we thought this was great. Billy used to have the practice like a military operation; it was like circuit training, different exercises on the ice.

Paisley Mohawks 1962/63. From left to right, back row: Jim McDougal, Joe Beveridge (treasurer), Dorry Boyle, John 'Jumbo' Milne, Bill Crawford, Ian Boggan, Campbell Forrest, Billy Miller, Matt Thomson (trainer), Tom Reid. Front row: Roy Collins, Billy Brennan (player-coach), Jim Black, Don Brown, Robert Stevenson, Ally Brennan, Dave Ferguson. (*Hockey Fan* photograph)

We did all that with the Mohawks. This was the Mohawks that had moved from Crossmyloof, wee Robert Stevenson, Dorry Boyle (who had played with Edinburgh Royals), these guys. We used to do all that, then they would have their scrimmage, and maybe slot you in an odd shift, and you were happy with that. I was about thirteen or fourteen at the time. I also played schools football and then in the Paisley and District Juveniles; one of the guys I played with, Gerry Sweeney, went on to Celtic and then Leicester City.

I left school at fifteen and went in to Babcock's as an office boy, before switching to start an apprenticeship with them as a turner. And then when I was sixteen I started playing hockey with the Mohawks.

When I first started playing for Paisley, we used to travel down to Altrincham who had guys like Spence, Forbes and Macdonald, Joe McIntosh; they used to travel down from Perth and Kirkcaldy, but they were paid for it. We used to get hammered, but that was a learning process for the likes of us.

Our Billy did a lot to keep the game alive in Scotland, especially on the west coast, in fact, the whole of Scotland. We used to fly down to London and play Wembley on the Saturday and Brighton on the Sunday, and you were playing against ex-pros, and I was only sixteen, but you learned.

My Dad, Bill, was fanatical about the hockey, but my mother would never watch me play; she wouldn't even watch me on TV! I was always her baby, being the youngest! I remember one time I had some virus and had been in my bed for a week. The Mohawks were playing Fife, who had Spence, Forbes, Macdonald and Sneddon, so my Mum and Dad were going to this game. I picked up Billy's two daughters, who were young, and took them round to the rink. As we were going in, the stick-boy told me that Billy wanted to see me in the dressing-room. I took the girls up to my Mum and Dad, and nicked down to the dressing-room. Billy

Alastair Brennan (left) and Billy Brennan (right), Paisley Mohawks, *c.*1968. (Bill Brennan archive)

> said to me: 'You're playing. Campbell Forrest'll run you up to the house to get your kit.' So, by the time I got back and got ready, the warm-up was finished and the game was about to start. I skated on and took the face-off with Jimmy Spence. He asked me how I was doing, and I told him that I had literally just got up from my sickbed to play! My mother, of course, couldn't believe it when she saw me, and spent the whole game walking about the corridors of the rink!

Alastair's rapid development received a surprising boost in February 1965 when, having just turned twenty, he was off to the World Championships with the Great Britain team:

> Then I went to Finland in '65 with the British team for the World Championships. Again, it just shows you how you get the breaks. It was a television game on *Grandstand*, Great Britain *v.* The Rest, down at Ayr. Lawrence Lovell was the centre, Roy Collins was on the left wing, and I was on the right wing for The Rest. We got beat 3-1, and I got the goal.
>
> But Ian Forbes withdrew from the British team; he told them before the game he couldn't make it for Finland, workwise. Big Jumbo Milne, the manager, 'phoned Bunny Ahearne, because they were leaving the following week for Finland, and he says that they'd need to get somebody to put in. Ahearne asked Big Jumbo if he'd any names and he says: 'Alastair Brennan'. Ahearne says: 'Oh?' Big Jumbo says: 'How, have you got a problem with that?' And Ahearne was a dictator, and he replied: 'No, have you got a problem?' John Milne said: 'No, he's good enough to go, but some people might think he's only getting picked because Billy's the coach.' Ahearne says: 'If there's anything about that, just tell them to 'phone me.'
>
> That was how I got my break for my first World Championship. It was funny, because I had a couple of pairs of Prolite skates that were hand-me-downs from Billy; fortunately he was the same size as me. My mother had asked him to bring me back a new pair of Prolite

> skates from Finland, and she was going to give him the money. Billy got the 'phone call on the Saturday night after the game to say that I was going. He 'phoned my Dad and said: 'See that money you were going to give me to get the wee fellow skates? Just give it to him and tell him to get his own!' And it dawned on my Dad what he meant!
>
> I was at the dancing in Glasgow with Roy Collins, because we'd just come back from Ayr. I came into the house, and I was lying on the settee talking about that day's game. My mother worked as a silver service waitress at functions at Paisley Town Hall, so she was out at work. I lay there in the living room, and my Dad's talking away to me, when my Mum came in with my sister, Ailie, who was also working there part-time.
>
> We're sitting talking away about the game on the television. After about a quarter-of-an-hour my Dad says to her: 'Oh, by the way, see that money we were going to give Billy to get him skates? Well, just give it to him, he can get his own.'
>
> I sat up and went: 'What?' He said: 'You're going to Finland next week.' He'd sat there for over two hours and never said a word!
>
> I had to go in to the work on the Monday and tell Babcock's, but they were great about it, they really were. The following year [1966] we went to Yugoslavia and, again, there was no problem. For some reason, the BIHA stopped sending a British team to the Championships for five years. So, in '71, when we went to Holland, I was established at Babcock's by then. That year, the works Union Convenor asked me if the company paid me when I was away with the British team, and I told him that I got unpaid leave of absence. He told me to leave it with him, as union members in England got paid by Babcock's in similar circumstances. And the company paid me for all the time I was away with Great Britain after that, no problem.

On the domestic front, Paisley Ice Rink closed its doors in the summer of 1970. Alastair and a couple of his teammates joined up with Ayr Bruins, who were being coached by their former Paisley colleague, Jackson McBride. Alastair and Jackson were close in age and went on holidays together.

With Great Britain re-entering the World Championships in 1971 after a five-year absence, both Alastair and Jackson were setting their sights on a trip to the Winter Olympics the following year; but they were to be disappointed:

> The Olympics were '72, and there was no British team. We were really cheesed off, because in Holland in '71 we had just failed to qualify for the Olympics by a point or something. I think it was Bulgaria who finished above us, but they withdrew from the Olympics because they couldn't afford it, which should've meant that we'd automatically go up. But the powers that be said that because we didn't qualify on our own merits we were not going. And what a trip that would have been, to Sapporo in Japan.

A road accident on Sunday 19 March 1972 nearly ended not only Alastair's hockey involvement and then-girlfriend Jean Scott's figure-skating career, but almost cost them their lives:

> It was coming back down from Aviemore to play at the old rink in Ayr that we had the crash. Jean was just back from the Olympics in Sapporo and was skating at some show at Aviemore on the Saturday and we left the next day to drive down. Jean was driving; it was her Mini. I was in the front passenger seat and another girl, who skated for Britain, was in the back. Just out of Kingussie it rained, and the windscreen was greasy. So, I told Jean to stop, and I got out and cleaned the windscreen. I jumped back in the car, and in those days it wasn't compulsory to wear a seat belt; we came round this bend, and there was a guy coming round it on the wrong side of the road and ploughed into us. I went through the windscreen.
>
> When I came to I was lying in a puddle up the road, but I didn't realise how badly I was hurt. Jean nearly lost an arm; she got forty-eight stitches and had a bad cut on her leg. I

kept complaining about my back and my neck, and it wasn't until they got me to Raigmore Hospital in Inverness they discovered the damage. That was me for seven months, with a brace on my neck.

That he was able to return to such a physically demanding sport as ice hockey in such a short space of time is a remarkable testimony to his courage and ability. But his return would mean a change of club, as the Ayr rink had closed in April 1972:

I'd met Norrie Boreham of Fife on two or three occasions after the accident, and he asked me if I was going to get back into playing again. I told him that I'd started practising at Crossmyloof, so he went back to Fife and told Harold 'Pep' Young, their coach.

The next thing was I got a 'phone call from Norrie asking me to go through and see them. I met 'Pep' Young and Tommy Horn, the rink manager, and they asked me to come and play for them. I told them they were taking a chance, because every other rink I've went to has closed (meaning Paisley and Ayr)! So, I ended up signing there and then. My first season at Kirkcaldy was 1972/73, and I had seven seasons there until 1979.

The time I spent in Kirkcaldy was, I would say, the best hockey I played in my life. I made so many friends through there that I still keep in touch with. The first year I went through, I was driving to Kirkcaldy on a Friday night for a late night practice, then driving back to Paisley, then driving back to Kirkcaldy the next day for the game. And I'd drive home on the Saturday night, and then we might have an away game on the Sunday night. So, this is what I was doing every weekend, and I was still working in Babcock's as well.

One of the boys in the team, Rab Petrie, him and his wife kindly invited me to stay with them on the Friday night, and I'd drive home the next day after the game. I did that for two seasons, then Rab's mother and father in law, who were great hockey fans, invited me to stay with them, as they had a big bungalow just down from the rink. So, I stayed with them for the rest of my time in Fife, practically, and I used to call them Auntie and Uncle!

Big John Taylor, he was my best mate through in Kirkcaldy; big 'Slack'. Him and I used to run about all the time; I used to go through and spend the summers in Fife, going to the beach at Kinghorn. John had three brothers who all played hockey: Jim was a goalie, who went with the British team to the World Championships in Holland; there was George, and then an older brother, Hugh, who had played before I went to Fife.

John Pullar took over from Jim Taylor, and he was a good goalie; daft, but then again, most goalies are!

These guys all came down for my wedding and they still all keep in touch, as do my 'Auntie and Uncle', and it's twenty-six years since I left Kirkcaldy. Big Joe McIntosh was at my wedding as well. Joe never changes; Joe still thinks he's thirty!

When at Kirkcaldy, Alastair moved back to a defensive berth, and went to Poland with the Great Britain team for the 1976 Pool 'C' World Championships as a blueliner:

We went to Poland in 1976. I remember that Jackson McBride and Jimmy Young from Ayr went on that trip. Jimmy Young was a hell of a laugh. We were in Gdansk, and oh, it was cold! Typical BIHA, they never think of anything about trips. They took us on a sightseeing trip to the shipyard in Gdansk; this thing was right on the seafront, and the sea was frozen. The ends of the buildings were all open, and the guys are working lathes with big parkas on – and we're standing about freezing! I'm saying: 'This is like me back at work!'

After the tournament, we were leaving, and we had to go right across Poland to Warsaw to get the 'plane home. This train journey was just something else! There were three bunks on top of each other in each compartment. From that tournament on, Les Lovell from Fife, Terry and Kenny Matthews from Whitley Bay, and myself always went about together. So, with three bunks, we were wondering who was going to get left out!

We had been warned about changing money, and to make sure there were two or three of us. Big Jumbo Milne was the manager, and he was laying this off to us. And who got mugged changing money? Big Jumbo! He lost about £100, and he chased them! I wouldn't like to have been one of them if he'd caught them! He was an awful size of a man; his hand could hold a pint tumbler and you'd only see a tiny bit of glass at the top.

That season, Ayr Bruins, coached by Alastair's old pal Jackson McBride, upset the strong-going Flyers in the British Championship:

Ayr beat Fife 8-1 at Limekiln Road in the semi-finals of the British Championship. At that time, whichever team won the northern section would go on and win the Championship, because you were playing against the likes of Southampton, who weren't strong. In fact that might have been Jackson's greatest hour! Jackson had two Canadian brothers, the Nelsons, who were good, and that was a right turn up for the book when they beat us. They had a good, young Canadian goalie as well, Jim Graves, who was a hell of a nice guy.

That result would be bought up a couple of years later when Alastair was contemplating a return to the West Coast club:

Sandy Reid was the Ayr chairman and approached me up at Kirkcaldy, when he knew that I was moving down to Ayrshire to live. The first time he came, I said no. But the following season, it was just before I was getting married, and I decided that I couldn't keep travelling up to Kirkcaldy. And Sandy always reminded me of that time Ayr beat Fife in the semi-final, he kept saying it was the best bottle of whisky he ever drank! He'd got a bottle of whisky from behind the bar at Limekiln Road and walked into the dressing-room. He said he took off the cap, threw it in the bin, and told Jimmy Young and Jackson that they weren't leaving till they'd finished it! So Sandy always used to cast that up to me! It was a shock, but they deserved to beat us.

I came down to Limekiln Road in '79, and Sandy asked me if I'd coach, which I didn't really want to do, as I'd rather just have played. It wasn't the best experience of my life, really.

Not only was the team not that strong, but I'd have liked somebody else coaching. In fact, I even asked wee Archie McCallum, who was coaching the juniors, if he would just coach from the bench, even if he didn't travel. But he wasn't for having it.

It didn't help me, trying to be a player-coach; I'd rather have just played. I was player-coach at Ayr, and I had a run-in with a member of the Committee, who shall remain nameless, round about Christmas '82. All the players helped scrape the ice before every practice at that time, except for one, who seemed to think that was beneath him and always turned up after all this work was done. A lot of the guys, rightly, resented this attitude, so I told him one night to go home; he wasn't getting to practise because he hadn't helped prepare the ice. A member of the Ayr Committee wasn't happy that I'd done this, despite having told me that, as coach, I had total responsibility for the playing side. So, they relieved me of my coaching duties – but still wanted me to carry on playing for them! Needless to say, I left!

Next thing was I got a 'phone call from Tom Stewart of Dundee, saying that he'd heard I'd stopped playing at Ayr, and he knew the circumstances. He asked if I'd like to play with Dundee. I wasn't sure about the travelling, but he told me I wouldn't need to go to practices, just to play for them. I told him I'd go up and see him, but that I'd need to speak to Jean.

I told Jean about Tom's offer, and she was raging about what had happened to me at Ayr, so she told me to go.

I went up, they were playing Murrayfield, and Tom took me in to the dressing-room, and Roy Halpin told me that him and Chris Brinster had asked Tom Stewart to sign me, because apparently Halpin had a hard time playing against me, although I didn't know that at the time. Tom announces to the players: 'Alastair will be signing for us.' So, that was me, I hadn't much choice after that!

Tom was another one of these larger-than-life characters, with his Rolls-Royce and suits of armour in the hall of his house! He went bankrupt umpteen times! He took the whole Dundee team to New York – that was where he got the idea of the New York Rangers uniforms – because they went to their training camp!

What I will say for him, though, it was him who started to bring a decent standard of import, with Halpin, Brinster and Leblanc. Leblanc came from a wee fishing village where they didn't speak English, and his English was really poor; Halpin's family were all French-speaking, although he spoke English with a Canadian accent and you'd never have known he was French-Canadian; and Brinster came from New York, the Bronx, but he went to Concordia University in Montreal with the other two.

I joined Dundee halfway through '82/83, and we won the British Championship at Streatham – and I broke my ankle in the final! It was comical, because Billy flew down from Aberdeen to London to watch me, and I broke my ankle in the first period! And I didn't know it was broken till I got to Ninewells Hospital in Dundee the next day! It was a Canadian goalie that Durham had, Katernyuk, and we were on a powerplay. I was standing beside the net, and he just whacked me with his stick right across my ankle. I just collapsed. Wee Alex McWilliam, who was the referee, never saw it, and he told me that I should've let out a roar! But I went off, and they wouldn't let me loosen my boot. At the end of the period I got in to the dressing-room and got my boot off and my ankle was all swelled up. Anyway, they put ice on, I got my skate back on, and was taped up. But I'm struggling to try and skate, and there's our Bill, flew down from Aberdeen to see me play about a period, all told!

The next day, we travelled back up by coach to Dundee. I went to the hospital and got told that my ankle was broken. So, that was me, a cast, the crutches, back to the ice rink.

Dundee's three imports that season – Roy Halpin, Chris Brinster and Al Leblanc, all came from Concordia University. To me, over the years of that era, big Brinster was the best defenceman I've seen; everything came from him. Halpin was scoring all the goals, but Brinster was setting up all the plays, breaking up plays; a great player, and a big, strong, hard man.

I remember each of them lost their driving licence for drink-driving in Dundee! They all shared the one car, and Brinster lost his licence first. Then, a few weeks later, Halpin got caught, and he lost his. So then they've got Leblanc driving. They'd been out in Dundee and they're going home one night, and the car was obviously well known to the police, who stopped it. Leblanc says to the police, in his pigeon English: 'For what did you stop me?' The cop says to him: 'Because you went round that roundabout three times.' Leblanc says: 'I new here, got lost, couldn't find road.' To which the cop replies with: 'If you had put on your effing lights you'd have seen where you were going!' 'Cause this was about two o'clock in the morning! So that was Leblanc lost his licence as well. Tom, who didn't drink, ended up having to chauffeur them about.

Again, though, they were good hockey players, and it didn't interfere with their hockey.

The following season I came back to Ayr, when we had Paul Bedard, Kevin Murphy and 'Worm' – Derek Watt. Wee George Richmond 'phoned me during the summer and asked to meet me. He told me that he knew what had happened the previous season, but said he was running the Ayr club now, and there'd be no hassle. He said it was daft me living down here and travelling to Dundee, so I should come back to Ayr. He also told me that he'd got three Canadians who were from Concordia University, who were the same calibre as Halpin and co. So, I thought about it, thought about retiring, but decided to go back and give it a go. And Jackson McBride came back as well, although he didn't play the full season.

I knew Kevin Murphy, because I had played against him in a tournament in Dundee, when he played with Concordia. What I remember was that Murphy fell out with everybody on the Concordia team! He came down one morning for breakfast, in the hotel

Alastair Brennan, Ayr Bruins 1983/84. (*Ayrshire Post* photo)

where all the teams were staying, and sat in the corner himself, despite all the rest of his teammates being there!

What a hell of a hockey player Paul Bedard was. I mean, could you imagine him playing in a really good team? He made the Canadian Olympic squad; okay, he never made the final cut, but to be good enough to get into that, from university, says a lot for him. Paul was a hell of a nice guy, he really was.

Ayr went to the first of the Heineken Championships to be played at Wembley at the end of 1983/84. Alastair scored early in the third period of the semi-final against the Murrayfield Racers to put Bruins ahead 4-2, only for goals from Tony Hand (2) and Jim Lynch to edge them out 5-4. Alastair retired from playing after this match and it is fascinating to think that his career bridged some of the great names from different eras of Scottish ice hockey over the past sixty years; from stars of the forties and fifties, like Bill Sneddon and Ian Forbes, to modern-day giants, such as Tony Hand.

The next season [1984/85] we had Steve Slaughter in place of 'Worm', and I ran the bench for Paul Bedard. By then I was starting a new job as Maintenance Engineer in the big Paper Mill that was opening up outside Irvine, and I just couldn't travel; it got to the stage where you were away every second weekend.

George Richmond did a wee bit for hockey in Ayr. There were quite a few, actually, at Ayr who did a lot for hockey and never got any recognition, or thanks for it. Guys like wee Archie McCallum, who was great with the juniors at Ayr, and guys like Alastair Reid and John Kidd really spoke highly of him as a coach. Wee Archie was a comical guy, and he was like that when he played; wee short skating strides.

His brother, Alex, was undoubtedly a far better player. Alex McCallum and Andy Pyper from Ayr guested for the Mohawks in the first game I played down in England, at Altrincham. Andy Pyper was a good player, until he got an eye injury; then I felt he became a bit nervous, understandably.

Alastair's most memorable trip, for several reasons, as captain of the Great Britain team, had come when he was with Ayr in early 1981. It was to be his last international appearance, and it involved a trip to China:

Big Jumbo Milne would arrange the outings when you were away with the British team, and some of them were, well, like the Gdansk shipyard I've mentioned! When we went to China in '81 one of the day trips was to a Renault garage in Peking! [It wasn't Beijing then] Can you believe it?

But China was an experience never to be forgotten, it really, really was. We went to the Great Wall, it was a long bus journey, but on the way we were passing life-sized statues of elephants in granite; amazing. And the Wall is unbelievable; when you're on it and see it stretching away over mountains, you just can't imagine how it was built by manual labour.

The food, however, was atrocious! At that time, I used to be around ten stones, but at the end of a season I'd be down to nine stones with all the skating and playing. I lost a stone in weight during that fortnight in China; you just didn't have any energy, because the food was so bad. I even tried eating snake, that's how bad it got; you'd eat anything! We even went in to the British Embassy and were getting food parcels; digestive biscuits and cakes of chocolate! Again, it was down to the BIHA.

I knew a couple of the Danish boys from playing in Copenhagen in the Pondus Cup, and by the second week they were giving us a couple of boiled eggs off their plates at breakfast because they felt sorry for you. These teams had all their own food with them, whereas typical BIHA, we were just sent away there without any thought or preparation, having just to eat the food supplied by the hotel where all the teams were staying.

They were expecting you to play a strenuous game, and we weren't getting fed. But it was a great trip for seeing the country, and the ice rink where they held the tournament was excellent, different class. It seated 15,000 or 18,000, and Elton John had done a concert in it about a month before the tournament. In the stadium control room, you could watch them press buttons and the floor would come out from under the seats to cover the ice-pad; things you'd never seen before, and that was back in 1981.

But it wasn't westernised then; there were no McDonald's or anything like that. There was one big store in Peking, the Friendship Store it was called, and it sold everything. Everything was dirt cheap, except the one thing that my mother asked me to bring back for her! She wanted jade earrings, which were about £400 even then!

I even brought back four bits of the Great Wall for paperweights! There were guys working on bits of it when we were there, and lots of small stones were broken off it, so we collected some to bring back. Every time somebody asked me what I was doing with a stone on my desk for a paperweight, I'd tell them it was a bit of the Great Wall of China! Those were the daft things you did!

At the time of writing, Alastair has the record number of appearances for the senior Great Britain side (102) and has played against twenty-two countries in eight World Championships. It's a tremendous record of which he is rightly proud; but his frustrations at the ineptitude of those running the British team are evident more than twenty-five years after he last captained his country:

My auntie used to make the Great Britain pennants for the World Championships; she was a brilliant seamstress. The two captains used to exchange pennants before the game. Our Billy got her to do this, because he was fed up being embarrassed by not having anything to give over to the other team's captain. Typical BIHA, again; the team captain had to get his own pennants done, because the BIHA wouldn't do it!

The Mohawks got plain Chicago Black Hawks jerseys, and Billy designed all the 'Mohawks' lettering across the chest, and the numbers on the sleeves, and my auntie made all these and stitched them on.

When we went to Finland in '65, Billy and big Jumbo did a bit of looking around in Glasgow, and they got us quilted anoraks, and my aunt stitched Union Jacks on them. But the BIHA wouldn't do anything. Even these anoraks were red, white... and black! They were Firestone Tyres jackets; that was the British team jacket! But Ahearne was at all the tournaments; although he wasn't staying in the hotels we were staying in, he was in five-star luxury!

When I went with Great Britain to Yugoslavia in '66, there were fourteen Scots and six English. The English boys were like Terry Matthews, Derek Metcalfe, Mike Jordan, and they had to come up to Renfrew Airport, as it then was, to fly out with us. The team jackets were bought, and we had these car-coat things, which were air force blue with a tweed collar. But they couldn't get twenty of them, so the Scots boys had these coats with the tweed collars, but the English boys' coats were all tweed! That was how bad the BIHA's organisation was.

We were definitely the poor relations. At another tournament we got green v-neck sweaters. The British team in green? They were bright, emerald green, with the Union Jack stitched on. Ellis Firestone, the trainer from Crossmyloof had got them (Ellis was a Jewish guy with contacts in the clothing business). One of the boys noticed a loose thread at the badge, and he started to pull it. The badge came off, and underneath was another badge, of a trophy and 'Celtic Football Club!' This had been a load of sweaters all made out for 'Celtic, Scottish Cup Winners' – and they got beat! So Ellis had got these as a job lot for the British team, and stuck a Union Jack on them. It was embarrassing.

Another time, big Jumbo's wife worked in the Buchanan's Distillery, where they made Black and White Whisky. He got them to give him boxes and boxes of miniatures of whisky to give as gifts to the other teams at a World Championship. So, other teams are giving you a nice souvenir of the tournament, and we're giving them six miniatures of whisky! You're saying: athletes? Don't get me wrong, some of the foreign teams enjoyed getting something like that, but at least Big Jumbo was trying, whereas the BIHA never gave you anything. It was embarrassing, especially at closing ceremonies, when all the other teams were dressed up to the nines, and we're there with Firestone racing jackets – or green jumpers!

But it was part of growing up, and part of hockey, and I wouldn't change it. Well, I would change it – there wasn't the money then there is now! But I've seen a lot of the world, places that I would never have gone to if it wasn't for hockey.

The question of payments for players is an interesting one, given that the period covered by most of Alastair's career is viewed as an 'amateur' era, as he explains:

The Mohawks club got money every home game, and the committee decided on a scale of payment for the players. Us young boys, I think we were lucky if we got £2; but nobody got a lot of money, because you'd to buy equipment, sticks, everything. It cost you money to play, really.

The first time I really got money was when I went to Fife, but, again, it wasn't anything to write home about; especially as I was doing all the travelling. Don't get me wrong, not everybody at Kirkcaldy got paid; it was the likes of the two Lovells, myself, Joe McIntosh, John Pullar – but, again, these guys had to travel. You were getting your petrol money and a few quid extra, but by the time you bought your beers and whatever – it wasn't costing you money to play, put it that way.

Of the British players he played with or against, Alastair rates the following five as the best of his contemporaries:

> Terry Matthews at Whitley Bay, Pete Johnson at Durham, the two Lovell brothers at Fife and Jackson McBride at Paisley and Ayr.
>
> Of the older ones, I was fortunate enough to play with Bill Crawford and Dave Ferguson, and fortunate to play against guys like Jimmy Spence, Ian Forbes, Sammy Macdonald and Bill Sneddon – 'Red Bill'. I remember Bill Sneddon on the television news, on a boat on the Forth, foghorn in hand, trying to stop foreign coal or something being brought in! I roomed with Bill Crawford at the '65 World Championships. Bill hated Canadian hockey players, and we were amazed when he told us that he was emigrating… to Canada!
>
> John Pullar was the best British goalie I played with. Billy Laird was not a bad goalie, too. I remember when the Mohawks went on a tour of Canadian Air Force bases in Germany; we didn't know anything then about slapping pucks. The Canadians were zinging them round Billy Laird's ears, and I don't think he was ever the same goalie after that.
>
> I remember asking our Billy how to slap a puck. I was a left-hand shot, he shot right, and he said: 'Just hit the ice behind the puck.' I used to practise and practise my slapshot, and Billy had set up like circuit training on the ice, and there was a bit with two pucks bolted together for shooting practice.
>
> Billy once sent me out to get four dozen sticks from a guy in Hillington in Glasgow, who had just got this consignment in. Before this we had got all our sticks from England. I went out with Roy Collins, and the guy tells us that some of the sticks must have 'warped' during the journey. My eyes lit up when I saw them, because here were all these curved sticks! The guy didn't know that they were meant to be like that, and he offered to give us the 'warped' ones at a discount! I played it as if I wasn't sure whether we wanted them, and he knocked more off the price! But it was the first time we'd managed to get a hold of curved sticks. Older guys like Bill Crawford, Dave Ferguson and our Billy wouldn't ever use a curved stick.
>
> There was a survey of all the players in the league as to who they thought had the hardest shot, and I got the most votes. When I first moved to Ayr in 1970, Jackson [McBride] had got a puck from Canada that was meant to measure the speed of your shot. I said to Jackson: 'I'm no' firing that.' But he said I had to. I said to him: 'Was it expensive, Jackson?' He asked why I was asking, and I told him: 'Because I'll break it!' So, I slapped it off the barrier and, sure enough, bits of this thing went everywhere!
>
> Wee Alistair McRae was a clever player, and he moved with me to Ayr when Paisley folded. But Johnny Carlyle only played him twice at the World Championships in Holland in '71; he felt it was too rough for him. Alistair was the West of Scotland Badminton Champion; wee 'Jamma'! He's living in Bradford, now. Alistair's father, Bob, was the trainer of Paisley Pirates, and also the physiotherapist of St Mirren Football Club, and wee Bob used to be great if you got any injuries at the hockey. The last time I saw Alistair was a few years ago at his Dad's funeral in Paisley.

Having returned to playing in just seven months following a broken neck, it is unsurprising that a mere fractured wrist would not keep Alastair out of a World Championship:

> Wee Jackie Dryburgh and Carlyle were good with Britain, and I enjoyed playing for Carlyle for the British team. I remember when we went to Holland in '73, I got a scaphoid wrist fracture playing for Fife on the Saturday, and we were flying out on the Tuesday. Carlyle 'phoned me and asked what I was going to do. I told him I would cut the plaster cast.
>
> We were over in Tilburg, and Jackson McBride, Joe McIntosh and me were sharing a room. Jackson held my arm, and I cut the plaster with a hacksaw, to give me enough movement to hold a stick.

Alastair Brennan, enjoying retirement, summer 2006. (D. Gordon archive)

At the warm-up before the first game, Terry Matthews was firing gentle shots at John Pullar. They were starting to clean the ice, so I was skating off behind the net. But Pullar had got a puck stuck in his catching glove, and he was trying to throw the puck out. It flew out his glove and hit me in the eye; I needed stitches at the side of my left eye.

So, that was me with a broken wrist and stitches in my eye! Then in the game against France, this guy upended me and I got a haemorrhage on my knee! I couldn't practise during the tournament as I had to go to hospital for treatment on my knee.

At the end of the tournament, big John Milne, the manager, came back from a meeting and told me I'd been voted Best Defenceman of Pool 'C'. I was quite chuffed with myself, considering the injuries I'd carried. All the teams were at the end of tournament banquet, and they're announcing the awards – and here the Best Defenceman award goes to a Bulgarian! Big Jumbo [Milne] was blazing mad, as they'd changed their decision without consulting him; it was all about politics at that level.

Alastair wed Jean Scott in August 1980 at Mure Parish Church in Irvine:

I've known Jean since she was fifteen from Paisley Ice Rink. She used to be down in Altrincham Monday to Friday with her skating, coming home at weekends. So, we drifted apart, but still kept in touch.

She was an only child, and her Dad died when she was seventeen. She was a European silver medallist, fifth in the World Championships and went to the Olympics in '72. She was the highest-ranked British skater since Sally Stapleford.

Jean and her Mum moved from Renfrew to Kilwinning when I was playing at Fife, and we still kept in touch. Eventually she told me that she thought we should get together for good; I said: 'Are you asking me to marry you?' Jean's mother's reaction was: 'About time!'

The move to Irvine also led to the end of Alastair's long career with Babcock and Wilcox:

> I was there for over twenty years, but when we moved down to Irvine I started getting fed up with the travelling, so I took voluntary redundancy. I then worked as a maintenance engineer for Caledonian Paper at their mill outside Irvine until 2003. Since breaking my neck, I've always had problems with the discs at the top of my spine, and I got a further spine injury at my work. The company were great, and I was eventually put on to light duties when I came back. Then I spent a while in an office doing computer work, covering for maternity leave, before taking early retirement.

The opening of a new ice rink in Paisley's Lagoon Leisure Centre saw Alastair briefly reacquainted with his first sporting love:

> Renfrew Council got me and Billy Miller to open the new Paisley rink in '92, and Billy and Jeanette came down from Aberdeen. I was asked to start up the junior coaching, and I got in guys like Jimmy Allen and John McLachlan to help. All the kids were getting new equipment bought by their parents and it really took off. They were getting more practices and more games, so I didn't really have the time to give it the attention it needed. I felt that I'd got a good committee to run it, so I gave it up.
>
> I played three or four games for the oldtimers at the new rink, but that was me finished with hockey.

Alastair's sporting activities are now confined to the golf course; sadly, his only connection now with ice hockey is watching on TV:

> I play golf at the Ardeer club, when Jean lets me! Because I couldn't play in any competitions due to my neck problems, I play off seventeen, but I'm hoping to get below that. Our Billy's a good golfer; he was playing off eight, and his son, Mark, plays off six up in Aberdeen.
>
> I met Jim Lynch in Prestwick when he was coaching the Ayr Scottish Eagles, and he wondered if I didn't come to the games at Centrum because it was all Canadians. That wasn't the case, and he left me tickets and I went once to see it. I enjoyed it, but I just didn't have any notion for it anymore. I enjoy watching the NHL on television. I record the games on Five and watch it at my leisure, but I'm right out of touch with the British scene. I thought I'd miss the game more than I did.

Career Record

	GP	G	A	Pts	PiM
Billy Brennan (Ayr/Paisley/Glasgow) 1951-1971 (Records unavailable for 1958-63;1965-67)	334	74	137	211	353
Great Britain 1953-1971	36	8	6	14	82

Career Record

	GP	G	A	Pts	PiM
Alastair Brennan (Paisley/Ayr/Fife/ Dundee) 1961-1984	423	361	307	668	766
Great Britain 1965-1981	47	7	3	10	29

10

A Gorbals Boy in Toronto: Bill Crawford

For those sportsmen whose careers straddled the years 1939 to 1945, it is usual to find a description relating to how they lost the peak years of their playing career to the Second World War.

In the world of Scottish ice hockey, that was sadly the case for the likes of Joe Collins and Tommy McInroy. Others, like Billy Fullerton, made the ultimate sacrifice.

Conversely, however, without the Second World War, the eleven-year-old Bill Crawford, from Glasgow's Gorbals, would never have taken up the sport of ice hockey, developing as an outstanding left winger on two Championship-winning Paisley Pirates' teams and culminating with his captaincy of the Great Britain team at the 1966 World Championships.

William Henderson Crawford was born on 7 January 1929, in his parents' tenement flat, at 42 McKinlay Street in Glasgow. His father, also William Crawford, was, in the parlance of the time, a mercantile clerk, running a greengrocers shop below the family flat. Crawford's parents had married in Glasgow in 1916. He was their second son, and was given his mother Annie's maiden surname of Henderson as his middle name.

McKinlay Street, off Pollokshaws Road, was located in Glasgow's infamous Gorbals district, and the five-year-old Bill Crawford started at nearby Abbotsford Public School at the end of January 1934.

Football was the game of choice for the young Crawford in the Gorbals of the late 1930s, but events on the international stage were to shape the direction of his sporting interests. Speaking in May 2005, Bill remembered how the outbreak of war in September 1939 led to his evacuation to Canada one year later:

> They made an appeal over the radio in Canada, for anyone who had relatives with kids in Britain. Would they take the kids for the duration of the war?
>
> The appeal was also made in Australia, New Zealand, South Africa, Rhodesia and the USA. The government was desperate to get rid of kids, because all they were doing was eating food and contributing nothing to the war effort.
>
> My mother had three unmarried sisters living in Toronto. My aunts heard this appeal, and sent a telegram asking my mother and me to go to Canada. My mother wouldn't leave my father, so I was to go on my own.
>
> I didn't actually know I was going until three days before I was due to leave. My elder brother was in the army when the war started; in the Field Artillery. I was sent down to Gourock when the bombing started, to live with another aunt. My brother was brought back from the army, because he was needed as an engineer in the Weir's factory. And when he came back, I was sent to Canada.

He was to be one of the last of the 'seavacs', the name given to British children evacuated to Canada under a scheme called Operation Hedgehog. Bill sailed in early September 1940, but a few days later, the *City of Benares* was torpedoed by a German U-boat, resulting in the deaths of seventy-seven of the ninety-six children on board. This tragedy saw the abandonment of the 'seavacs' scheme, as Bill recalled:

> The government paid for us to be brought out to Canada. I was one of the last to go, as the boat behind us was sunk, and they stopped sending kids after that.
>
> I was eleven when I got out there, and stayed with my aunts in their apartment in the east end of Toronto. They were super with me; they let me play with all the local kids.

The standard of living that he encountered in Toronto was in marked contrast to what he had left behind in Glasgow:

> I'd gone from a cold-water tenement, in the Gorbals in Glasgow, to a spacious apartment, with a tiled bathroom and a shower – I just thought it was marvellous, like being in Hollywood!

Crawford had arrived in Ontario at just the right time; the onset of the hockey season:

> I went to Withrow Public School for the five years I was in Toronto, and I started playing hockey in Withrow Park on an outdoor rink. I had never skated back in Glasgow, but I got a pair of second-hand skates and about ten of us went to play at Withrow Park at 7a.m. on a Saturday morning, just when it was getting light, and we were on until 10a.m., when it started to get really crowded.
>
> A couple of the guys were about a year older than me – Ray Timgren, who went on to play with the Leafs, and Freddie Glover, who played with Detroit – and they taught me how to play hockey. Timgren was a super hockey player.

Bill was fortunate in the choice of his new Torontonian friends. Timgren, four months older than Crawford, was to have six seasons on left wing for both Toronto and Chicago in the old 'original six' NHL. Glover was one year his senior, and would enjoy five NHL seasons as a centre with Detroit and Chicago, followed by a fifteen-year playing association with the Cleveland Barons of the American Hockey League, retiring in 1968 (Glover, sadly, passed away in 2001).

Crawford's wartime introduction to hockey in Toronto did not extend to playing for any recognised teams:

> There was no real organised hockey in Toronto at that time, just a couple of commercial or industrial leagues, and no real indoor rinks. There wasn't the same money in professional sports then as there is now, and there was no great kudos in being a pro hockey player. Just as I was leaving was the start of organised hockey for kids, when they formed the Young Leafs.

Arriving back in Glasgow at the end of the war, after a five-year absence, Bill was now aged sixteen, and soon was to get the opportunity to use his new-found hockey skills in his native city:

> I came back to Glasgow in 1945, and it was so strange going back; a whole cultural change. I was going to school at Shawlands Academy, which was just five minutes from the Crossmyloof rink, and somebody at school said I should go down. I wasn't particularly bothered, as I was playing soccer and rugby at the time.
>
> Jim Kenny was the coach when I started in 1945/46, and he got me to do a couple of skating drills, and then asked me to come out to a practice. He told me that at that time everybody and their brother, who had been evacuated to Canada during the war, were coming down to the rink and saying they were hockey players! Myself and Jock Ford

The Scotland team, 1951. From left to right, standing: Bert Smith (Fife), Ian Forbes (Perth), Johnny Quales (Paisley), Johnny Carlyle (Falkirk), George Watt (Perth), Bill Crawford (Glasgow). Kneeling: Johnny Rolland (Dunfermline), Lawson Neil (Ayr), Stan Christie (Ayr), Jimmy Mitchell (Fife), Tommy Paton (Falkirk). (Bill Crawford archive)

were the only two, though, who had learned their hockey as evacuees, that he took for the Mohawks.

Kenny was a Canadian and had come over to coach at Crossmyloof before the war. He was a good coach; he taught you the fundamentals.

It was a marvellous ice rink at Crossmyloof. It was a very long ice surface. We used to play English clubs there, and they would stay with us for a period, or a period and a half. And then from the second period on, it was all downhill for them; they just weren't used to the big ice, and we eventually leathered them.

It was a great rink, and a marvellous rink to play on. We used to go in and practise on a Monday and Tuesday night, and they used to have figure skating on one half, and you could practise whatever you wanted on the other half – it was all good skating.

The only problem was that you could only get about fifteen hundred people in it. They stood around on a balcony, and behind the players' benches, and that's really what killed it for senior hockey, as they couldn't get enough paying customers in.

Old man Stuart was the director at Crossmyloof. Old man Mitchell, who gave the Mitchell Trophy, was another director. Old man Frame was another director, but he wanted to throw the hockey out all the time, but Stuart kept us in there. And we had the Mustangs and the Mohawks at Crossmyloof, just to keep the league going, guys like Bobby Neil, 'Doc' Blackwood, Gus Munro, Stevie Patterson, Paul Logan.

When I started, there were guys still playing from before the war, like Dave Cross and Tommy Lauder. Most of the Mohawks were that bit older and had been in the forces during the war, like Gerry Collins, who had served in the Lovat Scouts. Gerry was a really good guy. I was a lot younger than him, and yet there was one time I was walking over to the rink at Crossmyloof. We lived in McKinlay Street, just in the Gorbals, and I was walking up Eglinton

Street and this car stopped and Gerry Collins jumped out, and said: 'How are you doing?' He would never pass you by, and there was a lot of years' difference. I used to feel like a fish out of water on the team bus, because they all had broads with them and, at that time, I thought girls were just soft boys! But Gerry was a really nice guy.

Frank Jardine was small; very hustling. He skated hard, and he was outstanding in our league. He married a girl called Grant, of Grant's the canning people; tinned foods and whatever. His folks were in the butcher business, so Frank was well geared.

Charlie Huddlestone was the goalie and he kept hockey going in the fifties and early sixties. He used to take teams down to Durham and Southampton – there would be a dollar in it for Charlie, of course!

Dave Ferguson was younger than me; I remember he used to work out at Hillington. Davie centred between Gus Munro on the right wing and me on the left for the Mohawks. That was a real good line at Crossmyloof.

I did two years National Service in the Air Force. I found it terrific; I did athletics, football and boxing. I was only on one operational base for six months, the rest of the time I was playing sport! I was supposed to be a radar technician. It was a wasted two years, but a good two years; I really enjoyed it.

Bill's step up to senior hockey came in September 1953, with the requirement by the SIHA that teams ice a minimum of four locally developed players, as Bill remembers:

There was a year when they said that all the British teams had to have so many homebred players, and Kewley went overboard on it. He had Joe Brown and Billy Brennan at Paisley already, and he got the Symes down from Dunfermline. He asked us to come out and try, and I thought it was a definite deal. It was to be £5 per week, which then was what a man was getting paid as a normal wage. And then he says to us that you would only get £5 per week if you were played. So then it was dog eat dog – and I made sure that I got my £5. And Billy [Brennan] got in there, and it was eventually Davie Ferguson that got squeezed out. It was too bad, because he was a good, smart hockey player. It always annoyed me that Davie got screwed on the deal, and that was his last year there.

I always felt that 'Tiny' [Syme] was very underrated; he was twice as smart as 'Tuck'. 'Tuck' was maybe a bit more agile, and could skate a bit better. 'Tiny' wouldn't do anything if he didn't see an advantage in it. He was a very smart guy – that's why he was a great poker player! I remember him telling me that he was really sad when he heard that Paisley weren't retaining Alf Lewsey; he said: 'That guy was worth an extra £10 per week to me through playing poker with him!'

'Tiny' was a good egg, a helluva player, and a good captain.

When I was in Canada as a youngster, everybody got the chance to stretch out a wee bit; but over here you didn't. The tenor of British life then was that you got a job as an apprentice or whatever with someone round the corner, and 'Tiny' just followed his father into the pit. Now, everybody's expectations are that they're going to go to university.

I always found 'Tiny' a terrific guy to talk to. You could talk to him about something, and he quite often took the opposing view to you, just to give you an argument; he was that type of person. But he would always come up with arguments that were quite sound, and you could see the brainwork ticking over.

'Tiny' Syme imparted so much knowledge to young players. He was a great guy in the dressing-room, and he would have made a good coach. 'Tiny' used to say to me that there were three types of guy you went into the corners with: there was the type of guy that you threaten, and then you never see again; then there's the guy that you threaten, and have to prove that you mean it, so you give them an elbow in the face or something like that; and then the third guy – he gives you the elbow back, and you know that you only have to worry about this one guy the whole night! A lot of the Canadians were like that; you could scare the shit right out of them.

By and large, though, we had good guys, like Tommy Lemon, Ernie Domenico and Al Holliday, the goalie. Eddie Lochhead was the goalie when I first played at Paisley – a bampot! I felt he was overrated. He was alright, but he had the Syme brothers and George Coulter in front of him!

Cece Slack and Hal Schooley were good guys. Cece married a girl whose father had a sports goods business and Hal was a scout for the Hamilton junior team.

I remember Stan Obodiac played at Ayr for a season. He went back to Canada and became the Publicity Manager at Maple Leaf Gardens. He was a great talker, Stan. He could have sold ice cubes to the Eskimos!

Ted McCaskill was a real good guy; he was our type of hockey player. Ted was a real hard-nosed bugger; I liked Ted. I played on a line with him until Ian [Forbes] and Jerry [Hudson] came. You got your money's worth out of Ted.

Des Moroney was a good guy, too – he went on to play and coach in Sweden, and married a Swedish girl. He was a university boy. I remember one of the times we went down to play Wembley in London, and Des asked me 'What are you doing?', because most of the hockey players then played poker or snooker; that was it. So I told him that *West Side Story* was on, and I was going to see if I could get a ticket for that.

We went down and there was a whole mass of people going to The Mall. There was some sort of parade on; I'd never seen one before, he'd never seen one, so we goes down and here it was, De Gaulle doing a state visit to Britain. They had all the Guards out, and the Queen and De Gaulle went past in the car, and Des was just blown away! He was enchanted with seeing that. Then we went up to the theatre, having already got the tickets for *West Side Story*, and it was the American cast – Chita Rivera and George Chakiris. If you'd never seen a stage show, that was one to blow you right out the seats!

Things like that were rewarding, but the numbers of these guys that had any brains... even the ones that went to college were stupid! I really didn't think too highly of a lot of them. I must sound very anti-Canadian! I just used to think that Canadian hockey players over here were getting a free ride. A lot of them were real toe-rags, and playing hockey was all they could do. A lot of them had the morals of animals.

Bill's first selection for the Great Britain team came with a visit to the 1951 World Championships in Paris, but it was a weakened British team, minus the Syme brothers and Bill Sneddon, as Crawford remembers:

All Star selections, and getting picked for British teams, a lot of it was once you were in, you were in. They had try-outs, and all that sort of thing. We beat the English team at Crossmyloof, and then beat them down at Ayr. We in Scotland were way ahead of the English at that time. I can't explain why guys like Bill Sneddon and the Syme brothers weren't in that team in 1951; I really don't know. Believe me when I tell you, we could've done with them, because there were so many dead bullets in that team in '51 it wasn't even funny.

I'm not trying to be vindictive, but you could've dropped Bert Smith and Jimmy Mitchell. Jimmy Mitchell was alright, but no more than that. Bert Smith would rather have a drink than a game. And Kenny Nicholson was so out of condition. Ken Nicholson was born in Canada of Scots parents who moved back here. He spoke like a Canadian, anyway! I never really got on with him, or never really got on with Canadian hockey players, period!

Johnny Rolland, I thought, was lazy, and you could never tell him. He would never give you a pass, and when you pulled him up he would always say: 'It's better to shoot than pass.' His old man, though, was a director of the Dunfermline rink.

And we didn't have coaches. Mowat from Ayr was down as the coach in Paris in '51, but he was really just the manager. He didn't say anything on the bench; we just changed lines ourselves.

> Davie McCrae from Ayr was a good player on that team and a really nice guy. I remember years later he had a carpet fitting business in Toronto. Johnny Quales was a great skater; one of the best ever. And when I say great, I don't mean good, I mean great skater. I remember he used to wear an old Pirates jacket all the time.

It is a sad reflection on British ice hockey's fall from grace that the 1951 tournament was considered a failure. Granted, GB only defeated Finland, and tied with a weak USA team and lost to Norway – both games they were expected win; defeats from Sweden and Switzerland, allied to a 17-1 humiliation by Canada, were obvious disappointments. But this was a British team still ranked fifth in the world.

Bill went to Switzerland in 1953 with the British team which picked up the silver medal in the Pool 'B' World Championship:

> Jim Kenny at Crossmyloof took us up to a level that we went to the World Championships in Basel, in 1953. I was on the team; Billy Brennan was on the team; Davie Ferguson. We had all played for Jim Kenny. Davie McCrae from Ayr was there, and Laurie Spence from Perth was the captain, but there were a lot of English boys on that team. Gordon English was the goalie; he ended up out in Canada. Johnny Murray from Wembley was a small, slight guy, but he could hold his own. He was a good manager.
>
> We did very well that year. The Czechoslovakian president had died, and it should have been Switzerland *v.* Czechoslovakia to open it, but it was cancelled. So it was Italy against ourselves, and they beat us 3-2. We blew it in the first period; they scored three goals, and we should've done better.

The British recovered from the opening reverse to defeat Switzerland 'B' 3-1, Holland 8-4, France 8-3, and Austria 3-0. Player-coach John Murray of Wembley considered Crawford the outstanding British player of the tournament.

Bill was an all-round sportsman in his younger days, and was a West of Scotland sprint champion:

> I used to be a sprinter, as well as playing hockey and rugby; I used to train down at Ibrox in the winter. They used to have a running track underneath the stand at Ibrox, it was 100 yards long. I had a manager/trainer, Davie Corbett, who had been trained as a sprinter by Bill Struth, the Rangers manager – that was how I got to train at Ibrox. I worked for Davie in his printing business. The best times I ever did were always on grass; that's practically all we ever ran on. The best time I ever did was 9.8 for the hundred yards. I used to think to myself, 'Jeez, I wonder what I'd have done now, what with rubberised tracks, these shoes that are like slippers?'

Dave McCrae (left), Bill Crawford (centre) and Dave Ferguson (right), with the Great Britain team in Switzerland, 1953 Pool 'B' World Championships. (*Ice Hockey World* photo)

Bill Crawford, Paisley Pirates, 1955/56. (*Ice Hockey World* photo)

And they are all on the juice now; everybody. We played the Russians one time at Paisley. We had just come back from Sweden, and I had the 'flu, as did half the team, and I had jammed my fingers in a car door, so my hand was all swollen! We played the Russians, and every time you turned around there was a red bloody shirt! And I thought to myself, 'what the...?' They beat us 10-1, but that was just because they had got us at the right time. After the game, we went in to their dressing-room, and we found a sort of bucket that had in it a whole lot of what were like test tubes. There was a spout came out the side of these test tubes that you snapped off, to get out whatever it was that was in them. Now, Bob McRae, our trainer, he took one of these and sent it to someone he knew at the hospital in Paisley to have it analysed. It turned out they couldn't analyse it, because there wasn't enough residue in it. But what were they taking then, back in the late fifties? That was when they were only starting to think about taking drugs, and that's what screwed up sport all over.

Bill always played his hockey hard and the Pirates of the 1950s had a similar reputation, as he explains:

Jimmy Spence used to always say: 'I hate playing at this bloody ice rink' [meaning Paisley], 'cause you guys only play the one way – tough.'

I remember playing in Paisley one night against the Czechs, and I had taken one of the Czech players and rammed him right into the boards. Somebody in the crowd shouted: 'Come on, Crawford, act the big man.' So I said: 'What the hell do you want me to do, kiss the guy?' You had a way of playing, and I know it used to annoy a lot of people.

A lot of the Canadians hated it, like Ernie Domenico, because you just never, ever left him alone. And a lot of these guys had never played much together, and didn't know how to handle this. I often say this to my grandson because quite often they'll do this to him; double-team him. I say to him that what you do is you go and skate with one of their guys. That means there's one or two of their players with you, on that one guy. You're screwin' up the whole thing. If they have no brains, they keep going with you, and if they have brains, they have to alter their game. And when they alter their game, things all open up for you.

Bill is saddened that the sport in Scotland did not develop the local talent that was undoubtedly strong at that time:

One year at Falkirk they had a whole lot of injuries and 'flu and what have you, and George McNeill, the coach, he ended up with his whole senior team made up of Falkirk Cubs, the juniors. And he played them against Ayr, as it happened, and they beat Ayr. But the supporters club in Falkirk went to McNeill and told him that if he wasn't going to get some back up for the Canadians that they had lost then they were going to withdraw their support!

They blew the whole thing then, because we had some great Scottish hockey players at the time, and they should have been moving towards professional teams of local players, but they just didn't get the support. Local players don't get a chance. It drives me crazy.

I did a television interview one time, on the ice, at Paisley in 1953. We had beaten Streatham, and it was the first time that Kewley had put on Billy Brennan on right wing, Davie Ferguson at centre, and myself on left wing. We beat them, and they seemed to think this was rip-roaring; I don't know why it surprised people. And this guy that was interviewing me asked if I thought they were ready for Scots kids to take over from the Canadians. I said not the way things were, but they didn't want to hear that. It's like soccer now.

There was one year at Paisley, they brought over from Canada a line of nice guys, but just not ready for this league. We had a practice, and young Danny Ballantyne was on with us. One of these three Canadians said to me: 'Holy Smoke, look at this guy.' And I said to him that there were at least a dozen other Scots guys out there as good as the four of us locals who were on with him. But nobody's going to pay to see that dozen, they're going to pay to see you, and you better perform! And they couldn't, and they were sent back to Canada. You had a lot of that to-ing and fro-ing back then. What used to save the leagues then was that, on the continent, they had only an eight-week season. So guys like Jerry Hudson would play in Scotland before they went to Switzerland, and then play when they came back.

It was totally unnecessary, but that was the nature of the beast. Everybody wanted to have a Canadian hero, and it was too bad they missed the boat, because Scots guys – like 'Tuck' and 'Tiny', Joe Brown, Lawson Neil – they were as good as any of the bloody Canadians.

Lawson Neil of Ayr used to have a terrific hip-check, a great hip-check, he swung right in. I always like to see somebody with a good hip-check, because it's all timing.

Lawson was great, but he wasn't alone. I would say that Jimmy Spence of Perth was the best hockey player ever produced in Scotland. Jimmy was a crafty, good player – and a good guy; and you had [Johnny] Carlyle and [Bill] Sneddon at Falkirk. Billy Sneddon was great. George McNeil at Falkirk had got in a couple of Canadians who were back from the continent. I don't remember who Falkirk were playing, or whether they won or lost; it's immaterial, but Sneddon felt these two guys weren't pulling their weight. As they were coming off, Billy Sneddon walked in the dressing-room door ahead of this Canadian guy. Just as he was coming through the door, Billy turned round and haymakered him – laid him out cold! Billy just got on with getting dressed! When the Canadian gradually came round, Billy said to him: 'When I skate, everybody skates.'

There wasn't enough of that. It was the same with 'Tiny'. 'Tiny' used to say: 'If I'm out there doing it, we're all out there doing it.' And that's what you needed, but we didn't have enough of it. Those are the guys that should've been coaches, at the next level.

I didn't care for Keith Kewley as a coach. He favoured Canadians, and you can say differently, but he played us because we were nice and cheap.

He had me on his Paisley team purely because I could out-skate practically anybody. Like when we went down to Ayr, he had me sit on Ernie Domenico. He told me: 'If he goes to the toilet, you go to the toilet.' People used to laugh about it, but that's what he paid me for, so he got it.

We had a lot of good kids who never really got a chance, though. Danny Ballantyne never really got a chance, and there were others.

In similar vein, Bill still retains a grievance that many of his Canadian teammates in the fifties were being paid around four times what he and some of his local colleagues were receiving from the Paisley management:

I got £5 per week at Paisley. I was a stereotyper. I did it as an apprenticeship. It's the making of rubber plates for the printing industry. That's how I went out to Canada, as a stereotyper. I was working at a company that was part of the Robinson Dickinson group in Glasgow that printed corrugated boxes. I had just joined them when that British team was going out to Colorado for the World Championships in '62, and that's why I couldn't go.

So I was getting £5 a week from Paisley, then I was getting my salary from the company, which was about another fiver per week.

Creasey, the rink manager, really did not like me, and I did not like him. I had the chance to play for Grindelwald in Switzerland, and the sonofabitch would not let me go. It was Lee Thorne, and it was out of the blue. He sent me a letter saying he was the one foreign player, and they allowed two per team, are you interested in coming over? I thought this was great, but this was when Creasey was intercepting my letters. I should've banged him right on the bloody head. And Ahearne was with it, when they said you can't go. They weren't going to pay me, but they weren't going to allow anybody else to pay me. That's the way they operated. They couldn't stop the Canadians; I don't understand why that was, or certainly they didn't stop the Canadians.

I always had arguments with Creasey about money, but when Bill Simpell came in as coach, he made sure I got the same money as the Canadians.

At that time Ernie Domenico's brother-in-law, Alec Smith, was a professional footballer with Queen of the South, who were one of the better teams in the 1950s. He was getting paid £12 a week as a full-time footballer. Paisley Pirates were paying their hockey players £20 per week.

When we won the Championship with Paisley in 1959, 'Eeny' Forbes from Perth was playing with us. There was Joe [Brown], 'Eeny', myself, and Bill Simpell and Gerry Corriveau. Simpell was the player-coach, and he was real good; the best coach we ever had. He had a right good mix, and he knew how to keep it all going.

I was on a line with Jerry Hudson and Ian 'Eeny' Forbes. Oh jeez, Jerry Hudson could go like a buzz-saw, 'Eeny' could go like a buzz-saw, and I could go like a buzz-saw – it was a great line to work on. Jerry Hudson was the best Canadian I ever played with. And when I heard recently that Ian Forbes had died, relatively young, a few years ago, my immediate thought was: 'It must have been either sex or alcohol that killed him!'

When we won the British League in 1959, we played Wembley, and beat them 3-2, at Paisley in the last game of the season.

Pirates needed to secure the two points in that game to lift the title; it was Bill who netted the late winner:

We played them in an exhibition game the night before, in Ayr. We played that game making sure nobody got hurt, so we were all skating like bloody mad, up and down. A guy from Paisley came up to me after the game was over and said: 'Jeez, that's the best game of hockey I think I've ever seen; fantastic!' I just thought to myself: 'What did you see, and what did you

The Great Britain team which defeated a Canadian Forces Select at the Empire Pool, Wembley, 15 April 1961. From left to right, standing: Jackie Dryburgh, Red Devereaux, Rupe Fresher, Roy Shepherd, Mike O'Brien, Bill Crawford, Joe Brown. Seated: Billy Brennan, Johnny Murray, Glynne Thomas, Jimmy Spence. (Bill Brennan archive)

> think you saw?' There you go, he just thought it was marvellous, because it was up and down and everybody was passing, and when you know you're not going to get hit you do things you don't do normally. We were doing all the wee, neat tricks and all the rest of it. And then the next night it was for real, and I think we won 3-2; it was a very close game.

The original Pirates' last ever match at East Lane came at the end of the following season, on Friday 29 April 1960, and Bill Crawford ensured that they went out with a bang. It was the first year that the British League had featured end-of-season play-offs, and Paisley faced Brighton in the two-legged semi-final. Brighton came north holding an 8-3 lead from the first game, and a Crawford hat-trick helped Paisley to a 5-3 win on the night, but an 11-8 aggregate defeat. Ironically, Tigers' three goals that night were scored by former Paisley favourite Hal Schooley.

Billy continued his hockey through the 1960s with the Paisley Mohawks. He captained the team under player-coach Billy Brennan and was the mainstay of a very successful side, using his experience to help develop a fine crop of emerging young talent:

> I played right up to the end of the Pirates in 1960, and then Billy [Brennan] and John ['Jumbo' Milne] kept the Mohawks going. Big John and Billy were good players, as were all the boys like Jackson McBride and Robert Stevenson. Robert was a good player.
>
> Billy Brennan told me that Jackson had died in 2003; it shocked everybody. Jackson was a nice big lad and a good player. If the opportunity had been there, a lot of those kids with the Mohawks would have done a lot better. There's no point in having talent, though, if you can't go anywhere with it; and there was nowhere to go in British ice hockey then.
>
> These guys could all check; there were some great skaters, and nobody ever acknowledged that fact. It's too bad that we haven't been able to maintain that sort of standard, or get the level of interest up.
>
> I remember Jackson had two aunties, who had a sweetie shop on Paisley Road West in Glasgow. Jackson used to always bring us in tablet from the shop to the dressing-room!
>
> Then there was Tom Reid, he was a good wee hustler. I remember he went bald prematurely! Dorry Boyle and Jim Black were a good laugh; they were like a comedy turn. They got up to all sorts of things while we were away. They had balls of brass, they really had!
>
> Peter Keenan put on hockey tournaments at Paisley in the sixties, but he just picked it up and dropped it. He made a buck out of it, and I guess our club made a buck out of it.

These kinds of things, you've got to find a niche and then go for it. We were all that honest. Everybody played the game true blue. And what you should be doing is going to play in Edinburgh or Ayr or wherever and nobody wins; the best you get is a draw – aim for the post! But if you want to play true blue, then go ahead.

Like a number of players of his generation, Billy was deprived of the opportunity to play for his country through most of the 1950s by the short-sighted policy of the BIHA to withdraw from international competition. The British came back into the fold in 1961, at the Pool 'B' World Championships, as Bill recalls:

1961 in Switzerland was the year we lost 3-2 to the Italians and got the silver medals. Tommy Paton from Falkirk was on that team; a good heavy skater, although Tommy was a quiet guy, never really spoke much. Falkirk always had good local players; there was Gus Adams, 'Red' Imrie – he was a real awkward guy to get past or round, he seemed to be all feet and legs, he could stop you. He was a real good player, and he went on to play with Brighton.

Billy Brennan, myself and a whole bunch from Paisley played in Finland in 1965. I captained the team in Yugoslavia in 1966. By that time you were getting screwed right and left, because I remember we played Switzerland, and Andre Girard was coaching the Swiss team. It was 2-2, going into the third period, and we were outplaying them. There was a Swedish referee, and we played that third period a man short, and they eventually beat us 3-2. And that's what they do to you. We played a tie with Yugoslavia; and West Germany, who won the Pool, only beat us 7-4, which was pretty good, as our legs were away.

The Swiss team were at the table next to us in the hotel, and Andre Girard asked me: 'How old are you now, Bill?' I said I was thirty-seven, and he turned to these young Swiss guys and told them they should be ashamed of themselves. And they should've been, because we had guys that were only getting one hour's practice per week.

The Yugoslav crowds were all for you, though; they came out and gave you a cheer.

Hep Tindale from Durham was a helluva guy for the girls, but a good defenceman and gave you 100 per cent. Terry Matthews was a good player, and so was Les Lovell – although I always felt that Les looked as though his mother had dusted him down with a flour bag! Roy Shepherd and Mike O'Brien were two real good guys and good hockey players.

I remember Andy Williams from Falkirk, when we played the Germans in Zagreb in 1966. Andy took a run at some guy; it was a collision more than a body-check. But Andy swung his skate, and it missed this German's face by two inches. I can still see the colour draining from his face – Andy was the Real McCoy!

During his time with the Pirates, Bill had wed Elizabeth McNeill, a bookkeeper. They celebrated fifty years of marriage on 16 June 2006:

My wife Betty and I had married in 1956 and we have two kids, Adam and Lyndsey. We emigrated to Canada in 1968. It was the weather that did it. It was March, there was wind and rain, I was working late and I took bouts of depression. I told my wife: 'We're going somewhere where there's sunshine.'

I got a job in Canada as a rubber cutter/stereotyper, and we moved to Toronto. I played some hockey in an industrial league in Toronto. 'Tiny' Syme had played Senior 'A' in Ontario, but it had folded, which was a shame, because a lot of those guys were as good as some that made it to the NHL. A lot of who makes it is down to the luck of the draw, who's coaching you.

I became involved with coaching kids. They were always on the look-out for coaches, and a Scots fellow – who used to watch the hockey at Paisley – offered me the job as coach of a team in a house league at the Ted Reeve Arena in Toronto. We didn't win a game until Christmas, but by then we had them coached, and we went on to win the play-offs!

The Great Britain team at Renfrew Airport, prior to departure for the World Championships in Yugoslavia, March 1966. From left to right: Sammy MacDonald, Lawrie Lovell, Joe McIntosh, Andy Williams, Les Lovell, Billy Miller (wearing Matt Thompson's spectacles!) Matt Thompson (official), Billy Brennan, Willie Clark, Glen Reilly, Bill Crawford, Robert Stevenson, John Milne, Derek Metcalfe, Hep Tindale (hidden), Alastair Brennan, Terry Matthews. Missing from photo – John Baxter and Red Imrie. (Bill Brennan archive)

I remember when I was assistant coach of a Don Valley Pee Wee team that won the All-Ontario Championship; we had these team jackets that we were expected to wear. I never was one for all that stuff. I only pulled mine on when I got into the rink, and took it off again before I got back into the car after a game. 'Spike' Bremner was another Paisley guy who always wore a hockey jacket, and put on a Canadian accent – an Argyle Street Yank! I used to take the piss out of them.

You talk about what sports do to you. I'm full of parts now! I've had a triple bypass and an aneurism in my stomach had to be removed. I've had two knees done, and one hip done. So, I'm full of bloody bits and pieces! One doctor, who was into sports medicine, asked me what sports was I in? I told him, and he said that it would have been the athletics that did it.

My daughter, Lyndsey, works for the City of Toronto in medical financial allocations. My son, Adam, works as a commodity broker in Toronto. He was okay as a hockey player, but he mainly played Canadian football. We've got one grandson and five granddaughters.

I retired in 1993, and we live down on what they call 'The Beach' in Toronto. We come back to Scotland for a month every year, to visit my sister-in-law in Erskine.

Career Record

	GP	G	A	Pts	PiM
Bill Crawford (Paisley) 1953-1969 (Records unavailable for 1960-1962;1965-1967)	467	187	216	403	564
Great Britain 1953-1966	27	12	4	16	6

11

Capital Gain: Scott Neil

Edinburgh's Murrayfield Ice Rink sits in the shadow of Scotland's national rugby union stadium. Since the extensive rebuilding of the rugby arena, the rink has been totally dwarfed by its giant neighbour, as if some massive, alien mothership has landed behind the Art Deco rink in the Edinburgh suburbs.

The Murrayfield rink has been the setting for many of Scott Neil's finest on-ice moments in the heyday of the Murrayfield Racers, and it continues as his second home in his capacity as owner and general manager of the Edinburgh Capitals Ice Hockey Club.

Andrew Scott Neil was born in Edinburgh on 1 August 1962, the youngest of three children of company director William Gordon Neil and Mary Stark McMorran, who had married at Leith, Edinburgh in 1954.

Growing up in Edinburgh, attending the rugby-orientated Royal High School, Scott initially harboured dreams of sporting success on Murrayfield's rugby pitch. That his aspirations were to be realised next door in the ice rink was Scottish and UK ice hockey's gain, although, given his family connection with the Murrayfield rink, ice hockey's good fortune was not entirely unexpected, as Scott explains:

> My family's got an involvement with the ownership of the ice rink here – it's been in the two families more or less since the start. My mother has got a shareholding in the rink at the moment.
>
> I more or less started through coming to public skating. I skated, but I never started playing till late – I was fourteen. But I played a lot of sport, very involved in rugby and football, so I took to the game fairly quickly and was asked to start playing with the junior team. At that time, there weren't too many seven, eight, nine-year-olds playing; we were all the same age group joining at the same time.
>
> I played a good level of schoolboy rugby for Edinburgh Schools. I played hockey and rugby for a number of years until it just got too much. My focus, my main kind of group of good friends were all mostly in the hockey fraternity, because I could've easily ended up playing rugby more seriously. I grew up playing for Edinburgh Schools with Gavin Hastings, who played for Watson's; he was our full-back. I played stand-off or centre. But most of my friends were involved in hockey, and when it came to a stage when I had to pick, hockey, at that time, seemed to have more interest.

A right-hand shot, Scott was to develop into one of the finest forwards in the British game; yet he started out as a defenceman in the Murrayfield junior programme:

> My first hockey coach was a chap called Gordon Inglis. He was a very good technical, tactical sort of player. He was a good coach, and I think we learned a lot from him in the early years.

The Scottish contingent of the Great Britain Under-19 team, 1980. From left to right, back row: Paul Heavey (Glasgow), John Kidd (Ayr). Middle row: Jim Dailley (Ayr), Iain Byers (Ayr), Scott Neil (Murrayfield, captain). Front row: Alastair Reid (Ayr), John 'Bernie' McCrone (Ayr), Kenny McKie (Glasgow). (Frank Dempster archive)

> I used to play defence when I first started, and I can remember sitting up on the terracing and watching him, how he played for the Racers. At that time there was a lot of Edinburgh-based players, and they had two good squads in the Racers and the Raiders, and a lot of good characters throughout both squads. Guys like Derek Reilly, Ally and Ronnie Wood, who also went to Royal High, so they were good friends of mine, and it was Ronnie who took me down to Sheffield eventually. Guys like Duncan McIntyre, Denis Clair, guys who'd look after you and tried to help you through the system.
>
> I seemed to accelerate through that system. From starting so late, it just seemed that I moved up the ladder relatively quickly.
>
> I had one call up to the Racers, when I was about fourteen or fifteen, when Johnny Carlyle was coach; but it was too quick. Johnny's always been a good character around the hockey; he still comes to this day. We then had Ake Alm as coach, and then Alex Dampier. But there have been so many good, good calibre guys, there was such a strong squad of players in Edinburgh at that time – Jock Hay, Bobby Hay, Stevie Hunter, Davey Mason; a good, strong base of guys, and characters, too. I have a lot of good memories of these early years.

One such memory is of his first senior goal for Racers, which came in auspicious circumstances. Billingham Forum, on 14 April 1979, was the venue for the 'Icy' Smith Cup final; then emblematic of Britain's national championship. A sixteen-year-old Scott Neil opened the scoring for Murrayfield against Streatham Redskins, setting up Racers for a 10-2 triumph and a record-breaking seventh 'Icy' Smith Cup [Scott finished with two of Racers' ten goals]:

> From there it moved fairly quickly. I had a pretty good sort of rise through the national programmes; I was playing for the senior Great Britain team by the time I was seventeen. I also went to a couple of championships with the GB Under-18s, in Bulgaria and Denmark; then I was out in China with the senior team.
>
> Bulgaria was a good trip. I don't think we did too bad, considering it was our first international tournament at that level and we didn't know what to expect. Terry Matthews was the coach and he was a good guy, and a very good coach.
>
> I captained the team on the trip to Denmark the following year. We had a few training sessions down in Billingham and up here to pick the squad; and I got told I was getting the captaincy. Again, I think we had a pretty reasonable tournament, although we lost to the Danes, if I remember correctly. I think there was definitely an improvement that year from the year before.

Scott's first exposure to the senior Great Britain team came at the age of seventeen, followed by a trip to China for the Pool 'C' World Championships aged just eighteen:

> There was an international tournament in Dundee that year [1980] and the GB senior team played against Concordia University from Canada and the Dutch national team.
>
> The China trip in 1981 was an eye-opener, because it was my first experience at that top level of hockey. We didn't really come close to any of the teams there. There were some good calibre teams, and it was an eye-opener for me, at that age, to see what good quality hockey was all about.
>
> Going to China was a great experience, because a lot of old, famous names went on that trip.
>
> There were a number of trials, because I can always remember wanting to make the team. I think I was having a pretty good season from a league point of view, but I wasn't convinced that I would make the team that year. I remember players getting cut at practices, so I was happy when, obviously, I got told I was going to go.
>
> What I can remember was that the food was awful. Other teams, more experienced, had brought their own stuff. Some of us didn't eat a lot – a lot of rice, and that was about it!
>
> It's a learning curve, and there aren't that many opportunities for players, even in today's game. Okay, most of the pro teams are on the ice every day now, but then, to get on the ice every day, practising every day, it just picks your pace up. It gets you more involved and interested in the sport.
>
> The unfortunate thing, for me, was that they closed down the national programme for the senior team after that. That was a big disappointment, for me personally, because it was coming right at the peak of my career, and having made the national team at that young age. It was disappointing, too, because there were a number of good, young British players coming through at that time. I think anyone who goes on these national trips do learn a lot from it; it is a good experience.
>
> I think the BIHA weren't sure if they could compete, and the finance wasn't there. But there was a good whack of British players who would certainly have developed from the experience then.

In what was then very much the exception for British players, Scott had an opportunity to play Canadian university hockey, as he explains:

> When I was nineteen, our coach here, Alex Dampier, had a connection with the University of Prince Edward Island in Canada, so I went out there. I had left school and started work for the civil service. This opportunity came to go, so I took off. I spent four years there. It wasn't so much a hockey scholarship, although I did get a small scholarship, as I didn't play for the university for the whole four years. The first two years I was there in the team full-time; the last two years it was on a squad basis.
>
> Again, I think I developed a lot there, but it was a big shock moving into that hockey environment. I was one of the bigger kids in the system over here, at the time, for my age. Over there, I think I was about the smallest player on the team. You were playing a much faster, more physical style of hockey. I ended up actually playing a lot of football for the university team – I probably did better at the football than I did at the hockey!

Scott's achievements on the football field were not inconsiderable, scoring 37 goals for the Varsity soccer team between 1981 and 1984. He assisted the UPEI Panthers to the Atlantic University Sport Men's Soccer Championship in 1983 and 1984, being voted the League's Most Valuable Forward in 1984.

> With the hockey, I was always a third or fourth liner and latterly, with the university the main team on the island, they were bringing in a lot of guys out the OHL. So, by the end of it, I wasn't playing that much. I still trained, but it was a difficult level.

> I had no aspirations of professional hockey in North America. At that time there weren't that many pro teams. Now you've got the East Coast League, the United League, and the Central League. I can remember two American League teams coming to Prince Edward Island, to Charlottetown, to do an exhibition game. The standard was absolutely outstanding. I knew, from probably a month after getting there, that there was no chance of overtaking a lot of these guys at that level. At that particular time the Atlantic Coast University level was a good standard of hockey. There were one or two guys from Moncton University who went on to the NHL; there were quality players.
>
> It wasn't like the rinks I was used to here, with lots of space and ice. They were tight, compact little rinks, and it was a very physical game. We were used to skating, handling the puck. You didn't get two seconds on the puck over there. You got rid of it as soon as you got it otherwise you were picking yourself up off the ice. It was a big change in just the environment and the style and speed of the hockey.
>
> It took a while to adapt, and physically too. The kids over there were much more advanced as to their physical requirements for the sport. I managed to probably catch up with them on that. I was in the gym and worked out, but there were a lot of big kids.
>
> I took a business course, and through that I was going to go on to education, go back and do a teaching qualification, probably majored in history. But hockey was beginning to take off over here when I came home that summer and I thought that maybe now was the time to come home.

His Canadian experience means that Scott is better placed than most to offer an opinion on the decision taken by Tony Hand not to pursue a North American hockey career after being drafted by Edmonton in 1986. That Tony is a former teammate, and a relative, adds weight to his views:

> Tony and I are related; it's not just Tony, it's Paul and a whole family connection, through my mother's family.
>
> I don't think I was giving Tony any advice at that time, he was out there and he had to make his own decisions as to how he felt he was doing and where he thought the game was going to take him. He's made his own decisions there and, in the circumstances, it must have been a very difficult thing for him to do.
>
> You have to remember, when you're in that environment, the junior hockey leagues out there, that their whole preparation, from joining a Major Junior 'A' team at age sixteen, is a process for them to prepare these kids both mentally and physically for pro hockey. Tony was plucked out of obscurity from a small Scottish ice hockey league and put in the big time. Going to any training camp in the NHL you're there with some proper men, big guys; they know the system and know what to expect and he doesn't have anybody out there really holding his hand or giving him a lot of advice.
>
> From all accounts, he had a very good camp with Edmonton. If things were different, even in today's environment, he'd have a lot more support mechanisms and people to take advice from who could maybe route a proper path for him. I think he was homesick and missing life back in Scotland and that was a good factor in why he came back. I think, in hindsight, he might've thought he maybe should've given it a year. Anyway, Tony's made his decision, and he's had a great career here.

Scott particularly enjoyed the hockey on his return to Murrayfield in the mid-1980s, as he relates:

> After the four years, I came back, and the sport was beginning to take off a wee bit here, with Heineken involved. I started playing again with the Racers. I was here for seven or eight years again, before I went to Sheffield.

Scott Neil in action for Murrayfield Racers against Durham Wasps in the Norwich Union Cup final at Basingstoke, 2 December 1989. Murrayfield won 10-4. (*Ice Hockey News Review* photo)

I enjoyed that time of the hockey. There was a good level of competition and there was a good rivalry between all the clubs. Most of the players knew each other pretty well. They were civil, and there were a lot of good friendships, which have lasted even to this day. But when you got on the ice, there was a good rivalry and a good will to win. From a fan's point of view in those days, I can see a lot of these games being fairly highly charged and emotional and being a good spectacle.

The live TV coverage then was certainly a big boost for the sport, and it certainly misses that now. We were lucky then; I think there was a football dispute over TV coverage and hockey managed to take advantage of what was going on. Things came on pretty quick through that era and Scottish hockey was strong. We had a lot of good teams that created good rivalry and it was an enjoyable period. They had Wembley going and that developed into a great tournament. I think we only won it once with Murrayfield. We were there every year, apart from the last year – we missed out on what would've been my last year of playing for the Racers.

The national programme started back up again. That developed, and I got right the way up. I was pushing on in age a bit, I was thirty-two/thirty-three when we won promotion to Pool 'B', and from Pool 'B' to Pool 'A'.

I didn't make the team for Pool 'A' in '94, and that was a disappointment. Part of my problem that year was that I had injuries most of the year, I carried them, and I didn't deserve to make the team, to be honest. When it came down to it, I didn't have a good enough season, through various things. That's just something you've got to accept, but it was a disappointment not to play at the top level in the World Championships, when you'd been there starting off in Pool 'C', as it was, back in China.

But it was a good experience overall, I enjoyed the trips.

The landscape of British ice hockey was to change at the beginning of the 1990s, with the opening of the Sheffield Arena and the advent of the Sheffield Steelers. Scott joined up in 1992, and looks back with great affection at his five playing years in South Yorkshire:

The year that the Racers never went to Wembley, a consortium came in to take on the team. I had a chat with them and had a chat with Fife, and then Ronnie [Wood] took me for a look at Sheffield. I had turned thirty that year and I just thought that if there was a chance of me leaving Murrayfield, I was wanting to move out the area altogether. If I'd played for Fife, I would've always wanted to come back and play for Murrayfield. It wasn't just a money thing going to Sheffield, because Fife actually gave me a better offer than Sheffield.

I looked at Sheffield, and it was a fantastic facility, and I've no doubts that I made the right decision, because I had a great time in Sheffield. We had a very successful team; I was there five years and, apart from getting promotion the first year, we won something every year from then on in.

It was good to see the sport rise so dramatically there and that's, ideally, what we'd like to see back in Edinburgh again. It was a meteoric rise for the sport, and I think the people of Sheffield really took to it and really got behind it. The profile of the sport, the following, it was quite incredible, bearing in mind that we were playing in a league the level below what the Racers were playing in at that time. I was never really a full-time hockey player till I went to Sheffield. I really enjoyed it there, although it would've been an interesting one had I gone to Fife!

I played one year of Superleague with Sheffield. I wasn't getting much ice time by then. I stuck it out; I still enjoyed it. I was there for the team when they needed me; they did go through a little injury crisis when I came in, and I thought I played pretty well, after sitting on the bench for so long! But I knew I was coming towards the end of my career. You've got to accept that the calibre of the sport was increasing and I was getting older.

I was probably training as hard as at any time in my career, I'd do extra training to try and keep up. Once you get to a certain age, when your performance is going down, and the overall calibre of the game is going up, reasonable people will accept what's going on, and I think I did. The other thing, too, is that you've got to look at kids coming through the system. I could've stayed and held up the system for a year or two, but it was time to move on.

I've kept in touch with a lot of people at Sheffield, and I still regard it as my second club.

Indeed, Scott even had a spell as general manager of Sheffield in the inaugural Elite League season of 2003/04 – while continuing his owner/general manager role with then BNL Edinburgh! Unsurprisingly, this dual role took its toll and he relinquished the Sheffield job after a couple of months.

Earlier, however, at the age of thirty-five, in 1997, Scott headed back to his native city, with some misgivings:

I came back to Edinburgh and played for the Royals for a year at the beginning of the BNL. I had a pretty good playing year, was top scorer on the team, but it was a tough year – we didn't compete very well. It was hockey, but it wasn't Sheffield.

From that year the rink decided that they weren't going to operate a senior team, and that's where I stepped in, along with a couple of other backers, to try and take the team forward.

I'm the owner and general manager. I've also coached the team as well, which I enjoyed. It's a hard grind, but it was a lot more enjoyable than being general manager! It's been frustrating and difficult. We've moved on steadily as a club, maybe not as quickly as we hoped. The last two seasons we came last in both leagues, yet still managed to build our crowd base, which is a positive. But, having played and worked in Sheffield, we are light years away from the Sheffield organisation and a lot of the other clubs in the league.

I think we have to be very, very clever. It's a big challenge promoting, developing ice hockey in this city. Further down the line I think a new facility will come to Edinburgh, and I think that'll help the sport. I still think this facility serves the city proud. We've probably got the best ice surface in the league, but to move things forward we need to be able to take advantage, like other clubs have, of shiny, new facilities.

The hockey club is, technically, a tenant of the rink. We try to work as closely as possible, but there are issues, like in any relationship. Going back through the ownership history of the rink, old Mr Kerr was very keen on his ice hockey, and old Mr Kerr's son, Willie Kerr, played hockey at a good level, so there was always a soft spot for hockey and for the team. The rink has been supportive of us, in trying to help us get going, and I think it also brings benefits to the rink, too. After the demise of the Racers, the rink understood the benefits that a good hockey team can bring to it, through publicity; kids coming in to play, secondary spend etc. I think it is an important factor of any ice rink; if you've got a good team playing out your rink you'll get spin offs from it.

There have been a lot of good, famous players who came through the development systems here, and I think a big bonus also for Edinburgh was the involvement of Smirnoff. That was a fantastic sponsorship, and that can help turn clubs around. There have certainly been a lot of people involved in the management at Murrayfield who have either been hockey players or they've certainly got a keen eye for it.

In terms of the outstanding British players of his era, Tony Hand is top of Scott's list:

Tony [Hand] is the outstanding talent I've played with. Tony was on my wing for a long time, and if I could get space, Tony would find me the puck. I must have scored bundles of goals off Tony's assists. Jock Hay was on our line as well, and we had one good, solid British line there for a number of years. Jock didn't maybe get as many goals or as many points, but he was as equally effective on that line. He played his part.

At Murrayfield, Paul Hand was a strong player to have at the back; Moray Hanson and Martin McKay were strong in goals.

Of the guys we played against, I'd rate Johnny Iredale, Alfie Miller and Terry Matthews from Whitley; Paul Smith, the Johnsons, the Coopers from Durham. When I came back from Canada, the Woods were up in Dundee, so that created a bit of rivalry; John Kidd, Ally Reid, 'Bernie' McCrone from Ayr. And there's more! I'd have to go through a list of them. Again, looking for characters, guys like Charlie Kinmond, Jimmy Pennycook, John Pullar, Mike Ward – stacks of them. There was a big core of real hockey names throughout Scotland at that time; a good community of hockey players.

From imports, Chris Kelland and Alex Dampier probably stand out; Rick Brebant was a strong player; Mike O'Connor; Hilton Ruggles – a lot of good calibre imports came through the system in those early years. Going latterly, the Sheffield era, Ken Priestlay was an outstanding talent; Jason Lafreniere, arguably the most talented player I've played with, and a bit of a character, but certainly a quality, quality guy, and a quality player.

I think, too, if you look at the guys that have lasted the test of time, guys like Rob Wilson, who's got a Championship-winning team now and seems as if he's been in the country since forever. Ron Shudra; he's still playing in Sheffield. In saying that, however, I think that if the ISL had maintained its level, you'd probably have seen a lot of these guys drift out the system.

Scott can speak fairly authoritatively about the sport, given that his perspective encompasses wide experience as a player, in both the UK and Canada, GB internationalist, coach, manager and owner. When we met during the summer of 2006, the sport in Britain was again suffering from internal strife and self-interest, with the Elite League having lost its London franchise partway through the season just finished. A lack of strong leadership from the sport's governing body, the absence of major sponsorship and limited television exposure were just some of the tribulations bedevilling the sport. His views on the way forward are interesting and challenging:

I think the sport's got to be fairly shrewd in understanding where the market is and what it can sustain. If one or two owners want to come in and treat it as a bit of fun, they're going to disrupt the whole sport.

If you look at some sporting models in the States, the NFL for example, the whole thing is about sharing; it's about creating a product that everyone can benefit from and grow. I think if we could grasp that focus, and agree that that is the way to develop it, then I think the sport can flourish.

I'm not so sure that teams have to be subsidised to huge amounts. There are always going to be teams that are going to spend less than the big teams; but if you can produce a competitive team at a lower budget, it still keeps the league sustainable and afloat. We're looking after our business, but the league itself, the bigger teams, can't be too dominant.

If you look at the structure of British ice hockey, you have the big arena clubs – most of them are fairly big successful clubs – but they've got to try and hold the reins on themselves, because they could charge off and put the wage limits and calibre of their hockey way above what the rest can sustain. That will ruin the product overall. I think where the Elite League have had success over the past two or three years is in starting to control finances, but being aware that the product has to be as good as it can be; but we can all grow at a certain level, and produce a certain calibre of hockey. I think we will get sponsorship back into it, and I think we'll get TV back interested. I think that's key for the sport in this country; that we can produce a sustainable league that can give good, competitive games, that can provide opportunities for some of our home bred players to develop into quality national players, and I think that's beginning to work.

I think we're beginning to move on again. What's also encouraging, and also disappointing – and this is where we're probably not getting it right – is that there are more and more kids leaving these shores and going to hockey academies. That will benefit British ice hockey, because a lot of them will return, but the sad thing is that we should be doing that in our own country, producing that level of service.

Even when I was at Sheffield, with 8,000 or 9,000 people coming to games, there was very little input from the senior team into the development system, and I found that disappointing. When there's that sort of money floating around the sport at that level, it's almost a sin, because that is where the future of the sport lies.

The Sheffield mentality was that they had to produce a better product all the time, and the product became too high a level for the sport to sustain. It took it out of the reach of most of the kids coming through.

In comparing the UK to Germany, you have to look at the demographics of Germany. I think a lot of their good players come from Alpine townships where the kids are in a good development system. More importantly, it comes down to cash. They have got some serious sponsorship in German hockey, whether it's through TV or major companies investing in the sport. Switzerland has had a recent bit of success because, I think, they got sponsored by Swiss banks, and they have invested that in turn, rightly, into their youth development systems and their national programmes.

That could happen here with the right funding and the right people. I remember Ivan Matulik, for example, he stayed with me when he first came down to Sheffield. He told me that the system in Slovakia wasn't about thousands of kids playing hockey; their top band kids were selected and pushed through a system – twenty or thirty kids in each age group were being focused on and worked on. It is an elite sort of way to go, and I don't totally agree with an elite project, but I think there are ways where we need to target our best guys and offer them more education, how to eat, how to train – give them that little bit of a carrot to develop to a standard.

Throughout Germany, they've got the DEL, which is a pretty high-paying league, and there are a few German guys going up there. But the Bundesliga, and some of the regional leagues, also give German players good employment opportunities. So there is a fair amount of money swirling around the system. What they've managed to do is kept the product good at the different levels. I think now there are a few other European countries which are beginning to build their hockey base.

There is a sort of perception in the British media that hockey is somehow alien to the psyche, with no understanding of the sport's strong tradition here. Again, I think what will help long term will be the advent of arenas. If major cities can all get a nice facility, I think that will help the sport develop – as long as there are also ice rink facilities in that city. I think that can help focus media attention, because a lot of the old rinks are just not glitzy and fancy enough; they're generally a bit tired looking.

He doesn't, however, see the sport's failure in the largest arena to host ice hockey in Europe, Manchester's MEN Arena, as an indicator that arena-based hockey cannot work in the UK:

With Manchester, I'm not sure how many people were paying when they were getting 17,000, but it was a fantastic marketing job, regardless. What I didn't think helped Manchester's plight was the instability in the rest of the league. The arena operator mentality is different perhaps from our ice rink operator mentality, and I'm not saying you need to shovel ice rinks out of the way, but there's got to be a happy balance. Coventry, for example, is an ice rink, but it's almost an arena, and they've got very good management that do a good job there. So, there's obviously a market for something like Coventry.

I think Manchester was probably too big for the sport – at any time. If I was to build a new rink in Edinburgh next week, am I building a rink or building an arena? You'd maybe want to build something in between that you could offer to concerts etc. The bottom line for hockey in Edinburgh, I think, is a new rink 3,000-3,500 capacity. If you build a 10,000 or 15,000-seat arena in Edinburgh, you're not going to fill it for hockey. Not within my lifetime, I wouldn't think.

The cities of Edinburgh and Sheffield themselves are similar-sized populations, around half a million, but Sheffield's catchment area's enormous. Edinburgh, I think, is not an easy city for sports. I think something similar to what Ayr's got (or had) with the Centrum would do fantastically well in Edinburgh. It could be as simple as that. Edinburgh needs an arena facility that would be well-used, for the Festival and other events; we don't really have any 7,000 to 10,000 seaters for concerts. If you had a 4,000-seat rink, floor off the area, you're up to about 5,500, 6,000 – that would serve a concert. That would be a big bonus for hockey, although I think we'd certainly lose the atmosphere we have here at Murrayfield. When this place is full there are few rinks, and I don't think any of the new rinks, can match the atmosphere here. Unless you've got a big rink that's full – Sheffield had a great atmosphere when full. Coming down to my last year in the ISL, attendances were dropping off, and you could noticeably see the atmosphere dropping off.

I think they've got to wake up in Britain, because the North American leagues are going to a European style, and that's the way I think it will continue to develop. We need more goals into the game, more excitement.

As an investor in the sport, Scott has obvious concerns about the way the game is administered in Great Britain, but especially in Scotland:

What's frustrating for me, since coming into ownership, is that you have got people who can get themselves into a position of authority and know nothing about the professional game. They just do not understand what you need to do to run a club, what are the risks and consequences and, traditionally, it's the senior club that runs the development programmes, or creates development systems. I think you need more professional people involved in running that system; people who have put their money where their mouth is in trying to run and develop the sport.

There is, certainly, a lot of distrust, and maybe rightly so, from past experiences. I might be controversial, but you will get representatives on the Scottish Ice Hockey Association (and on Ice Hockey UK through the SIHA) purely by votes from recreational teams and parents of junior players. The way it's set up in Scotland, recreational hockey can vote-in whoever they want because they've got more votes. They don't even go to the meetings, they just get proxy votes. That just gives it no credibility and doesn't give me confidence. I've put a lot of money into developing this club, and when I see some of the things happening, or things

Scott Neil receives the Capital Foods Scottish Cup, following Murrayfield's 13-4 win over Cardiff in Edinburgh, 11 March 1990. (*Ice Hockey News Review* photo)

being voted on, sometimes I just shake my head. They just don't seem to know what the consequences are for people who are trying to develop the sport and give it credibility at the top end.

We're getting more newspaper coverage than at any time throughout the history of hockey in Edinburgh. Our column inches in the *Evening News* are quite considerable. And that is profile for the sport as a whole, not just the Capitals.

Scott gives of his own time to coach the Under-12s at Murrayfield, so the development of the British player is a particular passion:

Your old school, and to an extent I'm in the old school, will be saying that the senior level is too high, and you've got to create opportunities for the British kids, reduce your imports etc. We are now competing with, and we've got a right of free movement as Europeans, all these continental nations. We've got to produce players that are on that par. We've got to do that, so we've got to invest. It's not about necessarily the top senior level; it's about the junior levels. We've got to make sure that these juniors are actually developing at such a rate that they're good enough to either play in another country or push guys out at our senior level. We've got to develop the core, rather than wait until the calibre of the senior level is lowered so our kids can get a chance.

You'll still only develop two or three through that system. The traditional way only ever developed, in any one club, two or three strong British players. What they have to do is develop fifteen guys coming through the system that are strong players.

I did an article in the *Sheffield Star* in '95, and I had a good go at the IIHF, the BIHA at the time, about their whole system. I had a real dig at them. It was the time that they really opened the doors for imports to come in, and it was actually the wrong time to do it, because there were a lot of good British players about. I said then that a lot of British kids are wasting their time in playing hockey, or focusing on it, because the development systems then, and now, are not strong enough to get these kids into that calibre of hockey. You'll get a few through the system, but not en masse. They've got to think on a mass target.

The Under-19s in Scotland, that should be the priority league for the SIHA, yet they play only something like sixteen games per year – it's pathetic. And a lot of the games don't even get played. These kids should be playing forty or fifty games per year. I had Ole Jokinnen, the captain of the Florida Panthers, over here at a hockey school once, and he told me that a lot of our kids at fourteen or fifteen were as good as Finnish kids at the same age. So it's the next age group that they need to develop; it's these kids that need the preparation and the focus. In Canada, the OHL is the breeding ground for the NHL, or in Europe good kids will be snapped up by a senior team.

I'm a believer in developing the British game. Our top leagues have to give opportunities for our top players to play at that level. But what we are not doing as a nation, and where I think we often take our eye off the ball, is helping our kids come close to attaining the levels they need to attain at a younger age group.

All the funding, generally, goes into the top tier squads. They play their little game and very little goes down the way. A lot of other small nations – Slovakia, for example – they're investing top to bottom, and bearing in mind it's a big sport in Slovakia, so there's a lot of interest and a lot of funding.

What we have to do is raise the level of playing and coaching for our kids so there is not a big jump from coming from Under-19s into the senior squads. Around the nations, there are a lot of good athletes at eighteen, guys like Crosby in the NHL. It's about creating that level of professionalism, if you like, at the younger levels so that our kids are, hopefully, on a par with the rest of Europe. It may be pie in the sky, but unless we start focusing on developing that, we're never going to get stacks of kids playing at the top flight, if we want a product that can compete with the rest of Europe at our top league level.

Scott and his wife Jill live in Edinburgh, some ten minutes up the road from the Murrayfield rink. They have three children, Cameron (nine), Lucy (seven) and Zak (three). And a dog! Trying to maintain a work-life balance while running a pro hockey team is problematic:

I try to keep in shape; I golf now and then, but I just don't get the time.

His fitness programme is obviously effective as, at the age of forty-four, he looks no different from his 5ft 10in, 185lbs playing days.

With an involvement in hockey now stretching over thirty years, Scott is adamant that junior development is the crucial issue for the sport in the UK today:

The game in this country has changed so much since I was a kid – more and more foreign players in the system – so there is less opportunity for kids to come through and play at the higher level.

So, we've got to find funding, and the means and the will, for development systems – to stop just playing at developing – and actually get seriously behind it. We need to put a lot of time, effort and resources into the kids that are involved in it.

Career Record

	GP	G	A	Pts	PiM
Scott Neil (Murrayfield/Sheffield/ Edinburgh) 1979-2002	687	694	588	1282	329
Great Britain 1981-1993	37	23	12	35	18

12

Family Business: Martin and Colin Shields

'The Draft' is a uniquely North American sporting phenomenon. To the uninitiated observer, it has the appearance of a strange hybrid: part American political convention, part showbusiness awards ceremony.

It is an alien concept to the British, and throws up an unusual dichotomy, as its equitable distribution of emerging talent on an annual basis, where last-placed teams get rewarded with first pick, is representative of the almost egalitarian approach of professional sports within the unrestrained North American free market. It is in stark contrast to the avaricious British football industry, where the wealthiest clubs lay claim to an ever-increasing slice of the pie, with their financial pre-eminence effectively destroying meaningful competition.

As with its counterparts in basketball and football, the National Hockey League's Entry Draft has become an annual event, moving from city to city. Although televised live, it is hardly the type of entertainment to attract the casual viewer over its two days' duration. Even the die-hard hockey fan would find its funereal pace challenging, with team representatives making the same repetitive speeches offering thanks to the host city. In any event, most of the real drama takes place behind closed doors and in smoke-filled rooms, where trades are made, away from the media gaze.

The 2000 Entry Draft was no different. Hosted by Calgary's Saddledome, the home of the NHL Flames, the major talking point was the decision of New York Islanders' general manager Mike Milbury to select American goaltender Rick DiPietro as the number one pick.

With nine rounds, and 293 players selected, it was a protracted process over a weekend. While Philadelphia general manager Bobby Clarke's major issue was trying (and failing) to arrange a trade for concussion-prone superstar Eric Lindros, he had approved the Flyers' fourth pick of the Draft, coming in the sixth round. With that selection, Colin Shields' NHL rights were to become the property of the Philadelphia Flyers.

Back in East Kilbride, Scotland, just south of Glasgow, the delighted Shields family learned of the news via the internet. Twenty-year-old Colin's selection was an achievement only shared by one other British player in fellow Scot Tony Hand. Without denigrating Hand's own considerable achievement, his last pick of the final round in 1986 by the Edmonton Oilers was, in comparison, a mere afterthought.

Colin's road to the Draft had started some eighteen years earlier at Glasgow's old Crossmyloof rink, where his mum Margaret had taught him to skate. But his Crossmyloof lineage actually goes back to the early 1960s, when his father Martin started out on his own hockey career, which would see him develop into one of the finest centremen in the British game of the seventies and eighties and an award-winning coach in the nineties.

Martin Shields was born on 13 January 1954 at Lennox Castle Maternity Hospital, north of Glasgow. He was one of three children born to John Shields, a leather storeman, and Jean Martin, who had married in Glasgow in 1947.

Martin Shields, *c.*1964, Glasgow juniors, at Murrayfield Ice Rink. (Martin Shields archive)

He grew up in the Govanhill area of Glasgow's southside, not too far from the city's Crossmyloof rink. It was there, during 1962, that he was to be introduced to ice hockey by Sam Stevenson, a man who had been involved with the sport at Crossmyloof since the great days of Billy Fullerton and Joe Collins, as Martin remembers:

> The first involvement I had with hockey was through Sam Stevenson. I always remember it was at the end of the skating session at Crossmyloof on a Saturday morning and the stewards were trying to get me off the ice! One of them said to me that the gentleman with the glasses and the hat wanted to speak to me. I thought I was going to get barred from the rink! There was a hockey practice on a Saturday morning and Sam took people who could skate. I was about eight or nine at the time.
>
> My brother and his pals had went up to the skating at Crossmyloof on a Saturday morning, and he took me up originally. He never continued, and I did. I'd no involvement at all with hockey; I didn't even know about hockey! It was Sam Stevenson that asked me if I'd like to play hockey and stay on for the practice; Sam got me involved and it went from there; that's where it all started.
>
> I was brought up in Glasgow, in Govanhill in the Southside. My mother separated from my father when I was about seven or eight. When I was about twelve or thirteen I took over my brother's milk run – he couldn't get out his bed in the morning to do it – and that was before I went to school and in between trying to get to the hockey! I went to Cuthbertson Street School in Govanhill; then I went to Calder Street, and when they closed Calder Street, which was just around the corner, we got sent to Queen's Park Secondary up in Toryglen
>
> There wasn't really a junior development, as such, in those days in the early 1960s. It was a right mix of ages and you couldn't call it even a junior or second team. There wasn't a league at that time and the senior team, the Glasgow Flyers with Charlie Huddlestone and these guys, were really winding up then.
>
> Then it turned into the Glasgow Dynamos when Robert Stevenson, Sam's son, got involved. He played with Paisley at that time, and his brother Barrie also got involved.

Martin, a right-hand shot, played centre, but was small in stature:

> I was the whipping boy of the practice at that time; it just went on from there, and I stuck it out. I then got the opportunity to play with the Dynamos when I was about fourteen or

fifteen, and that was through default because some guys couldn't make it. Nobody liked to go to Durham or Whitley Bay and probably your worst introduction to senior hockey was going to Durham!

In fairness to Robert Stevenson, some of the older guys were at the end of their careers, and he was trying to give some of their younger players a chance, like John Hester, myself and the guy Callaghan.

I played a lot for the Glasgow Redwings, who were the reserve team. There were a lot of older chaps in there, but they were good enough; they were great people and it was like a weekend away with all the boys! There was no badness with any of these guys; they always looked after you.

One of the times we went down to Whitley Bay with the Dynamos and we decided it was cheaper to buy a bus than to hire one! We got the opportunity to buy this old bus, really old. We were driving down the old Roman road when the engine started knocking going down a hill; Ellis Firestone, the trainer, he was actually driving it with Sam Stevenson as his co-pilot; going up the next hill the engine blew up! Ellis says to Sam, deadly serious, 'Do you think we should put more oil in it?' Robert Stevenson says 'Put more oil in it? Half of it's just lying behind us!'

When I was sixteen I went to Canada, which was an education, to be the biggest and best thing that ever hit Canada in hockey! But when you first move away from home you realise that there's more to life than hockey; you've got to put food in your mouth!

My elder brother John had emigrated to Canada. I originally emigrated at sixteen when my brother sponsored me. At that time [1970] it wasn't hard to get in and I was there for eighteen months.

I worked on building sites as a carpenter when I was there. I started my apprenticeship with Sam Stevenson before I went; he had a building business in Glasgow over at Cathcart.

The biggest thing when I went to Canada was that when you step on to the ice you think you can skate – and then you realise that there are another twenty-odd guys there that can skate as fast or faster than you can.

The number one lesson, one of many that I learned in Canada, was that you've got to eat! Realistically, once you're there, hockey takes second.

There was me and David Callaghan went at the same time. We just played catch-up hockey when we were there. David came back with me to Scotland, but he did go back to Canada.

You were looking to pay your accommodation; we were living in an apartment and there was no public transport, so you had to have a car. And if you're not working, you're not doing anything. You couldn't just jump on a bus. At that time we were in Mississauga, which was an up and coming place then, although now it's just about a part of Toronto. But then it had a lot of spare areas and you had to walk about five miles, with your kit, to get to the rink – anything to get out the house because you were bored!

I tried out for the Toronto Marlies, but it never came to anything. The try-outs were in Maple Leaf Gardens and I had no hockey equipment! I went to the try-outs and had to beg, borrow and steal off them to get on the ice!

My mother was then involved in a bad car accident in Spain. I came back to look after my mother, intending to return to Canada, and you never seem to get back; I never went back.

When I came back from Canada I played with the Dynamos right through until such times as myself and John Hester got the opportunity to play with the British squad.

I always thought Crossmyloof was like Edinburgh in that, because of the big ice, it made you a good skater. A lot of the clubs didn't like coming to play us at Crossmyloof because of the massive size of the ice.

It had a great atmosphere and everything else. But it was absolutely dying on its feet! The dressing-rooms were up the stairs and the opposition used to kid us on about taking the bulb out the light going down the stairs! They also said that we lifted the rubber mats so that by the time they got onto the ice they'd no edges on their skates! That was the ploy, although

Martin Shields in action for Glasgow Dynamos, 1971/72. (Martin Shields archive)

> it wasn't true, right enough! The management just wouldn't buy mats and bulbs! I've a lot of fond memories of Crossmyloof.
>
> Sam Stevenson started me off and his son, Robert Stevenson, in that league at that time, was slightly ahead of the way the game was played then. He had a really good, all-round game. I'd say Robert Stevenson was the best I played with at that time and the biggest influence. There were some other chaps there as well, though. 'Jumbo' Milne, in later days, came and coached the team; Billy Laird, the goalkeeper, came and coached; Mike Mazur came down from Perth, he was good; all these people had something to bring and all had some knowledge of hockey. That helped us all out.
>
> In those days you were fighting to get a stick. To get a new stick then was like getting a new pair of skates today; it was unbelievable compared to what hockey is now.
>
> I feel sorry, though, for kids today. When I look back to Crossmyloof, we could get on the ice five or six times a week; we'd a separate curling rink, and even when there was curling on the big rink you could get on to end-ice. They were very relaxed because the ice was that big; even if you had figure skaters on they'd let us on the end-ice.
>
> We talk about kids today not having the dedication but, Jesus, if the kids could get on the ice as much as we could I'm quite sure a lot of them would be dedicated.
>
> I think we used to pay half-a-crown each in those days for practices for the week – and it was ten shillings for a stick! It was a lot of money at the time, but not as expensive as it is today.
>
> John Hester and I had played for Scotland against England several times.

In the England *v.* Scotland international, at Billingham, on 16 February 1980, with the score tied at 5-5, Martin grabbed the winning goal for Scotland with one second remaining.

Martin's first outing with Great Britain was at the annual Pondus Cup, in Copenhagen, in December 1975. The British lost heavily: 2-10 to Denmark; 3-13 to Norway 'B'; and 8-13 to Bulgaria. Britain's leading scorers were Lawrie Lovell with four goals and Martin Shields with three. World Championship duty beckoned, as Martin recalls:

> Then we went to World Championships with the British team in Poland, Denmark and Spain. I had to pull out of the China trip in '81; I was self-employed at the time, and it was a three-week trip, and I just couldn't take the time off. In hindsight, I wish I'd went.

> The first thing that you noticed when we landed in Poland in 1976, and you stepped off the 'plane and looked round the airport, was that I'd only seen 'planes like this in films about World War Two! And everywhere you went there were armed guards, at the airport, at the railways stations.
>
> You'd see old women brushing the streets with big brooms; carts and horses; old trucks that looked as if they were from the 1940s. But the railway stations were magnificent.
>
> The whole carriage on the train, though, was heated by a coal fire, with two pipes running under each compartment!
>
> When we went to the rink in Gdansk we were really taken aback; it was a magnificent brand new ice rink. All the seating was tiered up one side of the rink; it must have held about 7,000. It was absolutely tremendous; it had a mini-sized pool for the players – facilities there that we could only dream about at that time.

The British team had finally arrived in Gdansk some twelve hours after flying out from Heathrow. After a few hours sleep, they had a brief training session, followed by lunch, then straight into the championship opener against Hungary:

> The first game we played there it was packed; they were sitting on all the walkways. We were amazed when we stepped on the ice.

Hungary defeated Britain 11-0 on 8 March 1976. Given their lack of preparation, it wasn't surprising that the legs gave way in the final period, when the Hungarians netted five times.

Things went from bad to worse. Austria were the opponents the following day and embarrassed the British to the tune of 21-2. It was scant consolation for Martin Shields that he scored Britain's opening goal of the tournament in the first period. After a rest day spent licking their wounds, Team GB responded with an improved performance against Denmark, albeit a 3-7 defeat.

The final game was against France and, although losing 1-5, there were further positive signs from the Brits, with Martin Shields grabbing the solitary goal thirty seconds into the third period:

> The place we were staying, it had armed guards at the gate and barbed wire round it! If you went there with £100 your money was worth four times that. We thought this was great and everything was getting bought. Then 'Jumbo', big Milne, he got done at the railway station. He was changing his money, handed it over, and the guy took off! Of course, it wasn't just 'Jumbo's' money, it was other guys' as well. It was illegal to change money, so he couldn't do anything about it!
>
> Spain in '79 was nice; we went to Barcelona. They took us to see the football when we were there – Barcelona were playing Ipswich Town in the UEFA Cup – and we got sitting right at the side of the pitch. These experiences were the things you'd expect of a professional team which, at that time, was quite nice.

At the Pool 'C' World Championships of March 1979, held in Barcelona, Martin Shields and Jimmy Pennycook were the leading British scorers, each finishing with 3 goals and 4 assists from 6 games:

> In terms of the hockey, technically we were way behind these other countries. I think physically they were way better prepared than us; they were a lot more professional in the way they did it. But with individual skills, I don't think there was a great deal of difference.
>
> I think, at that time, we were probably ten years behind them technically in how the game should be played. They were moving the puck and thinking how the game should be played; we were probably just guessing, and throwing five guys on.

With the Great Britain team at the 1976 World Championships Pool 'C', Gdansk, Poland. Martin Shields (left) and team manager John 'Jumbo' Milne (right). (Martin Shields archive)

> I think it was all about money. We had good players like Alastair Brennan and Jackson McBride, who I rated as really good hockey players; but these other countries could put five guys on and they all, basically, could do a job – they were all reading off the same page. I thought that when we put five guys on, maybe only three of them were reading off the same page.
>
> Preparation is everything, I suppose. At that time we just weren't financially in a position to do things like that. We got together for a couple of games and half a dozen practices, max, before we went; that was it.
>
> Hockey then, the majority of the teams were from Scotland and the majority of guys on the British team were Scottish. No disrespect to George Beach, who coached us in Poland, but he didn't know any of the players. Hockey's turned around now and there's hardly a Scottish guy in there; that's what's happened to hockey over the last twenty years.
>
> It was disappointing at times, but everybody wanted to play for their country. Today, though, hockey isn't that high in the pecking order for sport in this country. I feel sorry for the kids that are playing now. There's not enough money being put into it and there are not enough opportunities for them. After the age of nineteen they just disappear because there's nothing for them.

Although the Heineken-sponsored decade, which began in 1983, is viewed nostalgically now as some kind of renaissance period for British ice hockey, it actually signalled the end of hockey in Glasgow, with Dynamos consigned to lengthy road trips as the sole Scottish representative in the new national Division One:

> I think at that time a lot of people, like myself, looked at it and those that worked for somebody just couldn't give it that time, travelling up and down the country every weekend. Plus, you don't enjoy it the same. If you're travelling down to London and all these places every other weekend you've got to ask if you can give that time; and the answer to that, nine times out of ten, is no.
>
> Once that happened, I came out of hockey for about two years, and you never come back the same person; your standards drop and your whole attitude changes.

Martin's last playing season was with the ill-fated Glasgow Saints in 1990/91. He was an All Star during 1975/76. A history of back injuries, however, also hastened the end of Martin's playing career:

> I remember when I was fifteen we went to Durham and I got put into the boards by some big guy. I got taken to the hospital because I could hardly move my legs. They X-rayed

me and this gentleman threw me about the bed, said I was alright, on you go! They took me back up to Glasgow and I was on crutches for two weeks. I started back at work and I was still in a lot of pain; I came in one night and my mother told me I was to 'phone the doctor's right away. The doctor told me I had to come in the next morning. I went in, and the doctor asked me how I was feeling. I told him I was still in a bit of pain. He told me I was a lucky man; and when I asked him how that was, he said that I had a hairline fracture at the bottom of my spine!

They hadn't picked this up at Durham, and it was only noticed when the X-rays were sent up to Glasgow. That was why the doctor said I was lucky, because I could have been left paralysed if I'd done anything to it.

I was also involved in a car accident on the M74, so by the end of my hockey career my back was going into spasms. I remember playing at the old Ayr Ice Rink (the wee one, at Limekiln Road) and I went into the corner for the puck; there was a Canadian playing for Ayr who was about two feet away from me, just as we turned my back went into a spasm and I went down. Everybody was calling this Canadian for everything and he'd never touched me!

The imports that came at that time, one, two and three, certainly brought up the standard of hockey; but it also put an imbalance in there. The only guy I've seen that's matched up to that is Tony Hand. Tony's proved to everybody what can be done.

Tony was very lucky in that he came into the game just as I was going out; I can remember first seeing him and thinking, 'Jesus Christ, this boy can play!' Just at that time they started bringing imports in and that lifted Tony's game; all these people coming into Edinburgh and Tony being there at the right time. He was a gifted player anyway and he's carried that right through. He's maintained that standard; even today [2006] his game's good. And that was him playing in the bottom team in the league! Colin was always saying that he wished he was playing with Tony; that he wished Tony was on their team! I just can't believe that there were people criticising the guy.

Martin took over the coaching duties of the Dynamos in October 1985, after American imports Jack Bestle and Bill Kirk decided to concentrate on playing following a disastrous opening to the Norwich Union Autumn Cup when Glasgow shipped 77 goals in their first 5 matches:

I got involved with coaching at Crossmyloof, player-coach, at the latter end of the Dynamos; but that was a big mistake.

Then I got involved with the Summit Saints, which was a disaster. It was one season, but it's the old saying: don't go into something that you're not prepared for. The money ran out, players were getting angry, a catalogue of things.

We went from that and I got involved with the junior development at the Summit Centre. They didn't have a programme, and Peggy Smith asked me to come in and have a look at it. We got that going and after that Paisley opened up.

Richard Harding, who was the then-manager, asked me to come over there. That was when the district council had big ideas about wanting to reinstate hockey in Paisley to what it was in the days of the Pirates.

They had that first year when we were in that Scottish League with imports when nobody else did. In fairness to everybody else, it didn't take much to win it. We were turning up on the night with professional hockey players and we'd siphoned off the best of the Scottish players that we could, because we had money to spend at that time.

Then we went to the British Division One. The first year we went in there, the council physically ran it. Guys that were getting £400 or something – it was actually costing the council £800, because they had to get all the rights of a council employee! It was out of hand.

That came to an end in '96 when the councils were reorganised. Budgets were cut, and it was time for us to move out of there. That was their decision and it was something we didn't want to be part of. Unfortunately, that team went bust, because the budget was halved overnight, and there was no way we could continue, quite rightly. Other people, though, thought it could still be done at that level, so we said, 'you carry on'.

It was an unfortunate end, as Martin had been voted the British Division One Coach of the Year for 1994/95.

Martin's hockey connections had been strengthened with his marriage to figure-skating instructress Margaret Wilson, at Glasgow's Shawlands Old Church, in September 1977. Margaret's sister, Norma, was manager of the Crossmyloof rink and her Dad, Norrie, was chairman of Glasgow Dynamos. Her younger brother, Colin, was a teammate of Martin's on the Dynamos, and would himself have a long playing career with Dundee, Fife and Ayr. Curiously, Colin Wilson's stepson, goaltender Stephen Murphy, would become a Great Britain colleague of Colin Shields in later years.

I'd known Margaret from way back, when I was really young, from the skating at Crossmyloof. We drifted apart and then met up again in our early twenties – at the ice rink! It just went from there.

After we got married our first boy was Colin. He was skating very early at Crossmyloof; then he was out of it for a while after Crossmyloof closed and got back into it at the Summit Centre.

I think it's an unfortunate thing that anybody thinks that they've got to send their kid abroad to develop as a hockey player. The situation at the time was that I had to think about how far he wanted to take his hockey. The realisation is that if you send him there you hope he'll get the opportunity. He's been reasonably successful.

Looking back to where hockey was at that time when Colin was here, and the limits to what he could achieve here to progress his game, he had to get on the ice more; he had to get into a more professional organisation and that's when we finished up sending him to Notre Dame when he was fourteen.

I've no regrets in thinking it wasn't the right thing to do for him. It's made him a stronger and better person out with the hockey as well. I'm a great believer in not looking back in life and saying 'I wish I had' because it very rarely comes round twice. That's how Colin finished up going to Canada.

He was at Glasgow Academy here, and Glasgow Academy didn't recognise his ice hockey as being a sport. I remember they wanted him to give up the hockey and go into rugby at the time. But, of course, Colin wasn't for having that.

It was costing us money to send him to Glasgow Academy and there wasn't that much of a difference financially to send him to Canada to what we were paying in a fee-paying school here.

There was a short period when he went to school in East Kilbride while we were getting all the paperwork in order for him to go to Canada and waiting for the acceptance from Notre Dame. I think you had to make a commitment to Glasgow Academy for the full year, or half-year, so we took him out of there for the short period before he went to Notre Dame.

It was tough for him; it was tough for any kid at that age. I never went out the first year to Notre Dame, but Margaret did once or twice. At the time Colin was at Notre Dame there were no mobile phones or email. Through Terry McCutcheon we managed to get him moved to the east coast, just outside Toronto, and that made it a lot more accessible.

Martin and Margaret branched into the hockey equipment business at the same time:

> Margaret used to run the shop in Crossmyloof, so she knew all the suppliers and we opened a shop at the Paisley rink. The initial period of time with that was quite good; it was 'happy hour' with new ice rinks opening at Paisley, Dumfries and some fun rinks. As time went on, though, the internet killed that stone dead, so we thought it was time to come out of that. With me sharpening skates at Crossmyloof, and carrying that forward, that helped.

Colin's younger brother, David, just turned sixteen in 2006, is also, not surprisingly, a hockey player:

> My younger son, David, he's been quite fortunate in that there's been a junior development programme since he's been involved with hockey. When Ayr opened the Centrum, he managed to get down there; that was great for him. He always wanted to play in goal, but I wouldn't let him because I felt he was too good a skater to play in goal! But he always wanted to be in goal; I was away seeing Colin play and I got told over the 'phone that David was playing in goal at the rink that night. That was it. And when he was playing out he wasn't the toughest kid on the block; if he was going to face a man on the point he'd always lift his leg out of the way of the shot, yet in goals he's the opposite, I don't know how that can be!
>
> He's also heavily into golf so, whether there's anything available in America in the next couple of years we'll just need to wait and see. He's at Belmont House School in Newton Mearns just now; although David might not be the strongest hockey player, or strongest golfer, because he can do both there might be a wee niche there. Kristy, Colin's fiancée, her brother got a college scholarship for hockey and golf.

Martin's coaching days are now at an end:

> I've got no involvement with hockey now. I've been asked a couple of times, which is great to have been asked, but the way things are at the moment with the business I just couldn't give it the commitment.
>
> It did take a big commitment when I was last involved with the junior development at Paisley a couple of years ago; it was every weekend and, in fairness to the kids, to be there every Monday night, or twice a week, it's a commitment I just cannot give.

Martin and wife Margaret have a nylon extrusion company, based in an East Kilbride factory unit:

> We make nylon sheeting for industry, whether it be for cars, washing machines, cookers, stuff like that. We also supply window companies down south as well. I only got involved with it lately. I'd been helping Margaret out here and there. Margaret originally worked for a plastics business up in Stirling; it went defunct, and she'd worked there for six months before that. She thought there was an opportunity there and that's how she became involved in it, knowing a lot of people in the industry.

Martin is quite categorical in what is required to try and turn around the current poor standing of Scottish ice hockey:

> They need to get some heavy funding, because there's less money being put into junior development now than there's been in a long time. At the moment I've not seen any change in junior development, and it's not the kids' fault. We're not going to produce hockey players on twenty games a year, that's for sure. If we can't get the kids on the ice at least twice a week, and playing at least one or two games per week, then we're kidding ourselves on.
>
> That's okay if we want just to play in our own backyard; but if we want to go outside Britain then we need to get a more professional approach.

They keep building these fun rinks in Scotland which are unsuitable for ice hockey. Or else they build a proper rink but it's unsuitable for a spectator sport like senior hockey. At the moment we've got this scenario where they're quite happy to take the kids off the streets at the age of eight or nine, and then they reach nineteen and we just drop them. And we wonder what happened to these kids and why people are staying away from it? Some of these Under-19s teams only get fifteen games a year; it's ridiculous. How do they expect to keep kids involved?

They've got to get government funding. How do you get all these people like Tony Hand and Scott Neil that are involved in hockey to spend more time. Whether it's somebody like myself, who's out of the picture totally now, or anybody that knows about hockey, they've got bills to pay like everybody else. You need to pay them. You need to have a professional group. At the moment, and no disrespect to the people that are running it, it's certainly not a professional organisation in any shape or form. You can only go so far with volunteers. That's the problem with it – it was volunteers when I started and it's still volunteers today.

We need to put in serious money and we need to start paying people, just like all the other sports they keep telling us about; we need to regionalise it and put in coordinators and regional coaches. And we need to start playing abroad, because you certainly won't learn unless you're playing abroad.

In fairness, I can agree with the fact that spectators are not going to wait ten years to see decent hockey; the spectator that's paying his money wants to see the best that they can possibly bring to him. Our problem is that we don't have any government funding and all these council rinks were built with public money – so why were they all built wrong? If we want to employ people to keep kids off the streets, and that's the sport we want to do, then we need to get government funding, and it can't be a twelve-month stint. You're not going to get people to leave good jobs, to come in for something that's got funding for two years and then gets the plug pulled on it. You still need volunteers, but you need to put a professional body there. Hockey in Britain, I've no doubt, could be taken to a far greater level.

One of my strong arguments is that forty years ago, when I was a kid playing hockey, I had more freedom in an ice rink and I got more ice-time than these kids are getting today – and we're supposed to have stepped forward. We haven't; we've stepped back and it's not the kids' fault.

Who are the players he's played with or against who stand out in Martin's memory?

The best player I've ever seen has got to be Tony Hand, there's no doubt about that. Everybody can argue about where you've played your hockey, but at whatever level they've managed to produce over the last twenty years in Britain, Tony's played at the very top of it. He's number one, definitely.

Going back, other players that I'd rate highly are Alastair Brennan and Jackson McBride. From Glasgow, guys like John Hester, Neil McLennan. Neil's now a great golfer. He came out of hockey; he got to that time in his life when he looked at other things and decided he didn't want to commit the time hockey needed anymore.

There were a lot of good hockey players across the board in the seventies. It was more played for fun rather than professionally at that time. I played a couple of years at Crossmyloof with Jackson McBride, who joined the Dynamos when Ayr shut. A lot of people didn't like him, but I got on fine with him. He was a big, immaculate looking man, always well turned out, as we used to say! Sometimes he could be abrupt, and people maybe took it the wrong way, but I never had any problems with him; he was a really good player.

I met a lot of good guys through the hockey, like Johnny Gibson from Ayr, who are good friends of mine; a lot of guys from Billingham and Whitley Bay that are good friends, too.

There were always characters in the game, like John Kidd and these people that played for me at Paisley. I probably met more characters coaching than I did playing, guys like John and Bobby Haig that came through from Fife.

> I remember asking Alex Koulikov at Paisley how he'd become so good. He told me that he practised twice a day and played a match at night. I asked him how many days a week did he do this: every day, he told me! That was expected then, when they were still behind the Iron Curtain. People like Dino Bauba, who was young at the time; I used to laugh when he first came over and kept saying that he didn't understand – but they all understood pound notes!
>
> When you're playing you only want to see one side, and that's the dressing-room; whereas when you're coaching you see what's in the dressing-room and you see what it takes.

When son Colin joined the Belfast Giants during 2005/06, the local media made great play on his having 'Irish grandparents', but Martin can confirm that the press were stretching the truth just a little:

> My father's grandfather was from Donegal and my mother's grandmother was from Belfast, so there's an Irish connection on both sides, but it's like Colin's great-great grandparents!

Irrespective of how far back one needs to go to find any Irish antecedents, Colin Shields, despite now possessing an unsurprising mid-Atlantic drawl, is most definitely Scottish, being born on 27 January 1980 at Rutherglen's Maternity Hospital. Technically, this is outwith the Glasgow City boundary, but is so much a part of the continuous Glasgow metropolitan area that it would be pedantic in the extreme to take issue with those reference books and databases that list 'Glasgow' as his birthplace!

Growing up in Glasgow's affluent southern suburbs of Giffnock and Newton Mearns, before moving to the 'new town' of East Kilbride in his early teens, skating and hockey were a part of his life from an early age:

> When I was really young, my Mum was teaching figure skating at Crossmyloof, and my Dad was playing hockey there, so I think I was on the ice aged two or three. I only skated till I was five or six, and that's when the rink there shut down. My Mum stopped teaching figure skating, and my Dad wasn't so involved with the hockey, and we got away from it.
>
> It was when I was around nine or ten; we were actually going bowling at a new place in Finnieston, out by where the Summit Centre rink was. We got lost, and came across the Summit Centre. John Hester, who'd played hockey with my Dad, was the manager and he gave me a pair of skates. I went skating there for about a year, once or twice a week, before we went to Canada to visit my Dad's brother, near Toronto.
>
> We were at the beach, and there was a hockey camp starting the next day, so I said I wanted to go. We went and bought the full gear, and I'd only ever messed about on the ice with a stick before; I'd never played on a team or in a league, as I didn't have any hockey gear, just whatever my Dad had laying around the house. That was the start of it, from there. I went back every summer till I was seventeen or eighteen. The first year I'd go for two weeks; then four weeks the next year; then the year before I went to school in Canada, I spent about seven or eight weeks at different hockey camps all over Canada.
>
> I just stumbled across hockey; first with the skating, and then with the hockey camp at Wasaga Beach, just north of Toronto. I started playing hockey at the Summit Centre in Glasgow from when I was ten until I was thirteen. Then when my Dad started coaching at Paisley, I'd practise there but still play with the juniors at Glasgow.
>
> When I started in Glasgow they only had an Under-16s team. I was ten years old and there were a couple of other kids really young, and they said they'd get an Under-14s team. But we were only ten or eleven, playing against fourteen year-olds; and I was playing for the Under-16s, too. I'd play a full Under-14s game, you'd have a five-minute break, then the Under-16s would play right after! We didn't have a lot of players, so some games I'd play the whole game. My last year, we had an Under-12s team too; so I'd play Under-12s, Under-14s, Under-16s! A lot of

Colin Shields, Paisley Pirates, 1994/95. (Martin Shields archive)

times the Under-12s wouldn't be with the 14s and 16s, so you'd be one place in the afternoon and then you'd have to drive somewhere else for evening games.

After the 12s, I still had two more years at 14s; so I'd be playing 14s, 16s and 19s by that point, and then I'd go on the bench with my Dad's team at Paisley and go on the warm-up and stuff.

The amount of ice time Colin was able to clock up as a youngster was considerably greater than that which would normally be available to other junior British hockey players, and this helped in his development:

Obviously that helped a lot, because I'd be getting on the ice games and practices on the weekend with my Glasgow team; then the Pirates would practise at Paisley Tuesday/Thursday, and they'd have extra ice Tuesday morning and Friday at lunchtime. Because my Dad was with Paisley, I'd practise with their juniors, too; and I'd practise with the recreational teams at Paisley – so I was getting on the ice every day.

At that time, my Mum and Dad had a shop in the rink at Paisley, so a lot of times I'd just come from school and go right there. I went to private school at Glasgow Academy from I was five till I was thirteen; the last year before I went to Canada I went to a state school, Duncanrigg Secondary at East Kilbride for a year, because we'd just moved there at that point.

What were the factors that influenced Colin's decision to move from Scotland to Notre Dame, a boarding school in Wilcox, Saskatchewan, to further his hockey development?

I was playing for three age groups; I was getting on the ice a lot with my Dad's team, but, basically, it was like it is today for any Scottish kid at sixteen or seventeen; where do they go from there? Either you jump into the Elite League or go to Scottish National League or English Premier League; there's no mid-point there.

I thought it was important for me to go to Canada or the States at that point, because Grade 9 is the start of High School and I needed a chance of better hockey. The last year I played Under-14s in Glasgow I had ridiculous points; I can't remember what it was, but it was something like 300 points in less than 40 games! There wasn't any opportunity for me here.

My Dad was coaching Paisley, and there were Canadians and Americans playing for him, and somebody had said to him about Notre Dame being a good possibility for me, because it was all in a secure environment and you can stay right there; you didn't have to worry about finding a family to stay with.

It's like a boarding school; they have all kinds of sports there, but it's mostly famous for hockey because a lot of NHL players have went there, like Vincent Lecavalier and Brad Richards of Tampa Bay; they were in my year when I was there. You can go further back to guys like Rod Brind'Amour, Curtis Joseph, Kent Manderville.

It's in a small town of 400 people, with one store, right in the plains of Saskatchewan; there's nothing out there. It was a bit of a shock at first, but for me it was good, because there was hockey, and you'd practise every day. At that time they had eighteen different hockey teams, ranging from bantam (which is like Under-16) to Single A all the way up to Junior A. They have girls' teams as well; basically, ninety per cent of the people are there for hockey.

It was great. There were a couple of little ponds where you could skate outside. It's all about hockey there, and that's what I was looking for at that time. At the start it was definitely tough; not so much for the hockey, because I felt that I fit right in with the hockey. It was a lot tougher than I was used to, but I felt that with my skills and my skating I'd fit in no problem, as I was just as good as, if not better than, a lot of the kids at my age as far as school went. It was more off the ice, because I'd went from living in a city like Glasgow, or in Paisley, to going to a town with 400 people! That was definitely a shock, and there were a few long 'phone calls, that's for sure!

The school shuts down for two weeks at Christmas; you'd come home and see all your friends, and when you're young you don't really know what's best for you. You think about it, and you miss your parents and everything. But I'm certainly glad I stayed.

I went there because I wanted to get better; even at fourteen I knew all about the NHL, all about pro hockey and everything about it, because I'd been with my Dad's team and you learned a lot from all the older pro players who came through in that league. That's all you're around and that's all you want. I think, definitely, in the back of my mind, pro hockey was always my goal in going there.

I played golf quite a bit growing up; I had lessons when I was pretty young, before I got into skating and hockey. I play golf in the summer all the time now. But I'm not any good at football!

After a season with the Notre Dame Hounds, Colin moved east to spend 1995/96 with the Midget team of the Midwestern Ontario Junior 'B' Kitchener Dutchmen:

I went to Notre Dame for one year, and I came back home for the summer. Terry McCutcheon, who played at Glasgow and Paisley, was coaching the Kitchener Dutchmen, a Junior 'B' team in Ontario, and he asked me to go over there for a tournament for players who were interested in playing in that league, and the coaches could all go and look at them. I played in four games and had six goals. I was still only fifteen, pretty young and pretty small for Junior 'B', so they asked me to come back and play for their Midget team, which is Under-17 or 18.

I went back and got hooked up with a family there and played for the Midget team. I ended up staying with Terry McCutcheon the second half of the year, which was fun; I'd always been good friends with him and his wife when he played for my Dad's teams. That was a good experience.

Every year until I graduated high school I was in a different school! I went to two schools in Kitchener; I went to St Mary's that year, because it was in the area I was living. It was a bit of a change being a Scottish kid going to Canada and having to change schools so much; you

Colin Shields, Notre Dame Hounds, 1994/95. (Martin Shields archive)

don't really get to keep a base of friends; you're always trying to meet new people. That was definitely tough and that year was probably one of the toughest years I had. At Notre Dame, the kids that live in your room are the kids that are in your class, or on your hockey team, or in the dining hall; you make friends really fast and there's always a lot of people around and you're never really lonely, as such.

At Kitchener, I think there was only one kid off my team went to the same high school as me, and he was older. It was tough, because I'd have to take the bus to school by myself; then come home by myself, and Terry and his wife were working. I'd go to practice, and come home, and Terry would be busy; so I'd be on my own a lot, so it was tough to make friends. It's not easy when you're a young kid like that, in a different country.

That year there were a few times when I wanted to come back, and I actually played six or seven games for the Pirates that Christmas when I was home in '95/96. I did okay, and I wanted to stay, but my Dad talked me into going back.

I went back to play for the Dutchmen, and they were notorious for having a really old team with nineteen and twenty-year-olds. I was still sixteen, and they said they'd try and slot me in around the fourth line. I didn't want to play Midget again; I wanted to play with older guys; I wanted to move up.

A guy from a Junior 'C' team, the Caledonia Corvairs, called me and asked me to come play for them. I went down there, and I didn't know much about the team or the league. It turned out they were the last-placed team in the league for the last five years! I got there, and I thought: 'What have I done?'

But it turned out to be, at that point, probably the finest year I had. They had a great group of guys; all the guys that played on the team went to the same high school and the younger guys were all from around the same area, so it was a lot of fun.

Caledonia was half-an-hour south of Hamilton, Ontario. I played there and I got Rookie of the Year for that league. Caledonia was out of the play-offs, and the regular season was over by February. Glanbrook Rangers was in first and they said they would trade for me and I could play for them in the play-offs. I went there, and we ended up winning the All-Ontario Junior 'C' title. I played 34 games in the regular season, and something like 36 in the play-offs;

> we played six seven-game series in the play-offs! I can't remember who we played in the final, but it was a lot of fun; I got a championship ring and all that sort of stuff, even though it was only Junior 'C'. They had a small rink, but they just jam-packed it. It was a good experience and I got to play a lot, and did pretty well in the play-offs.

He picked up the League's Rookie of the Year award and was named an All Star. He also earned a first call up to the Great Britain junior teams during that season; making two contrasting visits to Romania. Firstly he spent the New Year with the Under-21s in a hotel with no heating – and temperatures dropping to -25°C. Little wonder GB could only finish fourth out of eight in the World Pool 'C' tournament. It was a more successful trip in March 1997, when the Under-19s won the European Pool 'C' gold medal.

Colin was to return to Kitchener for 1997/98, but this time he was on the Junior 'B' team:

> I went down to Strathroy, near London, Ontario, and played three games for the Strathroy Rockets in Junior 'B'; but I didn't really like where it was going there. So I went back to play for the Kitchener Dutchmen that year, for Terry McCutcheon. We did pretty well, second or third in the league, and I was third on the team in points; I did good that year and it was a good stepping stone for me. I think that was my second-last year at high school, and it was a good experience. It's a pretty good league, even for Junior 'B', with a lot of younger guys, and it was a chance for me to play a lot. I lived that year with a family whose son used to play on the Dutchmen. He had moved out, but the lady and the gentleman were really great for me; she made all my meals and took care of me really well and that was definitely a really positive experience.

The 1998/99 season would see the now eighteen-year-old Shields with another new team and at another new high school, but this time south of the 49th Parallel:

> One of the guys who used to run that hockey camp way back on Wasaga Beach was an assistant coach in Cleveland, Ohio, in the North American Junior Hockey League. He asked me to come down and play for them. They're only allowed two non-Americans on the team, and they already had one guy from up near Thunder Bay, Ontario – and he used to go to that same hockey camp in Wasaga Beach, too! He called me and told me to come down.
>
> Me and my Uncle drove from Toronto down to Cleveland; it's about six or seven hours, and they showed us the rink and stuff. I agreed to go and play for the Cleveland Barons.
>
> In my first season we didn't have a very good team, but I ended up playing on the top line with another guy who ended up leading the league in scoring. I had something like 60 points in 55 games and I think I got a Second Team All Star. Then I played in the All Star game and did really well; I got some college interest at that point.

Colin spent the last night of the twentieth century in Nagano, Japan, along with his teammates on the GB Under-20s team. He led the British scoring (4 goals, 5 assists, for 9 points from 4 games) to help secure a bronze medal in the World Pool 'C' tournament:

> My first year in Cleveland was my last year of high school. I went to Kenston High School, which was half-an-hour outside Cleveland; that's where I lived at the start. I actually only needed three or four classes to graduate, but because I moved to the States, I had to take a bunch of other classes because in the States they had certain requirements like US History, US Government.
>
> That year I stayed with a family for half the year, and I stayed with the assistant coach in an apartment the second half of the year, because it was a lot closer to the rink. Where the Barons played was twenty minutes outside Cleveland, just south. I liked being at the

rink all the time at that point – still do – but where I was staying was just too far. The assistant coach lived just half-a-mile from the rink. So that way, I'd come back after school – I had to drive half-an-hour in traffic out to school and back – but after that I could just spend all night at the rink; there was always stuff going on – kids' games, so I spent a lot of time at the rink.

In my second year there I led the league in goals and points, and got First Team All Star and all that stuff. I think we finished second; we had a good team that year. That's the year I got drafted, too, after that season.

His two seasons with Cleveland in the North American Junior Hockey League saw Colin produce 155 points in 110 games (76 goals, 79 assists), earning the offer of a hockey scholarship for the following four years from the University of Maine, at Orona. The close season of 2000 was to see the highlight of his career to date when, on Sunday 25 June, Philadelphia selected him as their fourth pick (195th overall) in the sixth round of the NHL Entry Draft:

I didn't have an agent at that point. All these people were telling us that you need to get an agent; but I'd seen the Draft things and I was pretty low down in the European rankings. My Dad kept saying that I was going to get drafted; but it's not worth going to the Draft, even now, unless you're going to go in the first two rounds. I've known people that have gone and they've sat there for two days; and some guys not even get picked. Or some guys were rated first or second round, and they've sat there till the end of the second day and get taken in the eighth round. It's just disappointing for the kids and I know a lot of people who've went through a lot of disappointment.

I came home after the season was finished and started working out, because I knew I'd be going to Maine. I think I signed in early signing period, October/November '99. I knew I was going there, so I was already back home training and golfing.

I was checking on the Draft back and forth. It was an eight-hour time difference; I got up in the morning and checked it, and I saw that I got drafted. I remember being in contact with somebody, I think one of the Assistant GMs at Philly contacted me a few days later to congratulate me. Later they sent me a packet and told me they wanted me to go to college and that they'd still be watching me through college and keeping in contact.

I don't think at that time there was any doubt in my mind that I'd go to college; I had a full scholarship from Maine. At the start of my last season with Cleveland I was getting a lot of calls and offers from different schools for scholarships. There are basically two or three signing periods; I think October/November is the early period, then you can sign again in March/April, and there's another period in the summer.

I knew that I wanted to sign early and get it out the way, because I wanted to focus on hockey during the season; I didn't want to be worrying about picking a school. Cleveland won the Compuware Fall Classic in Plymouth, Michigan, that year. I think I led the tournament on points; there were a lot of schools at that tournament, and after it I was getting a lot of calls from schools – Michigan, University of New Hampshire, Michigan State, Western Michigan, University of Miami, and Maine.

Maine really pursued me hard. I went on a visit to Maine at that point, and the coach was Shawn Walsh, who actually passed away my second year there. He was just an unbelievable guy. I went on a visit to a couple of other schools, and it was usually an assistant coach or a trainer would pick you up and take you all over. But at Maine, the airport in Bangor is twenty to thirty minutes away from where the school is in Orona, and the head coach, Shawn Walsh, picked me up; he showed me around, and I met with him for a couple of hours. When you go on a visit you'll watch a game, then they'll cart you around and show you all the facilities and all the things on campus. The other places I went to I felt they just pushed you off; but I felt that Shawn Walsh really took the time to show me that he really wanted to have me on his team and to be a big part of the programme.

> That meant a lot to me, and his character certainly made me realise that was going to be the school for me. But that's definitely a tough decision. Basically you're making a decision that's going to impact somewhat the rest of your life; not only where you play hockey, but where you get your degree from, and the people that you meet in college are probably the people that you're friends with for the rest of your life.
>
> In the States, especially for an athlete, that's probably the biggest decision you'll ever make. I don't regret my decision; the only disappointing thing was that I had to sit out my first year of hockey.

Unfortunately, Colin had fallen foul of the National Collegiate Athletic Association's (NCAA) strict eligibility rules. Because he had enrolled in a full-time education course in Cleveland the year prior to attending Maine, the NCAA's rules stipulated that he had to pass a full year's coursework before he was allowed to play in Hockey East. Unfortunately, his course, which he didn't complete, was only an expediency to comply with the terms of his US visa. What appeared to be a minor technicality because of his British nationality meant that he was ruled ineligible for his first year of college hockey just as the season was about to open:

> When I was in Cleveland my second year I wasn't going to high school, but for me to stay in the States I needed a visa. The only way that we saw to get a visa was to go to a community college; I was told later that I needed to go to school full-time, twelve credits each semester, to be eligible for the visa. At the time I didn't know this, so I think I went to school the first semester, and then I dropped out after the second one, which started end of January, because hockey was over in March.
>
> I then came home; so I didn't think that had any direct relationship to the NCAA and Maine or wherever I was going. I never really thought about it; I mentioned it to somebody, and my coach in Cleveland didn't really know, and he said it didn't really matter. When I went to Maine I was all pumped up for the season; I was on the top line with Martin Kariya (Paul Kariya's brother); the coach had pumped me up as probably the top incoming freshman.
>
> Then two or three days before the first game against North Dakota, somebody from the Regulations Department of the NCAA went: 'Wait a minute, what's this?' They wanted to know where I went to this community college. This was the first week in October; I'd been there since the beginning of September, and I'd built it up for a year – because I'd signed back in October the year before. I was all ready for the first game; it was a huge disappointment.
>
> At that time I didn't know what to do. I got called by a whole bunch of agents saying that I should see what my best options were. They talked to Philly, and they thought that even if I turned pro I'd probably be playing, at best, in the East Coast League at the time. I also thought about going to play Major Junior in the OHL, as I had a lot of chances to go there. But after looking at that, they found out that I'd need to be an import, and they were only allowed two Europeans per team; but Europeans have to be drafted, so you can't just sign a European midway through the year, so that was out. Basically, it was go to the East Coast League – and I wasn't coming back to Europe at that point – or stay at school and work out and practise for the rest of the season. I ended up deciding just to stay at Maine.
>
> They said that my scholarship was secure; it wasn't like I'd screwed up in so far as I was going to lose anything, I just couldn't play in games. I could practise and train, so I ended up working out, training and practising a lot. It turned out good; I put on a lot of size that year, got a lot of experience watching a lot of games! It definitely prepared me a lot better for the start of my second year. By the time it came to second year, although I hadn't played a game, I felt I'd played a year already; I was a lot stronger, a lot faster, and a lot more prepared for the big jump from junior to college hockey, especially to a top team like Maine.
>
> My first year playing [2001/02] we went to the 'Frozen Four', the National Championships; we lost in the final game in overtime to Minnesota. It was in the Excel Center in Minnesota. There were 20,000 fans; about 2,000 were Maine fans and 18,000 Minnesota fans, so that was

Colin Shields, Cleveland Barons, with the Compuware Fall Classic Trophy, Plymouth, Michigan, October 1999. (Martin Shields archive)

an unbelievable atmosphere. Those are things that you can never experience again. College hockey is so huge in certain places, like Michigan, Minnesota, Maine, Boston – those are huge hockey hotbeds. For us to play somewhere like Minnesota, with hockey so huge there, and to come so close to winning, it was a huge disappointment; but at the same time you look back on it as a great experience you'll never forget.

At the end of his inactive first year in Maine, Colin headed to Ljubljan, Slovenia, in April 2001 for his World Championship debut with the Great Britain senior team, recording 6 goals and 2 assists for 8 points from 5 games, netting twice on his GB debut, a 6-2 win over Estonia on 15 April 2001.

In my last year at Maine [2004], we lost 1-0 in the final game of the 'Frozen Four' against Denver in Boston, with around 15,000 Maine fans and 2,000 or 3,000 Denver fans. It was the reversal there of Minnesota, but we were unfortunate we just couldn't get any goals in that game. It's definitely a different experience because of the crowd factor.

I played three seasons at Maine because I lost a year of eligibility; even though I didn't play that first year it still counts, because, in essence, I messed up! It basically came back to me because it was my fault; it wasn't the NCAA's fault. If I'd been injured, or if it was their fault through paperwork or something, then you wouldn't lose the year; but because of what happened I lost a year.

I started studying business, but then I ended up with communications, media, writing; all that kind of stuff. It was a pretty broad field, and I left it open for myself. When I'm done with hockey it's maybe something that I could get into; anything in TV or radio. I think hockey is such a broad sport, but it's such a tight-knit community; everybody somewhere knows somebody; doors just seem to open up for guys retiring out of hockey. People like hiring guys who've been involved in stuff like hockey, because you've grown up in a team atmosphere with guys who work hard; people like that when they're looking for somebody to hire.

Colin had three very successful seasons for the University of Maine Black Bears, and enjoyed playing for their fanatical fans in their home barn, the atmospheric Alfond Arena. He had 61 goals, 56 assists for 117 points in 120 games for Maine, earning a Hockey East All-Rookie Team selection in 2001/02 (when he was third overall in all US college hockey scoring). He led the Maine scoring in 2003/04, when he was honoured with both a Second Team All-American and Second Team Hockey East All Star selections:

I left Maine in 2004, and that was when the NHL lock-out started! I don't think there could've been a worse timing for me trying to get into pro hockey. With the lock-out, teams would sign really top Draft picks to deals early at the end of the season because no-one knew at that time what was going to happen, would these guys go back into the Draft or whatever. For a guy like me who went in the sixth round, and even though that's not a low pick by any sorts, Philly said they weren't going to sign me because they didn't know what was going to happen with the league. Their American League team was pretty stacked because anyone who'd played under a certain amount of games the year before in the NHL could play in the American League. And guys who didn't have contracts who'd played under a certain amount of games in their career could, basically, sign an American League contract and play there. American League teams that season had maybe four or five guys on their roster who are now playing in the NHL, it was unbelievable.

It was super-hard to get a job. I said to the Flyers that if they're not going to sign me then release me. They said they could sign me to, basically, an amateur contract, almost like a try-out contract, but I said no, because I felt that my chances in Philly were very limited due to the pretty stacked organisation that they had. I just didn't feel that my chances were very good at that time in the Philly organisation. They'd signed a bunch of guys before the lock-out even started, so I figured I'd take my chances as a free agent and I got my release. If the lock-out hadn't came, and I'd just became a free agent, there is no doubt in my mind that I'd have gotten something somewhere; but given the lock-out, teams just weren't signing anybody. I ended going on try-out to San Jose Sharks rookie camp; I played in the rookie tournament in Anaheim and, basically, I was trying out for a slot on their American League team, because guys weren't signing NHL deals.

San Jose said okay, you can go to our American League team in Cleveland. I got there, and they said that they really had only one contract to offer, and twenty-five guys trying out for it! They basically had all their guys signed up; they just wanted to take a look and string me along to fill up the spaces.

It's so out of your hands; you can only do what you can, and if one person says they don't like you, then all of a sudden ten guys say: 'Oh, he said he didn't like you,' and then it just snowballs.

After I was done at Cleveland I had to make a decision as far as where else could I go in the East Coast League. It ended up mostly being between Atlantic City and San Diego. The head coach in Atlantic City was one of the assistant coaches in Maine; so he was pushing really hard for me to go there, but I'd been living in California for two summers before this, so I decided to go to San Diego and give it a shot. They had a good team and had done really well the year before. But being a rookie in that league it just didn't work out for me in San Diego; I thought I did okay, but they'd a really old team that year and those guys got the first shot on the ice-time.

After that I got traded to Atlantic City, believe it or not! I did really well there; I think I had 18 points in 19. A guy got traded from Atlantic City to Greenville and he refused to go, because he said he had a concussion. So the league said Atlantic City had to send another player, and Atlantic City said no. Then the league said that Greenville gets to pick who they want; it was a big mess, and Greenville ended up picking me. So I had to go to Greenville by default, if you like, for the last nine games. I was injured pretty much the whole time I was there; I had a bad shoulder at that point, and it didn't really work out very well; basically, that was my first year of pro hockey! It wasn't a very good experience, but, at the same time, it was a learning experience.

Greenville held onto my rights and Alaska traded for my rights during the summer of 2005. They're a team that's got a lot of money; there are a lot of wealthy owners up there, and they're a team who wants to win the league championship. The year before they'd done really well; they had Scott Gomez, of the New Jersey Devils, on their team. They thought they had three or four guys that were going to crack American League line-ups, but these guys all came back. East Coast League teams keep ten or eleven forwards; and they already had ten forwards back from the year before! So I was sitting around thinking to myself, doing the math that they're not going to get rid of a guy from last year, especially not for some Scottish kid!

I went to the coach and asked him what the deal was. He said I was right, and we came to an agreement and he let me go. At that point I went back to California. I'd had such a sorry experience the year before and then, to have another bad experience the start of the year, I just felt my confidence was really low and I needed a change of scenery as far as hockey went.

I'd been contacted by a bunch of teams in the British Elite League; Ed Courtenay had called me a couple of times in the summer, before I'd even went to Alaska, to try and get me to come to Belfast; but I wanted to see how things went in the East Coast League. He called me again, and I got a call from London and a couple of other teams in the league; it was actually between London and Belfast, and a month after coming over, London folded – so I think I made the right choice in Belfast!

It was just important for me to get back on the ice and get some experience and confidence back playing again, because I'd lost the enjoyment out of it. I'd gotten away from the things that had made me successful in the past, and lost belief in my abilities.

The fact that a certain Theo Fleury was on the Belfast roster was also an influencing factor:

It was a bit of an attraction, too; anytime you get a chance to play with an NHL legend like that is definitely a good experience. Even though me and him didn't really play on the same line, we were on the ice here and there; but just to practise and be in the locker room with a guy like that brings a lot of experience to the team. That was definitely a real positive experience for me, coming to Belfast and having something like that.

It wasn't really too much of an adjustment for me, but Kristy had a bit of adjustment; she's from Canada. Coming back to the UK, some things are obviously a bit of a change; it's pretty rainy over there in Belfast! Some things in the States, it just seems so much easier because everything's at your fingertips, and no matter what you need or how you want it you can get it there; whereas in the UK it seems there are always so many more hoops to go through to get things!

Off the ice the transition wasn't too difficult for me as Belfast was a lot like Scotland – similar city and culture; on the ice it wasn't too much of a transition either. The hockey's not much different from the East Coast League; I think the standard's about the same, or a bit higher, but in the East Coast League it's a lot of younger guys trying to move up to the American League, whereas in the Elite League the top two lines are a lot of older guys who've played in the American League or East Coast League and who've been over here for a while. But it's a totally different game. The East Coast League is all guys between twenty and twenty-five, because they have a veteran rule limiting them to only three or four guys who've played more than 280 games. The top end guys in the Elite League are as good as the top end guys in the East Coast League; but the bottom end British guys, and nothing against them, but even the third line guys on the East Coast League are better than the British guys. Obviously, there are a few exceptions: Tony [Hand], David Longstaff, Jonathan Weaver. I think that hurts British hockey; but I think over time, once the British kids get to play more, I think it'll come up; who knows?

Who does Colin regard as the major influences on his hockey career?

My Dad obviously knew a lot about hockey and was a good coach, still is, and he's always been there for me; he's made a lot of trips to Canada and the States to help me out, so he's probably been the biggest influence on me. My Mum obviously helped me with skating when I was really young, she's always been there; she's a great hockey mum.

Like his father, Colin shoots right, but plays on the wing, whereas Dad Martin was a centre. Colin is a pure goal scorer with a deadly shot, but is also an excellent skater who moves the puck well. Colin is also much taller than Martin, standing 6ft and weighing in at 189lbs.

After that, probably Shawn Walsh at Maine was my biggest influence; I was with him for the one year, and then he got cancer during that year, but he was always around and then, sadly, he died in the second year. There were definitely some things I learned off him; not just hockey lessons, but life lessons that you'll take with you forever. He was just an unbelievable man and an unbelievable character; somebody I'll never forget.

Who are those that he's played with, and against, who have made the greatest impression?

In California in the summer I skate with all the NHL players, because there's a lot of them train there. I just go and skate and work out, and go to the beach! I try to save money, and make it last throughout the summer.

There are maybe fifteen to twenty NHL guys and a couple of college guys and me; I'm out there because I worked out with the same trainer that trains those guys in California, so I get to skate with those guys: Alexander Mogilny, Rob Blake, Sheldon Souray, Mike Conway, Dan Cleary, Glen Murray, Mathieu Schneider. Sidney Crosby was out there the last two summers because he has an agent in California; and Mario Lemieux was there as well. It's unbelievable getting to practise with those guys, because they're at a different level altogether.

Theo Fleury; he's a great player, and has an unbelievable history and a great career in the NHL. Though he's probably at the end of his career, he's still fun to watch, an exciting player; he's pretty chippy, always in their faces and into the game.

The best British player by far is Tony Hand. I'd seen Tony play when I was younger, but even at the age he is now he's still got the tools and he's unbelievable, the passes he makes. He just sees the ice so well and it always seems he's just a step ahead; he's got such a great head for the game. Even playing against him, when you're on the bench you watch him and try and pick things up and learn from him. I played with him in the World Championships the first two years I played with Great Britain, and you definitely pick up a lot of things from him.

Colin's California summers also allowed him to meet then fiancée Kristy, as he explains:

We met two years ago in LA where Kristy worked as a personal trainer. We're getting married this summer [2006] on 1 July, in Castlegar, British Columbia, Kristy's home town.

Given his own experiences in trying to reach the National Hockey League, is following the 'American [or Canadian] Dream' something he would recommend to aspiring young Brits?

I put in more time and effort, and my parents put in more money, or whatever, than anybody. I came close there, and there is still an outside longshot that I could go back and do something. But I don't know what the percentage of hockey players who make it to the NHL is; probably something like a hundredth of one per cent, when you look at the number of players in the NHL compared to all the players around the world.

There's nothing wrong with having a goal, or a dream; everyone that laces up skates wishes they could play in the NHL someday. But it's definitely a long road, and it's not easy. Not only do you have to work harder than anybody, and show it on the ice, but it's also so out of your hands, too, even if you're a top points scorer or whatever. I mean, I had 30 goals in my first year of college – and still didn't even sign; ended up not even getting the chance. It's all a matter of who sees you and who needs what, and at what time, as far as the line-up. There are so many hoops you have to jump through and so many things that have to go your way.

If kids want to go over and play hockey, they're going to get better over there than they are here; there's just more competition, more practice, more experience, more everything – and better coaching. In Britain, they're just not going to get the ice time or the things they need.

It's tough for British kids to go over and try to jump into hockey. I think I went at the right age. If you go at the age of entering high school [fourteen], at bantam, that's a great age. If you go at sixteen or seventeen, then you're looking at junior age. Nothing against Stevie Lyle, but he went over when he was seventeen or eighteen and straight into junior; that's tough, not only an outsider, but in the OHL the hockey's too different from here, it's too big a jump at that age. You go from being a big fish in a small pond to being one of like everyone else, and you're also an outsider, so you've got to be even better. If you're the same as a Canadian or an American kid, doing the exact same numbers or whatever, they'll always choose the Canadian or American. It's a fact of life; just the way it is. No one is going to do you any favours because you're from somewhere else; they're going to pick some home-grown person before they pick you.

It's definitely tough, and I would suggest that anybody wanting to go over should go earlier rather than later.

I think there's something missing in British hockey; whether it's coaching, ice time, commitment – I just don't know. There's just not the opportunity or the competition. I can't imagine that there are that many more people playing hockey in Germany, say, than in Britain. I'm sure there is, but obviously the DEL is one of the top five leagues in the world, so it helps with something like that, and kids can see that and they've got a chance to do it.

In Britain the kids just don't have the commitment to want to do it. Even now, in the Great Britain team, the guys just aren't committed; they're doing it to have fun. Why would any player in Britain want to play hockey full-time, and give up everything within their whole life, when the top thing they can aspire to is the Elite League and when the most as a British player they're going to make is £300 a week?

You'd have to be out of your mind if someone said to you that you'd got to give up everything – drinking, partying – you'd got to work out every day, you'd got to practise every day and just think about hockey; and all for £300 per week for the rest of your life. You'd have to be crazy; what's the point?

In Canada, or the States, there's a chance you can make $5 million a year; or in Germany there's a chance you can make €100,000 a year, or whatever. But here, there's no point in kids dedicating themselves to hockey; there's no incentive; that's the reality of it.

When it comes down to love of the game, yeah, we'll play it for fun; but probably seventy-five per cent of the British players in the Elite League have to have another job, too, because they can't afford to live or pay the bills. £200 or £300 a week for seven months of the year is not going to go very far.

I think that's a big part of it; no incentive. It's like there is no light at the end of the tunnel, so why would you bother? And stuff like the NHL and other pro leagues seems so far away that people just can't be bothered with it.

Hockey's not on the same magnitude as football, because obviously there are millions of people in Britain playing football, but it's the same thing as like that; every kid's playing football because they want to play for Manchester United or whoever. Maybe some players play hockey because they want to play for, like, the Sheffield Steelers; but they're never going to make a living until they're forty and then never need to work another day!

That's part of the reason there's that attitude around British players and around British hockey in general; people just don't take it seriously. But that's just my opinion!

As an articulate young man with a mature outlook, Colin's honest and forthright opinion on the current troubled state of British ice hockey should give pause for thought to the game's decision-makers:

> I'll probably get in trouble for saying this, but I don't care anymore; the general attitude of British players at the World Championship is that, well, we're not going to win anyway, so let's just go here and have fun, have a laugh; if we win a couple of games, good, but that's it. There's no commitment. The games we had this year [2006] were close, but I don't care what anyone says, France dominated us. It was a one-nothing game but they dominated us. If it wasn't for our goaltender, we'd have lost 10-0; the shots were like forty to twenty or something.
>
> In 2005 we had an older team, but we worked really hard, and I didn't think we were too far away. But this year, Kristy and I wanted to talk to some of the supporters and try and build a plan to make a qualifying bid for the Olympics in 2010; but after this year, I think it'd just be a waste of time, because we're so far away it'd be crazy to waste money on it. Why should all the fans and supporters put all their money and time and effort into it, and there's just not the commitment there? All the volunteers that go there on their own time, the supporters, the staff that are putting in time to try and help the team, they are all wasting their time if the players aren't committed.
>
> It's sad, because there are a lot of players in Britain that have great skills who could be a lot better than they are but, maybe, inside they're saying 'Why should I bother?' because what are they going to gain out of it? They might as well go to the World Championships and enjoy themselves because, basically, it's not really benefiting them; people don't even take British hockey seriously as it is, so it's not like there are teams from the DEL coming and offering contracts to these guys. Everyone just thinks British hockey's a joke.
>
> When my Dad played for the Great Britain team it was an honour for the home-grown players, but I don't think there's any honour left in it. It's sad, because it's all guys under

Colin Shields, University of Maine and Great Britain, 2002. (Martin Shields archive)

twenty-five that are on the team, and they just assume that because they're one of the top thirty players in Britain they'll go to the World Championships. They just feel that they'll try and get a bronze, or whatever. We lost the first game to Hungary [in 2006] so the attitude was like, 'Oh well, the tournament's over.'

I want to go to the World Championships and I want to try and win it. I want to go there and have a set plan and everyone to be on the same page; our goal is to try and win it; I don't care if Germany's there or Canada's there, we're going to try and win it. We're going to do whatever we can to try and win those games.

I'm not going to name any names, but I don't expect to go to a tournament and someone say, 'We want to give up the least goals we can against this team.' Anybody that's played hockey puts on the skates to win, not to try and give up the least goals they can because it could matter when we play Israel, in case we tie them. It's just disappointing and you feel like you're wasting your time. Anytime any team ever won anything, you always hear about how everyone was 100 per cent committed; everyone's on the same page. With the British team, it feels like not everyone's on the same page. Until that happens, we're not going to go anywhere.

Unless they do it right, and have a plan in place and some certain things set up, I don't think they're going to do anything. I mean, how can you have two of the best British players in the League [Hand and Longstaff] not going to it? They probably feel the same way about the things I've said. Tony [Hand] and David Longstaff are two of the best British players, and Tony's probably the best British player ever, and he's not there. Are you trying to tell me that some of those guys that went to the World Championships are better than him? Basically, he feels the same way; what's the point? Guys aren't committed, so we're not going to win, and he's getting nothing out of it. If we were right on the borderline, and there was a chance we'd get to Pool 'A', I bet Tony would be there; those are the types of things that players play for, not to go somewhere and just be average and put up with all the crap.

Some of the teams we were playing against were practising together for a month before the World Championships. I know guys on the Austrian team got €4,000 or €5,000 just for going; and then they get €500 per game incentives for winning.

There needs to be a bridge between professional and kids' hockey; minor hockey. There needs to be at least a junior league set up; almost like a Major Junior League in Canada or the States. When kids here are sixteen or seventeen they're going to an English Premier League team or an Elite League team. If they go to an Elite League team, they're not playing; at best, they're playing third line. They're getting to practise maybe a couple of times a week with that team, but they're not getting any ice time.

This needs a lot of money and funding, but it's definitely do-able. If you had a six or seven-team league, like a Major Junior League, where the players were semi-professional, where they got some money; if they weren't from that town, they'd get housing, or stay with families. They'd practise four or five times a week, maybe play two games a week; add in weight-training, all this stuff, because British kids just don't have that – in Canada and the States kids are working out so hard off the ice growing up.

You could have some affiliation between those teams and each Elite League team, with kids from sixteen to twenty in the junior team. There's too big a gap. Kids growing up here, they turn sixteen and if they're not quite making it, playing that type of 'Major Junior' hockey, I think you'd see a huge difference in kids by the time they were eighteen or nineteen, even with the off-ice training and stuff.

Basically, when you get kids between the ages of eight to fourteen, there's not that much difference between British kids and kids from elsewhere in terms of hockey. But when you get to fourteen/fifteen, boys start turning into teenagers and men, and that's when a lot of things start changing, and you need to develop those skills more in that bracket between fifteen and twenty, and I think then you'd see a huge difference.

Hockey in Scotland is even a different spectrum from England; England has got so many more rinks, there's no curling on the rinks, and they've got full-sized rinks that are suitable for hockey.

There is probably only one out of four rinks in Scotland that are suitable for hockey. The rink here in East Kilbride is in the middle of a shopping centre! I played there when I was twelve years old, and we had to play with plastic pucks! I played there two summers at something like ten at night; but that was something that was good, because we just got on the ice.

But Scottish kids just don't get on the ice. My brother gets on the ice once a week, twice a week, max, with his team. And that's better than I had; when I was growing up it would have been once a week, because in Glasgow it was curling all week, and hockey at weekends. There are just not enough rinks for hockey in Scotland.

It's a shame for Edinburgh, because they don't seem to get any fans, and it sucks, because that should be an area really popular for hockey; Braehead in Glasgow, and Centrum in Ayr, are two great facilities without hockey. It's a shame, because there is only the one Elite team in Scotland, which I think hurts, too, because there is basically very little light at the end of the tunnel for Scottish kids playing hockey.

Even in England, there's not much incentive, but at least there they have some options; but here there are not really any options. Maybe it's just that we're at the bottom of the cycle and it's going to come back around.

Colin's hockey career took another unusual turn in August 2006 when, after a season in Belfast, he returned Stateside, signing for the East Coast Hockey League's Texas Wildcatters, based in Beaumont, Texas. After attending the Wildcatters' training camp, Shields found himself traded on the eve of the regular season, being dealt to the Fresno Falcons. The Falcons, though California-based, also compete in the ECHL, and the move allowed Colin to team up again with Fresno head coach Matt Thomas, who had worked previously with Shields at both Maine and Atlantic City.

Although Colin Shields' selection in the 2000 NHL Draft may serve as an inspiration to young hockey players in the UK, it is also something of a cautionary tale. Despite his obvious talent, allied to selfless dedication and total commitment, and backed by the unqualified support of parents steeped in skating and hockey, he has yet to play in the National Hockey League.

His story serves as a reminder of the enormous obstacles which the aspiring British hockey player has to overcome in pursuit of the NHL dream. Even though Colin reached the heights of being a top player in a leading American college team, the NHL has still proven elusive.

It is a salutary reminder that, with more Europeans skating in the world's top league than at any time in the past, a British born and trained player has yet to join their ranks. Although a number of players from what might be termed the second tier of European hockey have made the NHL in recent years – from Germany, Norway, France, Switzerland, Poland, Lithuania, Latvia et al – it would appear that a 'true Brit' in the NHL is, sadly, even less likely now than it was when 'Tuck' Syme briefly became the property of the New York Rangers, on joining the Guelph Biltmores, back in 1948.

Career Record

	GP	G	A	Pts	PiM
Martin Shields (Glasgow)					
1969-1991	375	228	442	670	554
Great Britain 1976-1979	17	6	5	11	8

Career Record (in British Hockey)

	GP	G	A	Pts	PiM
Colin Shields (Paisley/Belfast)					
1994-2006	47	20	35	55	24
Great Britain 2002-2006	29	18	9	27	32